Digital India

Governance Transformation

Digital India

Governance Transformation

Kalyan Sagar Nippani and B K MURTHY (BKM)
Edited by: Amitabh Sinha

Vitasta

Published by
Vitasta Publishing Pvt Ltd
2/15, Ansari Road, Daryaganj
New Delhi - 110 002
info@vitastapublishing.com

ISBN 978-93-86473-12-7

Cover and layout by Vits Press
Printed by Vikas Computer and Printers, New Delhi

Arthasya Moolam Rajyam
(Prosperity and welfare of the people
depends on good governance of the state)
—Chanakya

CONTENTS

PART 2

e-Governance: Managing Change and Case Studies

Annexure–1

Annexure–2

FOREWORD

The book on e-Governance by B Krishnamurthy (BKM) and Nippani Kalyan Sagar is a comprehensive compilation of basic concepts and practices with specific inputs and practical tips in starting, monitoring and evaluating e-Gov projects. The book is timely and useful to a large number of people in the government, business, civic society and public at large. The e-governance initiatives were started in India during mid-1980s. Then the technology was in infancy and data connectivity was possible only through special satellite links for district headquarters. From there we have come a long way with large data centers, fiber optics links, cloud computing, open source software, laptops, tablets, smart phone and a lot more. In the process, e-governance has been continuously advancing by offering many interesting citizen services to millions of people all over the country. These services include income tax, passport, driver's license, birth certificate, banking, payments, education, health-care etc.

The book covers many of these aspects with interesting insights. The coverage on the global case studies widens the horizon of a practitioner with specific lessons that can be applied.

The guidance and tips for managing vendors, contracts and other legal aspects are covered in detail which are very valuable for the officers championing e-governance projects. Linking the current technology developments to digital governance, painting a picture of the potential future and suggesting futuristic business models are interesting thought initiators. Overall this is a good handbook that provides valuable insights.

The real benefits of e-governance relate to openness, accessibility, accountability, connectivity, democratization, decentralization and expediting the process of development. Now that India is a nation of 'connected billion' we can begin to use this connectivity to improve governance and increase people participation in managing and monitoring local developments. The key is to modernize age-old government processes left behind by British Raj to meet the needs of the people in the 21st Century, with focus on empowering citizens at all levels for active participation in building a real inclusive democracy.

I hope this book will educate and encourage a large number of young people on the e-governance and related potential to create innovative opportunities in business, education, health, agriculture, environment, energy and transport through new technologies related to big data, analytics, robotics, automation, smart devices, smart services and a lot more.

Sam Pitroda
Former Advisor to the PM of India
Innovator, Entreprenuer, Technocrat and Global Thinker

REVIEWS

It is a comprehensive book on e-governance at the appropriate time when the government is taking various initiatives under Digital India to transform the government service delivery to citizens. It is providing practitioner perspective to various stakeholders and extending very valuable tips on project management, monitoring and control. I hope the book will contribute significantly in efficient and effective execution of e-governance projects in the country for transforming the functioning of government entities and their service delivery model.

P K Purwar
CMD & Director (Finance)
Mahanagar Telephone Nigam Limited (MTNL)

An exhaustive body of work that still provides a concise introduction to application of digital technology in governance. A wide variety of topics are covered and this can become the treatise on developing digital systems in governance.

The treatment of project management is particularly fresh and will benefit every project manager in today's context. A novel way of treating the subject with exhaustive pointers to specific solutions. Well done.

Lakshmi Narayanan
Founder, Cognizant Technology Solutions (CTS)

PREFACE

We are very delighted to bring this book on e-Governance leading to Digital Democracy. The book is aimed to provide not only a thorough understanding of e-Governance concepts and practices, but also to impart valuable lessons on implementation of e-Governance projects from around the globe.

Almost all governments around the world would like to provide transparent, quick and easy to access services to its citizens. Good governance is a practice that has come to stay in most democratic nations. Improved process efficiency, good governance and inclusive development coupled with use of Information and Communications Technology (ICT) paves the way for e-governance.

Several nations have advanced in application of ICT in their governance and are reaping the benefits by way of improved economic activity, citizen centricity and providing a very conducive environment for businesses to operate. They attract investments from multinationals.

Though India has been a relatively late starter in this arena, the progress made so far has been encouraging, considering the expanse and diversity of our country. However, the speed of progress has hugely been accelerated with the launch of Digital India initiative. It is planned to bring with it a sharp focus for execution and synergizing disparate initiatives to reap the benefits quickly in a sustainable manner.

In order to survive in this era of digital initiatives around governance, it is imperative that conceptual and practical understanding is gained by the players involved in making it happen. This book provides the reader with a pragmatic approach to understanding e-Governance and its practical application leading to Digital Democracy.

The book is organized in such a fashion that it helps a variety of readers with differing interests. The table how to use the book guides the readers through different issues conveniently. Thus the authors sincerely hope that this compilation of information is not only educative but also practically useful.

Enjoy the voyage through digital governance!

ACKNOWLEDGMENTS

'If I have seen further, it is by standing upon the shoulders of giants', said Isaac Newton. These words also truly reflect all those who made this book happen. This book happened with the help and support of many important people and resources. It is our privilege and pleasure to place this on record and thank them wholeheartedly.

Much material cited in the book has been taken from various sources of Government of India, publications of National e-Governance Division (NeGD), National Institute for Smart Government (NISG), Department of IT and other State Government sources[1]. Wherever applicable all the sources have been duly mentioned (the copy rights belong to the respective organizations). We thank these organizations that have published these details and made them available in public domain. That

---

1 www.meity.gov.in, www.nisg.org, www.negd.gov.in, www.aponline.gov.in www.apit.ap.gov.in/e-pragati, www.it.telangana.gov.in, www.nisg.org/case-studies www.nic.in, www.gswan.gov.in/sitepages/E-Governance.aspx, https://vibrantgujarat.com

helped the authors to quote them to drive the learning points and compile this book for easy application on the job for the well-intended user.

It is really heartening to us, that the effort of compiling this book has been acknowledged by luminaries in the field –especially from those at policy level and who represent the telecom and IT fraternity.

We thank profusely Mr Sam Pitroda for taking time out from his busy schedule to give a Foreword for this book. He has sown the seed for rapid development of telecom infrastructure in the country and played crucial role in formulation of the game changing policy initiatives at the national level.

Our heart-felt thanks are due to Mr P K Purwar, the CMD of MTNL, and Mr Lakshminarayan, founder-chairman of Cognizant. The former is a proven telecom professional at the helm of affairs in the country and the latter has created strides in IT industry with significant and lasting contributions. The Foreword and Review comments by these stalwarts mean a lot to us. We place on record our gratitude to each one of them.

We thank our editor Mr Amitabh Sinha for his constant motivation and guidance during this endeavour. Thanks are also due to Mr Deepak Kashyap, for his encouragement and feedback from time to time. We express our thanks to the subject matter experts and senior officers of the Central and State Governments to whom we spoke on several occasions to get the ideas vetted or gain some points of learning and insights worth sharing in this book.

We thank the team at Vitasta publishing for their unstinted support through-out the project.

We wish to acknowledge the support of respective families all through the journey of writing this book.

B Krishnamurthy (BKM) & Nippani Kalyan Sagar

HOW TO USE THE BOOK

Purpose/Objective of the reader	Chapter No.	Title of the Chapter
Awareness of e-Governance	1	Introduction
History of e-Governance in India	2	Historical developments
Digital India, its components and details	3	Digital India
How to plan for e-Governance projects – what are the major steps involved	5, 6, 7, 8 & 9	Planning for e-Governance projects and so on.
Architecture of e-governance systems	4	State Enterprise Architecture
Formulating contract and dealing with third party vendors	7	Administering contract for e-Governance projects
Knowledge of legal aspects including the IT Act	8	IT Act and other Legal aspects

Specific project management aspect	9	Project Management
Change management	10	Change Management in e-Governance projects
Mobile governance	12	e-Governance to m-Governance
Digital Governance and beyond	13, 14	Application of IoT in Governance in governance and the digi road ahead
Implementing e-Gov projects and associated lessons	11	Case studies

ABBREVIATIONS

ADKAR	Awareness,Desire,Knowledge,Ability,Reinforcement.
AMC	Annual Maintenance Contract
BCA	Business Case Analysis
BOO	Build Own Operate
BOOT	Build Own Operate Transfer
BPR	Business Process Reengineering
CA	Certifying Authority
CCA	Controller of Certifying Authority
CCTNS	Crime and Criminal Tracking Network
CDAC	Centre for Development of Advanced Computing
CDSW	Custom Developed Software
CERT	Computer Emergency Response Team
CFST	Citizen Friendly Services of Transport Department
CIIP	Critical Information Infrastructure Protection
COTS	Commercial Off The Shelf Software
CSC	Citizen Service Centre/common Service Centre
CAPEX	Capital Expenditure
CTC	Critical To Cost

CTP	Critical To Process
CTQ	Critical To Quality
CVA	Customer Value Add
DPR	Detailed Project Report
DAR&PG	Department of Administrative Reforms &Public Grievances
DFSS	Design for Six Sigma
DISNIC	District Information System of National Informatics Center.
DIT	Departmental of Information Technology
DMAIC	Define, Measure, Analyze Improve Control
DMADV	Define, Measure, Analyze, Design, Validate/Verify
eGLC	e-Governance Life Cycle
ERP	Enterprise Resource Planning
ECV	Estimated Contract Value
EOI	Expression of Interest
EOL	End of Life
FBS	Fixed Budget Selection
G2B	Government to Business
G2C	Government to Citizen
G2E	Government to Employee
G2G	Government to Government
GFR	General Financial Rule
GPR	Government Process Reengineering
GPS	Global Positioning System
HOP	Hands Off Points
HOT	Hands On Time
ICR	Intelligent Character Recognition
ICT	Information Communication Technology
ILIS	Integrated Land Information System
IPR	Intellectual Property Right
ISDN	Integrated Services Digital Network
ISS	Information System Security
ITAA	IT Act Amendment
ITES	IT enabled Services

JV	Joint Venture
KPI	Key Performance Indicator
LAN	Local Area Network
LCS	Least Cost Selection-LI
LSIP	Large scale Interactive Process
M&E	Monitoring & Evaluation
MCA	Ministry of Corporate Affairs
MIS	Management Information System
MMP	Mission Mode Project
MoE	Measure of Excellence
MoP	Measure of Performance
MSA	Measurement System Analysis/Master Service Agreement
NeGD	National e- Governance Division
NeGP	National e- Governance Plan
NICNET	National Informatics Center Network
NLSA	National Level Service Agency
NPV	Net Present Value
NSDG	National Service Delivery Gateway
OCR	Optical Character Recognition
OMR	Optical Mark Recognition
PDA	Personal Digital Assistant
PKI	Public Key Infrastructure
PMC	Project Management Committee
PMU	Project Management Unit/Programme Management Unit
PPP	Public Private Partnership
PSC	Public Sector Comparator
QBS	Quality Based Selection
QCBS	Quality & Cost Based Selection
RA	Registration Authority
RAD	Rapid Application Development
RFI	Request for Information
RFID	Radio Frequency Identification
RFP	Request For Proposal

RFQ	Request For Qualification
ROC	Registrar of Companies
ROI	Return onInvestment
RMP	Risk Management Plan
SAP	Service Access Provider
SAAS	Software As A Service
SDA	State Designated Agency (Software Development Agency)
SDC	State Data Center
SDLC	Software Development Life Cycle
SeMT	State e-Governance Mission Team
SLA	Service Level Agreement
SLM	Service Level Management
SLO	Service Level Objective
SMART	Simple, Moral, Accountable, Responsive, Transparent with respect to Government. Specific, Measureable, Achievable, Realistic, Time Bound with respect to Goals / Objectives
SOA	Service Oriented Architecture
SOW	Scope of Work/Statement of Work
SP	Service Provider
SPV	Special Purpose Vehicle
SSDG	State e-Governance Service Delivery Gateway
STQC	Standards Testing and Quality Certification
SWAN	State Wide Area Network
TAT	Turn Around Time
TCV	Tender Contract Value
ToR	Terms of Reference
UAT	User Acceptance Test
UCID	Unique Company Identification Number
UID	Unique Identification Number
UNCI-TRAL	United Nations Commission on International Trade Law
VLE	Village Level Entrepreneur
VOC	Voice of Customer
WAN	Wide Area Network

PART 1

e-Governance

Concepts and Practices

1
Introduction

Role of Government

The role of government in any country is to formulate policies and enact legal regulations to take the nation on the path of progress and to ensure that every individual's right to freedom and equality is protected. Through both short term and long term planning, governments create internal focus on development and ensure growth with equity among all sections of society. It is the duty of every democratic government to ensure that basic amenities are available to citizens. While building vital infrastructure for the nation's growth, good governments ensure that both the public and the private sectors play a dynamic role. It is also the mandate of every government to maintain law and order and safeguard national security.

Government vs Governance

Government is defined as 'A group of people that govern the community, or unit. It sets up and administrates policy and exercises executive, political and sovereign power through customs, institutions and laws within the country'[1] (or state).

There are various types of governments namely republic, monarchy or dictatorship etc.

Governance is defined by the World Bank as 'the manner in which power is exercised in the management of a country's economic and social resources for development'. Governance is also defined as 'establishment of policies, continuous monitoring of their implementation, by the members of the governing body of the organization. It includes the mechanisms required to balance the powers of the members with the associated accountability and their primary duty of enhancing the prosperity and viability of the organization'[2]. This definition is applicable across several types of organizations–be it a company or a government. It is the process of governance simply.

In essence it can be said that the government is the 'structure' and governance is the 'process'.

In order to enhance governance, governments across the world have been embracing the following goals and objectives:

- Service orientation–to make government more customer-friendly and service-conscious. Instead of being focused only on government departments, a move towards citizen-centric approach is desired and in a way demanded!
- Productivity enhancement–being more efficient and effective and to provide more services without having the need to increase taxes. Review of key processes, eliminating and streamlining wherever possible, are undertaken.
- Market alignment–making use of market-style strategies (similar to the way private enterprises are managed) and

[1] http://www.businessdictionary.com/definition/government.html

[2] http://www.businessdictionary.com/definition/governance.html

incentives to drive public policy, privatization. This also is aimed at attracting the investments in the state or Country to boost economic activity.

- Decentralization–breaking up the bureaucracy, empowering smaller agencies for effective performance delivery.
- Separation of policymaking and service delivery–This approach eliminates a potential conflict on intentions and improves policymaking and monitoring implementation. The service delivery is driven with a specific focus on the customer or end-user satisfaction.

Once the above are in place, it generates a positive environment. The outcome would be driven by the existence of the following aspects that are critical.

- Accountability–This mainly shifts focus from processes and structures to outputs and outcomes. The government is accountable to citizens and the public in terms of results and benefits derived.
- Sustainability–The long term sustainability of initiatives are considered rather than quick fixes and populist measures.
- Transparency-Making government accountable by designing its operations more transparent thus reducing the opportunities for corruption and out of turn favors!
- Inclusive development–Providing development opportunities for all sections of society, especially benefiting rural and traditionally under-served communities across the country.

Incidentally, the above factors are a must for a democratic country. A country that is focused on economic development and the betterment of its society, would be keeping these as the main agenda for action in its fiscal development plan.

Stakeholders and their changing expectations

The government has various categories of stakeholders to whom it provides different services. These could be broadly classified as citizens (G2C), businesses (G2B), employees (G2E) and other governments (G2G).

Citizens: One of the main stakeholders is the citizens. The citizens have a greater awareness and better access to information due to various technology advancements. Thus they have expectations of effective services from the government. Additionally, due to the demographic profiling, India is a country having a large number of younger population, which is preferring online services and quick turn-around for their needs.

Businesses: The business environment is extremely dynamic and they keep evolving in line with global developments. Indian businesses are no exception. There is a need from the businesses for a faster turn-around time for starting up business or for normal operations, one stop solution and an encouraging environment for growth of businesses. Various gtate governments compete with each other in ensuring to provide a 'business-friendly' environment in their state, to attract investments.

Employees: The government has to employ, engage and enhance its employees for better performance and effectiveness in service delivery. All the services the government provides right from pre-recruitment to, post retirement cycle for its employees would be covered under this category. It even extends beyond the lifetime of employee, as the Government provides widow pension and medical benefits etc.

Governments: Government to government services could be under several categories: Interactions can be between the departments of the same state government, between state government and central government, between governments of two countries etc. These services may be in the forms simple information exchange to major bilateral agreements for strategic cooperation.

The expectations and the need for the stakeholders are changing continuously to more effective ways of governing. This means there needed to be a paradigm shift in governance from a vicious circle of systemic issues-complexity of operations-inefficiency-high cost to a more virtuous circle wherein reduced complexity-affordability-sustainability play a vital role. In order to achieve these, it is important not only to carry out the administrative reforms but also use technology as an enabler for faster turn-around – thus giving birth to e-Governance (e-Gov).

e-Governance defined

The principle of e-Governance may be the same, but several bodies have defined it using different languages. For the sake of academic understanding, it is good to look at some of them.

It is the transformation of government to provide efficient, convenient and transparent services to the citizens and businesses through Information and Communication Technologies.

e-Governance is the transformation of public sector internal and external relationship through Internet-enabled operations, information and communication technology in order to optimize government service delivery and governance.

e-Governance or 'electronic governance' is basically the application of information and communications technology to the processes of government functioning in order to bring about 'Simple, Moral, Accountable, Responsive and Transparent' (SMART) governance[3].

World Bank defines it as: 'e-Government refers to the use by government agencies of information technologies (such as wide area networks, the internet, and mobile computing) that have the ability to transform relations with citizens, businesses, and other arms of government. These technologies can serve a variety of different ends: better delivery of government services

[3] Paragraph 83, Report of the Working Group on Convergence and e-Governance for The Tenth Five Year Plan (2002-2007), Planning Commission, November, 2001

to citizens, improved interactions with business and industry, citizen empowerment through access to information, or more efficient government management. The resulting benefits can be less corruption, increased transparency, greater convenience, revenue growth, and/or cost reductions.'[4]

UNESCO defines it as: 'Governance refers to the exercise of political, economic and administrative authority in the management of a country's affairs, including citizens' articulation of their interests and exercise of their legal rights and obligations. e-Governance may be understood as the performance of this governance via the electronic medium in order to facilitate an efficient, speedy and transparent process of disseminating information to the public, and other agencies, and for performing government administration activities.'[5]

The words described to define e-Governance may differ from one another. However there are certain key elements that are common and that actually qualifie e-Governance. The key elements are given below:

- Delivers key and tangible business benefits (e.g. reduces the overall cost for the stakeholders, enhances revenues for the department etc)
- Involves new operational framework (e.g. improved processes and organization structure to deliver services like Public Private Partnership (PPP) models)
- Fosters efficient and effective communication internally and externally (e.g. transparency)
- Application of information and communication technology and use of electronic delivery channels (e.g. Internet/mobile or applicable emerging technologies)

---

[4] http://go.worldbank.org/M1JHE0Z280 (extracted on 18.08.2008)

[5] http://portal.unesco.org/ci/en/

It is important to note from the above that e-Governance is not mainly about computers and internet but it is about bringing in a change in the operational framework and thereby delivering tangible benefits to the stakeholder. In that process, use of technology becomes incidental.

Benefits from e-Governance

The basic premise of e-Governance is to bring in effectiveness in service delivery to the stakeholders. In view of this, the advantages are many and these often occur over a period of time depending on the way e-Governance is administered and sustained. Figure 1 gives an overview of such benefits, in a nutshell.

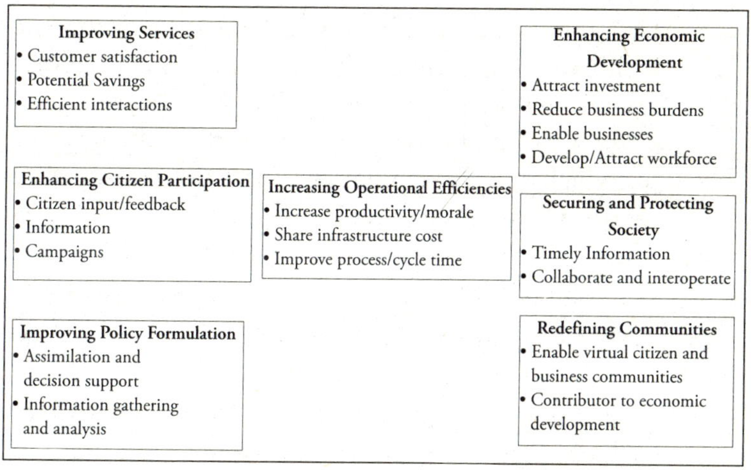

Figure 1 Benefits from e-Governance

Government service categories

The government in general may be considered to serve four types of stakeholders. These are:

- G2C (Government to Citizen): This deals with the relationship between government and citizens. G2C allows citizens to access government information and services instantly, conveniently, from everywhere, by use of multiple channels.

- G2B (Government to Business): This consists of e-interactions between government and the private sector enterprises. The opportunity to conduct online transactions with government reduces red tape and simplifies regulatory processes, therefore helping businesses to become more competitive.
- G2G (Government to Government): This may be at several levels – between departments within the State, between different states or between state government and central government or between two government agencies, one in the country and the other abroad. Governments depend on other levels of government within the state to effectively deliver services and allocate responsibilities. In promoting citizen-centric service, a single access point to government is the ultimate goal, for which cooperation among different governmental departments and agencies is necessary. G2G facilitates the sharing of databases, resources and capabilities, enhancing the efficiency and effectiveness of processes.
- G2E (Government to Employees): This covers the relationship between the government and its employees – spanning from pre-recruitment to post retirement including the family pension benefits.

Good governance and e-Governance

Governance itself is defined as 'the process of decision-making and the process by which decisions are implemented (or not implemented)'[6]. Having defined governance this way, the cited paper goes on to list the characteristics of good governance. The characteristics are participatory, consensus oriented, accountable,

[6] Yap Kioe Sheng, What is Good Governance, UNESCO

transparent, responsive, effective and efficient, equitable and inclusive and follows the rule of law. It assures that corruption is minimized, the views of minorities are taken into account and that the voices of the most vulnerable in society are heard in decision-making. It is also responsive to the present and future needs of society. Figure 2 indicates the eight characteristics of good governance for ease of understanding. Thus good governance and e-Governance are closely linked and depend on each other in some ways.

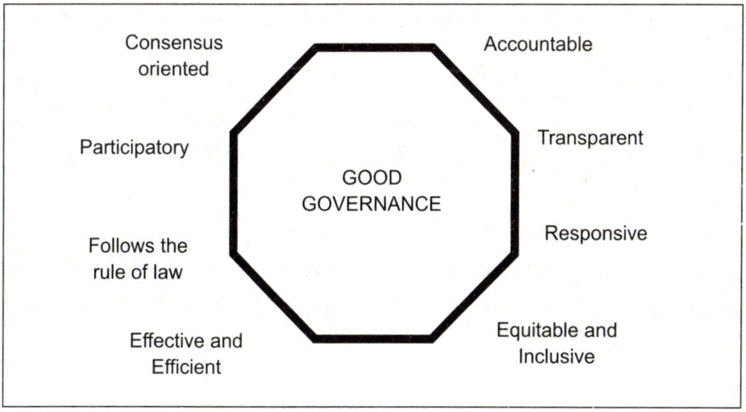

Figure 2 Characteristics of Good Governance.

The four pillars of e-Government

e-Government is to be built on a strong foundation with all relevant elements to make it function effectively. As it is said, e-Governance is effective governance, easy governance and also economical governance. The foundation of e-Government has to be on strong legal and policy framework. The four pillars on which the e-Government would rest are people, process, technology and the resources. The same is depicted in Figure 3.

In general, whenever an e-gov project is taken up or executed these four pillars and their corresponding needs have to be addressed. As the legal and policy framework is the foundation,

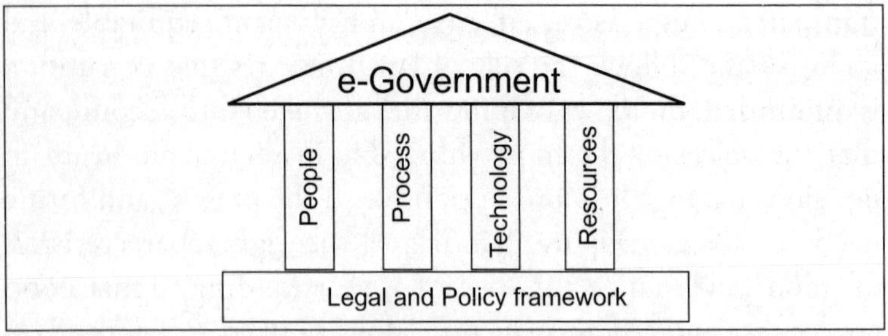

Figure 3 Benefits from e-Governance

adapting them to suit the requirements of e-Governance is essential. These processes would be covered elsewhere in the book.

e-Governance evolution model

Evolution of e-Governance has been closely linked with the development and evolution of internet. It is also not out of place to mention that the evolution between the two have been almost parallel in some sense.

Figure 4 gives the evolution model of e-Governance. As depicted in the Figure 4 the first stage of e-Governance is just

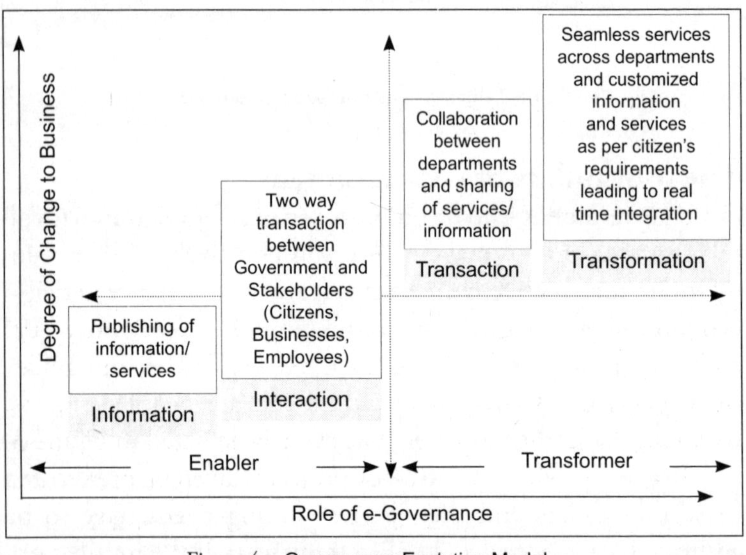

Figure 4 e-Governance Evolution Model

publishing of information about the department. It is a one way communication – just to pass on the information. It is as good as a notice board, but electronic in nature.

The next stage is where there is a possibility to send a query and get a response, leading to an interaction stage. The example could be in the website of Indian Railways, someone is seeking information of a train between two locations on a particular date and the portal would display all the trains between the two locations. If one train and a particular class of travel (II AC) is chosen, the portal would display the availability of seats, thus the Interaction.

The next stage of evolution includes cash transaction between the user and the department offering the e-Governance service. Continuing the same example of railways above, the user may book for travel based on availability for which the payment will have to be made through an online transfer. This is a case of transaction in e-Governance application. Under this category, there are a lot of departments that enable payment through online modes – like the utility services (state electricity boards, water consumption charges, property tax etc).

The advanced stage of evolution is the transformation stage. In this stage, multiple departments are seamlessly integrated to provide service to the citizen. For example, suppose a citizen is accessing the portal of the tourism department of a state to plan the vacation. Once the citizen chose the location to have the vacation and booked hotel through the state tourism portal, the portal may re-direct to the state transport for booking the travel and then to a taxi hiring portal for local conveyance etc – all these under one sign-on in the state tourism portal. Here several departments like the tourism, transport etc are accessed – thus easing the job of the citizen for his requirement.

Typical challenges confronting e-Governance

As described all through, e-Governance is likely to provide a lot of advantages to the stakeholders and enables the government in multiple ways. But it is not without its own challenges – that are unique sometimes. Typical challenges are briefed here.

Process challenges: e-Governance necessarily involves process improvement, as part of the reforms. This would actually ensure the benefits for the user community, be it businesses or citizens. It actually translates to reducing the number of steps that are involved in rendering the service, making the entire process simple etc. Sometimes, the process improvements will also involve amendments to the prevailing rules and regulations. Thus the basic requirement for e-Governance is the process improvement and it takes time to get this done. But it is not impossible as seen by the results thus far in the implementation of e-Governance programs.

Lack of preparedness: Transforming the governance to e-Governance requires a lot of changes associated with it. This may be in the form of changing the way of working, way of doing the transactions and building in revised systems to provide the services. In terms of all these the preparedness plays a major role. Referring to Figure 3, the preparedness spans across all the four pillars of e-Governance, namely the people, process, technology and resources.

Proper and detailed planning, executing and monitoring of e-Governance project would help to overcome the preparedness challenge. Appropriate change management plan and capacity building activities will take care of the people dimension to a large extent. Carrying out process improvement and amending the prevailing rules and regulations to suit the revised way of working will address the process angle. To address the technology aspect, efforts should be taken in respect of choice of technology, ensuring connectivity and associated areas. The last area, namely resources may refer to the funding and having the right people to do the transformation agenda. This may be addressed by resorting to seek funding by creative means (public private partnership, funding through World Bank etc) while for the people, enlisting the expertise from private consultants from the industry.

People challenges: The people challenges refer to not only the employees of the departments of the government but also the users and other stakeholders in the entire exercise. Whenever such e-Governance programs are rolled out it creates an uncertainty in the minds of the employees about their future and 'fear of the unknown'. This can be addressed by their involvement in the project right from early stages, which may make the transition easier. With respect to the other stakeholders, an appropriate planning has to be done after listing and analysing the stakeholder needs.

Rural challenges: India is a country with over six lakh villages. Various governments from the time of independence have attempted to address the growth and inclusion of the villages into the mainstream of the country, but with limited success. The challenges of rural Indian villages range from non-availability of potable water to not having electricity to absence of basic health care and so on. In the context of e-Governance the major challenges encountered in rural areas are mainly lack of connectivity of internet, absence of skilled / semi-skilled manpower, and electricity etc. These are being addressed by the government in a focused manner through several programs across the country.

Critical success factors for e-Governance programs

Some of the major challenges have been listed in the previous section. These have to be recognized and addressed while planning and executing e-Governance projects. However, based on the experience of several projects, some lessons have been captured as critical success factors that drive the e-Governance programs. These are listed below and details are provided where necessary.

- Strong political and administrative leadership– conviction and commitment from the leaders, make a defining difference. In many cases, it is one of the main factors that make the program succeed

- Clearly identified goals and benefits – in order to gain clarity quantification or qualification of the tangible and intangible benefits become mandatory
- Significant process reengineering required – improvement in the way processes are done and the new ways of doing them should be different – they need to be effective and efficient
- Detailed project management – drawing a detailed plan with specific milestones, deliverables and measureable outputs becomes a need. Not only monitoring of progress is enough, but also taking appropriate decisions at relevant points is essential
- Ownership by people who are most affected – involvement of relevant stakeholder's right from the beginning of the project and taking the necessary steps to address the concerns play a major role in enlisting the support to ensure success
- Adopt established standards / processes and protocols – minimize customization. Resorting to proven methods of working is preferred. This relates to choice and use of appropriate technology, standards and protocols while designing the e-Governance systems
- In-source analysis, outsource design, software development, data preparation, training, etc. – as needed, the expertise have to be taken from where it is best available – be it in private or government
- Manage change process-unfreeze, move, refreeze – this is a major activity and it needs a separate plan and execution
- Invest in training all stake holders on application and

its use – in other words, capacity building within the government department and also the user community is a must for the success of the program

- Explore Public Private Partnership (PPP) – with several development programs competing for resource allocation (funds), it is a challenge for the government to fund them all. New and innovative business model options have to be explored to fund the programs
- Create awareness of how things have changed for the stakeholders – communication of achievements, changes and the benefits gained thereof is of paramount importance. India being a country of multiple languages, the communication needs to be customized for different regions highlighting the benefits accrued
- Think big, start small, evaluate and learn, scale up and evaluate – keeping the big picture of national development agenda in mind, various programs have to be conceived. While implementing them, it is preferred to do a step by step approach so that the impact it creates can be assessed and next steps taken. This systematic approach helps to deal with the large scale departmental/ organizational change one step at a time – giving time for the implementors (government) and the users (stakeholders) to fine-tune, improvise and adapt to the new systems and processes

2

Historical Developments

National e-Governance Plan

Introduction

In this section, a brief but comprehensive history of e-Governance in India is presented. The seeds for e-Governance, not necessarily in the present form, have been sowed in India very early. The liberalization of electronic imports in the early 80s, setting up of National Informatics Centre (NIC) in 1977, providing connectivity between the State Capital and the district headquarters etc had been some initiatives in this context.

As the technology advanced and the society started moving towards Information and Communication Technology (ICT), different forward-looking state governments started some initiatives in this segment. One of the early birds was the State of Kerala that started the drive of one person per family to be 'ICT literate' (or e-literate). This was conceived and implemented in one of the districts and then later spread across all the districts to proliferate ICT awareness. The States of Gujarat, Andhra Pradesh (pre-bifurcation), Karnataka and others have embarked on their own ways, to bring about changes in the service delivery to citizens through electronic means by applying ICT. Several States followed suit.

Formation of NeGP Vision and launching of Mission Mode Projects (MMP)

In order to stream-line the initiatives that were largely in silos that were largely in silos and to bring in a unified approach, the government of India formulated the National e-Governance Plan (NeGP) driven by the department of information technology. Under its aegis, a vision statement was released in May 2006 and several initiatives were undertaken for its roll out.

The NeGP Vision states:

'Make all government services accessible to the common man in his locality, through common service delivery outlets and ensure efficiency, transparency and reliability of such services at affordable costs to realize the basic needs of the common man.'

As can be seen, the vision aims to reach the common citizen and provide government services with ease and transparency.

This NeGP Vision roll out had several associated actions. The government provided a common platform and had enabled several features that would be of immense use to the State governments for implementing their respective e-Governance plans and projects. In order to realize the Vision, 31 MMPs were also rolled out. These MMPs were chosen in such a way that they bring in the benefits to the stakeholders (mainly citizens and business houses) and cut across several departments or state governments. The list is presented in Table 1.[1]

The strategy to realize the vision of NeGP is stated briefly below.

- **Centralized Initiative, Decentralized Implementation:** The Government of India (GoI) set up the vision and created a slew of enabling infrastructure, so that the States may use them to develop their own projects on e-Governance. There was no mandate by the GoI specifically as to the projects to be initiated by the States. Several infrastructure aspects were provided by the government of India under the 'central

[1] http://meity.gov.in/content/mission-mode-projects

Table1 List of Mission Mode Projects taken up under NeGP

Central MMPs	State MMPs	Integrated MMPs
Banking	Agriculture	CSC
Central Excise & Customs	Commercial Taxes	e-Biz
Income Tax (IT)	e–District	e-Courts
Insurance	Employment Exchange	e-Procurement
MCA21	Land Records (NLRMP)	EDI For eTrade
Passport	Municipalities	National e-Governance Service Delivery Gateway
Immigration, Visa and Foreigners Registration & Tracking	e-Panchayats	India Portal
Pension	Police(CCTNS)	
e-Office	Road Transport	
Posts	Treasuries Computerization	
UID	PDS	
	Education	
	Health	

initiative' – namely State Data Centre (SDC) to be used for storage of data and hosting applications, State-Wide-Area-Network (SWAN) for connectivity, National Institute for Smart Government (NISG) for capacity building and training human resources etc. However, the choice of actual projects and their implementation were left to the specific State governments.

- **Focus on quality/speed of implementation of IT services**
  The state governments had to adopt methods to ensure quality of service and also implement the e-Governance services quickly. They were encouraged to use central quality control agencies like STQC (Standardization Testing and Quality Certification) for this purpose.
- **Delivery of services through Common Service Centres**
  In order to provide the government services to the citizens located far and wide, GoI envisaged centres or kiosks located close to the citizens – which means several such centres had to be set up. These centres have been named as Common Service Centres (CSCs) that provide a basket of services cutting across several departments of state and the central governments.
- **Ownership & role of line ministries/state governments**
  The projects have to be conceived, planned and executed by the respective departments or the ministries. They may be able to take assistance and guidance from the IT department but the ownership and budget need to be from the respective ministries.
- **Public-Private Partnerships as preferred business model**
  All projects require the resources – be it human expertise or funds to execute them. The demands placed on the government to provide the infrastructure and services at a fast pace are difficult to meet with limited resources. In order to get the developments going and exploit the expertise and competencies of the private industry, the involvement of private industry has been resorted to. This is called Public Private Partnership (PPP). One other reason for resorting to the PPP model of working is also for sharing the risks – thus reducing the negative impacts on the parties involved.
- **Connectivity up to block level through SWANs**
  The service delivery to the citizens have to be done using

ICT. One of the mandatory requirements is the internet connection to the cities and towns alike. While there is a fair amount of connectivity in large towns and cities, it is a challenge for small towns and villages. There was a concerted effort being taken to provide internet connectivity as a basic infrastructure to the block and village levels for ensuring service delivery through e-Governance.

Progress achieved through NeGP

With the specific focus on the NeGP, the government made significant investments. These have resulted in developments in various fronts. These are indicated below to get a historical perspective.

Common Service Centres (CSC)

- More than 100,000 tele-Centres in 600,000 villages
- Plan to have CSCs at all panchayat levels.
- Broadband internet enabled connectivity
- Implementation through PPP

State Wide Area Network (SWAN)

- Secured network for government work
- Connecting State HQs, District HQs, Blocks HQs
- Minimum 2 Mbps broadband connectivity

State Data Centres (SDC)

- State of art data centres at each of 35 States/UTs
- Housing all applications and databases
- e-Delivery of G2G, G2C and G2B services
- State Portals, State Service Delivery Gateways (SSDG)

Capacity Building Scheme (CB Scheme)

- Constituting State e–Mission Teams (SeMTs)
- Workshops for Political & Policy levels

- Specialized Training courses for Department level officers

Support for Mission Mode Projects

Besides all those described above, there is also enablement through policy, action framework and guidelines needed for the programs to progress. These have been provide for by the respective line departments or enabled by the Department of IT. The list of such departments and the support components they provided are indicated in Table 2.

#	Support Components	Line Ministry/Department
1.	Core Policies	Department of Information Technology
2.	Core Infrastructure (SWAN, NICNET, SDCs, etc.)	Department of Information Technology
3.	Support Infrastructure (CSCs, etc.)	Department of Information Technology
4.	Technical Assistance	Department of Information Technology
5.	Research & Development	Department of Information Technology
6.	Human Resource Development & Training	Department of Information Technology and Department of Administrative Reforms & Public Grievances
7.	Awareness & Assessment	Department of Information Technology and Department of Administrative Reforms & Public Grievances
8.	Organization structures	Department of Information Technology and Department of Administrative Reforms & Public Grievances

Table 2. Support Components and the respective Departments.

Thus by taking several concerted steps cutting across several areas, the Government of India embarked on the e-Governance journey right earnestly. These steps and the progress made thereof, have paved the way for the next Digital Revolution in the country.

3

Digital India

Introduction

As explained in the previous chapter, NeGP had been launched and sufficient focus was given to the electronic delivery of public services and there was spectacular progress across the nation. However there was a need to realign the overall program due to fast changing technology and the needs of the stakeholders involved. Thus a new 'avatar' was created for the e-Governance movement, brining several initiatives under an umbrella. This was named as Digital India.

'Digital India is a programme to transform India into a digitally empowered society and knowledge economy'.

It is aimed at preparing the country to become a digitally empowered society. The transformation is aimed to be achieved by combining the Indian Talent with Information Technology to make India Transformed (IT + IT = IT) for a better tomorrow. The transformational change is to be enabled by using technology in governance. It weaves together a large number of ideas and thoughts into a single, comprehensive vision so that each of them is seen as part of a larger goal. It is being coordinated by

Dept. of Electronics and IT (DeitY), implemented by the entire government – both at the centre and state. The weaving together makes the Mission transformative in totality.

Digital India

- Is the common branding of programs as it highlights their transformative impact
- Pulls together many existing schemes
- Restructures several schemes, gets them re-focused for implementation in a synchronized manner

Vision Areas

Digital India identifies three vision areas that cover the infrastructure, application of services and knowledge. The three areas identified are

1. Infrastructure as utility to every citizen
2. Governance and services on demand
3. Digital empowerment of citizens

The first vision area Infrastructure as utility proposes that people pay as per their use and it avoids the huge outflow of cash generally associated in large scale ICT programs. Thus the salient points are

- Storage and computing power using cloud
- High speed internet- Broadband and Mobile
- Unique digital identity- Aadhaar card
- Identity linked with mobile phone and bank account for ease of transactions
- Public Internet Access- Common Service Centre/Post Offices

These help the citizen access the government at ease with least effort. The governance and services on demand are at the core of digital India. It helps people to access the services of the government at their place and at their pace. The main elements in this are

- Services through online and mobile platforms
- Ease of doing business – either individually or as a business enterprise
- Financial transactions electronic and cashless

Many state governments have already embarked on this route and Digital India is only a catalyst to speed up the implementation. The third and final vision area of Digital India is digital empowerment of citizens. This helps to prepare the citizens for their 'digital life' which is inevitable. Though the main focus is educating the citizens on the use of these services, there is more to it as can be seen from the points below:

- Digital literacy and IT for Jobs
- Universally accessible digital resources
- Resources and services in Indian languages
- Collaborative digital platforms- (eg. MyGov)

The last point indicates that the citizens can voice their opinions on policy matters at the stage of the proposal itself to make it more appealing and applicable.

Nine Pillars of Digital India

In order to provide the necessary focus and to keep the implementation under track, the Digital India programs have been grouped under nine pillars. Obviously these pillars are related closely to the three vision areas that have been described earlier. The nine pillars of Digital India are depicted in Figure 1. A brief description of these pillar is attempted to provide a comprehensive understanding of the concepts. As can be seen from the description, each pillar has several program under implementation with strict target timelines and a department that is managing it.

Broadband highways is part of the infrastructure as utility vision area. This addresses the need of broadband highways for rural connectivity and broadband connectivity through virtual network connectivity for urban (new and existing). The nodal department implementing is Dept. of Telecommunications. The National Informatics Infrastructure needs to be provided across

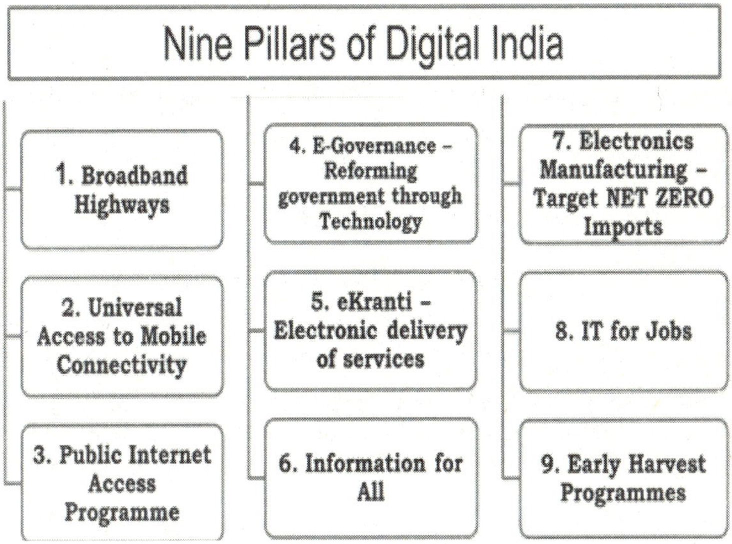

Figure 1. Nine Pillars of Digital India

the country which is addressed by Dept. of Electronics and IT. Universal access to mobile connectivity is the ongoing program to increase the penetration and spread of the mobile connectivity to the remaining villages. This program is managed by the Department of Telecommunication.

Public internet access program and rural internet connectivity is the next pillar. This aims to provide the accessibility to government and allied service across the country through common service centres and some post offices. In the long run, it is envisaged that post offices would become multi service centres. Under this scheme a total of 150,000 post offices are proposed to be converted into multi service centres. Department of Posts would be the nodal department to implement this scheme[1].

'e-Governance – reforming Governance through technology' aims to re-look at the processes of providing services with a view to optimize them for better customer experience. In essence process re-engineering (or simply process improvements) are being attempted followed by adopting them using ICT technology. Some of the steps being taken are simplification of forms, reduction of process steps keeping the core processes intact, use of online repositories for citizens, linking the Aadhaar identity to service provisioning ('aadhaar seeding'), integration of service platforms including mobile etc. All these are expected to provide a better and effective workflow, common data base and an effective grievance redressal system.

eKranti – the electronic delivery of services is at the centre of the Digital India movement. This is the link across the segments. Though this is not a totally new program, this program brings together the existing ones under one framework for planning, monitoring, tracking and ensuring that the benefits are realized. The major programs covered under the e-Kranti are use of technology for education, health, planning, agriculture, security, financial inclusion, justice department and so on. Several ongoing programs under NeGP have been regrouped or re-scoped for better monitoring and outcome.

There are 44 Mission Mode Projects under eKranti under various stages of development at the time of publication of this book. These are indicated in Figure 2[2].

Information for all, is an approach to have inclusive participation of the citizens in governance. At one end, it expects to provide all the information needed to the citizens and at the other end it also encourages them to participate in governance. The citizen participation in governance is enabled through

---

[1] http://pib.nic.in/newsite/efeatures.aspx?relid=115276

[2] http://www.digitalindia.gov.in/content/ekranti-electronic-delivery-services

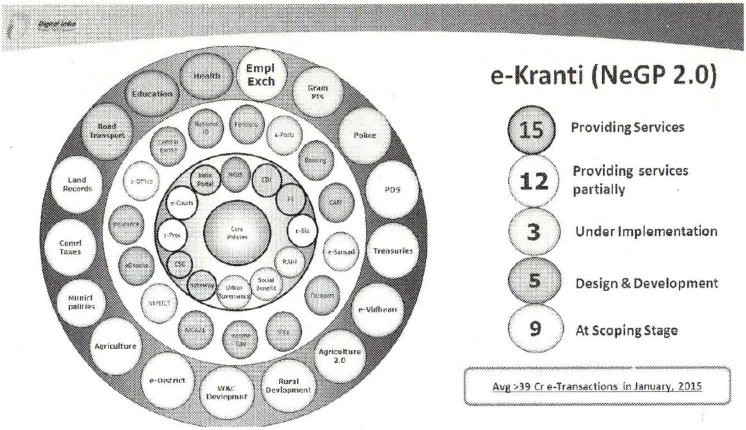

Figure 2. e-Kranti and Mission Mode Projects.

mobile apps and web based portals. There is also a process of engaging the citizens through mobile messaging on various developments and updates from time to time.

The next pillar is electronics manufacturing. This is an ambitious plan with an objective of net zero import of electronic items by 2020. The government targets to boost manufacturing of electronics within the country by creating a conducive environment to attract global and domestic investment in the Electronic System Design and Manufacturing (ESDM) sector. This is a program that encompasses several areas and sectors to increase the contribution to GDP from manufacturing sector. This involves initiatives like taxation incentives, providing economies of scale, ensuring ease of doing business in India, providing cost advantage etc. This aspect includes areas like fabrication at semiconductor chip level, satellite communication and mobile communication equipment, set top boxes, consumer electronics, smart energy meters, smart cards, micro ATM's and point of sale terminals and the like. On the human resources front, it has to address skill development and providing conducive environment for innovation and creativity by setting up incubators and accelerators.

In IT for jobs the focus is to upskill youth in the skills required for employment in IT and ITES industry. There are four components with specific scope of activities under this pillar:

(a) Train ten million students from smaller towns and villages for IT sector jobs over next five years

(b) BPOs (Business Process Outsourcing) to be set-up in north-eastern state to facilitate ICT enabled growth in these states

(c) Train three hundred thousand service delivery agents as part of skill development to run viable businesses delivering IT services

(d) DeitY (Department of Electronics and IT) has been designated as the nodal agency for all of the activities listed above

Early harvest programs is a different kind of pillar with a focus on achieving results quickly to create visibility and show success. There have been several quick shots that have been taken up and proved by the government. Some of them are listed below. The enlisting is not exhaustive though!

Biometric-based attendance system for government offices

Attendance of central government employees are marked through the biometric attendance system. The Biometric Attendance System (BAS) has been rolled out in almost all central government offices in Delhi with lakhs employees. Also, BAS is rolled out in 1,365 central government organizations outside Delhi involving over a hundred thousand employees. It is also rolled out in over half a dozen States across the country. While the application is simple to implement, the government of India has provided the platform in the cloud (Govt. of India cloud – Meghraj). This support has enabled the roll out quickly across the country.

Secure Email within government departments

The government e-mail infrastructure is being enhanced and upgraded. Thus in future e-mail to be primary mode of communication within the government. Under Phase I, upgradation of infrastructure has already been done for one million employees. Phase II to cover five million employees. DeitY is the nodal department for this scheme.

e-Greetings from government departments

The GoI has initiated the trend of e-Greeting trend against the earlier practice of paper greeting. E-Greetings portal has been started. The e-greetings are sourced using crowd-sourcing by the MyGov organization functioning under the DeITy.

Wi-Fi facility in all universities

All universities on the National Knowledge Network (NKN) shall be covered under this scheme. Wi Fi connectivity in Allahabad university has been approved as proof-of-concept and further action is being taken for execution of this project. Ministry of Human Resource Development (MHRD) is the nodal ministry for implementing this scheme.

Public Wi-Fi hotspots

Cities with a population of over 1 million and tourist centres would be provided with public Wi-Fi hotspots to promote digital cities. The identified Smart cities also would be provided with public wi-fi hotspots at specific places. This scheme to be implemented by DoT and Ministry of Urban Development (MoUD).

School books to become digital (eBooks)

The e-Basta has created a framework to convert all the school books into eBooks. Implemented as a portal, e-Basta brings together three classes of stakeholders with their respective roles

- Publishers can publish their e-content on the portal, for use by the schools.
- The schools can browse, select and compile their choice of resources from this pool, as a basta for different classes.
- Students can then download such bastas from the portal, and the schools can distribute them through media like SD cards, pen drives, etc.

Khoya-paya portal for tracking missing children

This is an attempt to help track the lost and found children. The portal will facilitate real time information gathering and sharing on the lost and found children and would go a long way to check crime and improve timely response.

The portal is being redesigned with ease of participation and use. It also support the mobile and web based portal formats. It has facility to integrate child services. Also use of social media to popularize the system/web portal is envisaged. The DeitY and Department of Women and Child Development (DoWCD) have been identified as the nodal departments under this.

Thus the early harvest program, had utilized the 'low hanging' fruits to prove the possibilities of using technology for the benefits of the citizens and other stakeholders.

Program management structure

A massive program of this magnitude needs not only vision and strategy but also a meticulous plan to execute. That would ensure the success and the realization of benefits to the intended stakeholders. As can be expected, the program governance is headed by the Hon'ble Prime Minister of India with appropriate levels of miniseries and bureaucrats nominated. A brief description and a pictorial representation of the program management structure is given in Figure 3. The representation of the institutional mechanism and the description that follows is as given by Dept. of IT[3]

A monitoring committee on Digital India under the chairpersonship of Prime Minister which was constituted with representation drawn from relevant ministries/departments to provide leadership, prescribe deliverables and milestones, and monitor periodically the implementation of the Digital India programme.

---

[3] http://www.digitalindia.gov.in/content/management-structure

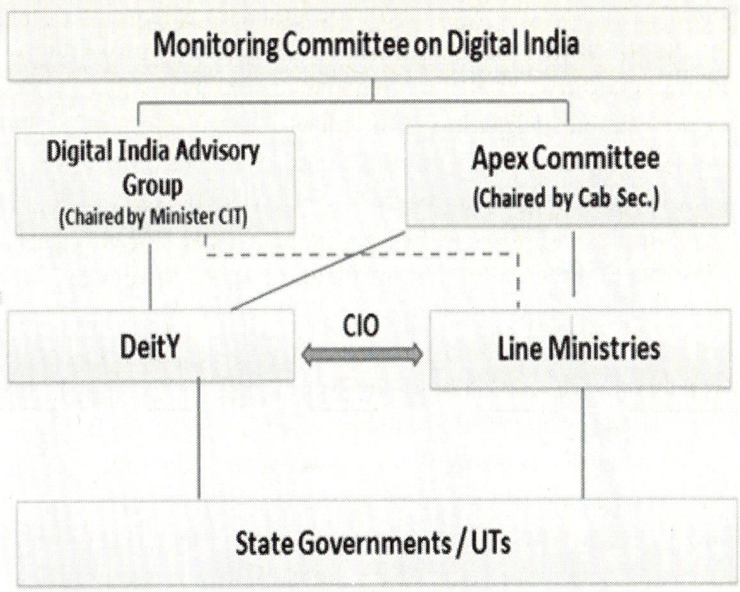

Figure 3. Institutional Mechanism at National Level to Manage the Digital India Program.

A Digital India advisory group headed by the minister of communications and IT to solicit views of external stakeholders and to provide inputs to the monitoring committee on Digital India, advise the government on policy issues and strategic interventions necessary for accelerating the implementation of the Digital India programme across central and state government ministries/departments. The composition of the advisory group would include representation from the planning commission and eight to nine representatives from states/UTs and other line ministries/departments on a rotational basis.

An apex committee headed by the cabinet secretary would be overseeing the programme and providing policy and strategic directions for its implementation and resolving inter-ministerial issues. In addition it would harmonize and integrate diverse initiatives and aspects related to integration of services, end to end process re-engineering and service levels of MMPs and other initiatives under the Digital India programme, wherever required.

Expenditure Finance Committee (EFC)/Committee on Non Plan Expenditure (CNE) to financially appraise/ approve projects as per existing delegation of financial powers. The EFC/ CNE headed by secretary expenditure would also be recommending to the CCEA the manner in which MMPs/eGovernance initiatives are to be implemented, as well as the financial terms of participation for states. A representative of the planning commission would also be included in both the EFC and CNE.

A council of mission leaders on Digital India headed by secretary, DeitY would be established as a platform to share the best practices in various existing and new eGov initiatives under Digital India and also to sensitize various government departments about ICT projects of DeitY. While the inter-departmental, integration and interoperable issues of integrated projects / eGovernance initiatives would be resolved by the apex committee on Digital India headed by cabinet secretary, the technical issues of integrated projects would be resolved by the council of mission leaders.

Further, considering the scope of the Digital India Programme and the need to look at issues such as overall technology architecture, framework, standards, security policy, funding strategy, service delivery mechanism, sharing of common infrastructure etc. at a programme level, it is proposed that the technical appraisal of all Digital India projects be done by DeitY, prior to a project being placed before the EFC/ CNE. This appraisal would cover issues relating to inclusion of adoption of standards, utilization of cloud and mobile platforms, consideration of security aspects, etc. The secretary, DeitY or his representative may also be included as a standing special invitee to all EFC/CNE meetings, which are appraising/approving MMPs. It may be mentioned that the DeitY has already set up a programme management unit, namely National e-Governance Division (NeGD) to provide support to departments in conceptualizing, developing, appraising, implementing and monitoring respective MMPs / eGovernance initiatives.

Institutional mechanism of Digital India at state level would be headed by state committee on Digital India by the Chief Minister. State/UT apex committees on Digital India headed by chief secretaries would be constituted at state/UT level to allocate required resources, set priority amongst projects and resolve inter-departmental issues at state level.

Since the "e-Kranti: National eGovernance Plan 2.0" is already integrated with Digital India programme, the existing programme management structure established for National eGovernance Plan at both national and state level had also been decided to be integrated appropriately with the programme management structure of Digital India programme at national and state/UT level

Progress on Digital India program

A program of this nature requires a constant monitoring and guidance form the powers that be. With specific focus on developmental efforts, there has been a rapid progress on several fronts on Digital India programs. The following paragraphs give a gist of the progress at the time of writing this book. (For the actual progress anytime, please refer to the website of government of India).

- Launch of the MyGov.in portal, with more than 1.9 million citizens interacting on it.
- Establishment of BharatNet for the distribution of broadband connectivity, using fibre cable technology. BharatNet aims to connect 2,50,000 gram panchayats across India. As per this scheme, the OFC pipe laid (till July 2016) is around 1,40,742 km (against 2,292 km in 2014), while the OFC fibre laid is approximately 1,12,871 km (against 358 km in 2014). It has offered optical fibre connectivity to around 48,199 gram panchayats so far.

- This campaign has managed to make the internet reach out to around 40 crore Indian citizens, while the number of broadband users has increased to 12.088 crore.
- Out of the 40,000 WiFi hotspots planned by Bharat Sanchar Nigam Limited (BSNL) for important locations across India, it has managed to commission around 2,504 WiFi hotspots at 1,227 locations.
- The number of Common Service Centres (CSCs) has risen from 80,000 (before this digital movement) to around 1,66,000.
- Digitisation of around 21,319 post offices has occurred, out of a target of 1,55,000 post offices.
- Training of 5.5 million people under the digital literacy programme and allotment of INR 6 crores for the programme, during the last budget.
- Enrolment of 1.5 million pensioners onto the biometric-enabled digital service, Jeevan Pramaan.
- Initiation of the e-sign framework to digitally sign documents.
- BSNL to undertake large-scale deployment of WiFi hotspots across India.
- Introduction of the Unified Payment Interface (UPI) by National Payments Corporation of India (NPCI) to enable citizens to carry out instant push and pull transactions without issues.
- Launch of an exclusive job portal dedicated to the differently abled people.
- Kick start of Mahila-e-Haat programme and encouragement of aspiring women entrepreneurs.
- Introduction of free "mobile TV" by a public broadcaster, Doordarshan, to air free TV content on mobile

phones across 16 cities initially (without any internet connection).

- According to the World Bank's doing business 2016 report, India has raised its rank by 12 places from rank 142 (in 2015) to rank 130 (in 2016), showcasing tremendous improvement rarely seen in an economy as large as India's and within such a short timeframe. The two major contributors towards this improvement in rank for India have been the greater ease of starting a business (through the elimination of the minimum capital requirement and the need of a certificate to start business operations) as well as greater availability of electricity.
- The extensive use of the eBiz portal (India's single window government to business online platform) helped to provide more eGovernance services on demand. The portal offers more than 16 services, against the 12 that it offered initially (as of April 2017). It has contributed to reducing the average time it takes to start a business in India.

The Digital journey has just begun and there is a visible change across several segments in the country. Given the size and diversity of India, it is a matter of time before the Digital Governance becomes an everyday affair and touches almost every sphere of life and livelihood of the citizens.

4

State Enterprise Architecture

Introduction

It is important and beneficial to have a view of the government as an enterprise, and that too a connected enterprise. The government is constituted by several departments and ministries that provide services to its stakeholders. In the current scenario each of them act as an independent pillar with their own data bases. This leads to avoidable duplication of stake-holder's data and more importantly, not interlinking of departments for leveraging the service provisioning in better ways. Thus the need is to build a comprehensive business-driven blueprint of the entire government. The main purpose and outcome of such a step would be to identify opportunities to leverage technology to-

- Reduce redundancy– of data among multiple departments of the state
- Facilitate horizontal (cross-departmental) and vertical (state and central governments) information sharing.

Enterprise Architecture (EA) is a well-defined practice for conducting enterprise analysis, design, planning, and implementation, using a holistic approach at all times, for the successful development and execution of strategy. Enterprise architecture applies architecture principles and practices to guide organizations through the business, information, process, and technology changes necessary to execute their strategies. These practices utilize the various aspects of an enterprise to identify, motivate, and achieve these changes.[1]

The following paragraphs detail the enterprise architecture in general initially and then bring in the context of government services into the fold and how it is connected.

UN Five-stage Evolution Model

The evolution of service provisioning by governments, as per UN-ASPA[2] may be depicted as given in Figure1. A brief explanation follows.

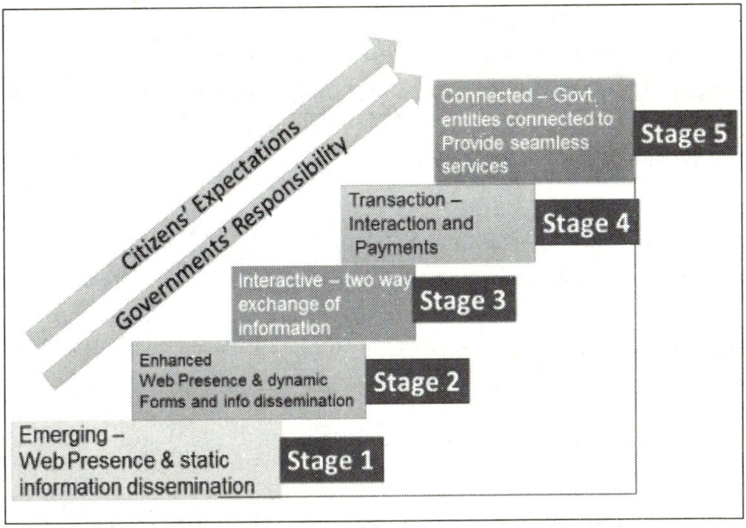

Figure 1. Five stage Evolution Model of e-Governance.

---

[1] Federation of EA Professional Organizations, Common Perspectives on Enterprise Architecture, Architecture and Governance Magazine, Issue 9-4, November 2013 (2013). Retrieved on November 19, 2013.

[2] unpan1.un.org/intradoc/groups/public/documents/unpan/unpan037470.pdf

Stage I-Emerging: A government's online presence is mainly comprised of web page and/or an official website; the links to service providing ministries or departments may/may not exist. Much of the information is static and there is little interaction with citizens.

Stage II-Enhanced: governments provide more information on public policy and governance. They have created links to archived information that is easily accessible to citizens, as for instance, documents, forms, reports, laws and regulations, and newsletters.

Stage III-Interactive: governments deliver online services such as downloadable forms for tax payments and applications for license renewals. In addition, the beginnings of an interactive portal or website with services are evident.

Stage IV-Transactional: governments begin to transform themselves by introducing two-way interactions between 'citizen and government'. It includes options for paying taxes, applying for ID cards, birth certificates, passports and license renewals, as well as other similar G to C interactions, and allows the citizen to access these services online 24/7. All transactions are conducted online.

Stage V-Connected: governments transform themselves into a connected entity that responds to the needs of its citizens by developing an integrated back office infrastructure. This is characterized by:

1. Horizontal connections (among government agencies)
2. Vertical connections (central and local government agencies)
3. Infrastructure connections (interoperability issues)
4. Connections between governments and citizens
5. Connections among stakeholders (government, private sector, academic institutions, NGOs and civil society)

Thus, in this case, ICT-based connected governance efforts are aimed at improved cooperation between governmental agencies, allowing for an enhanced, active and effective consultation and engagement with citizens, and greater involvement with multi-stakeholders regionally and internationally. It concludes that "An effective connected government is about a 'bigger and better' front-end with a 'smaller and smarter' back-end. This is nothing but the slogan of "minimum government with maximum governance".

Enterprise architecture defined

According to TOGAF (The Open Group Enterprise Architecture) Enterprise is - as any collection of organizations that has a common set of goals. For example, an enterprise could be a government agency, a whole corporation, a division of a corporation, a single department, or a chain of geographically distant organizations linked together by common ownership.

Need of an enterprise architecture

In order to understand this in a better manner, a look at how companies make use of it, will help. In general, the purpose of enterprise architecture is to optimize across the enterprise, the otherwise generally, fragmented legacy of systems and processes (both manual and automated) into an integrated environment. This is mainly to make it responsive to changing needs and be supportive of the delivery of the business strategy. Today's CEOs know that the effective management and exploitation of information through IT is a key factor to business success, and an indispensable means to achieve competitive advantage. Enterprise architecture addresses this need to a large extent.

Also, a good enterprise architecture enables the company to achieve the right balance between IT efficiency and business innovation. It allows individual business units to innovate safely in their pursuit of competitive advantage, while ensuring the needs of the organization for an integrated IT strategy are met. This also permits the closest possible synergy across the extended enterprise.

A more efficient business operation results in the following generally

- Lower business operation costs
- More agile organization – ability to adapt to changing needs
- Business capabilities shared across the organization
- Lower change management costs
- More flexible workforce
- Improved business productivity

A more efficient IT operation

- Lower software development, support and maintenance costs
- Increased portability of applications across divisions
- Improved interoperability and easier system and network management
- Improved ability to address critical enterprise-wide issues (like security)
- Easier upgrade and exchange of system components
- Better return on existing investment, reduced risk for future investment
- Reduced complexity in business and IT
- Maximum return on investment in the existing business and IT infrastructure
- The flexibility to make, buy or out-source business and IT solutions
- Reduced risk overall in new investments and their cost of ownership

Conceptually, there are four architecture domains that are commonly accepted as subsets of overall enterprise architecture,

- The business architecture defines the business strategy, governance, organization, and key business processes.
- The data architecture describes the structure of an organization's logical and physical data assets and data management resources
- The application architecture provides a blueprint for the individual applications to be deployed, their interactions, and their relationships to the core business processes of the organization
- The technology architecture describes the logical software and hardware capabilities that are required to support the deployment of business, data, and application services. This includes IT infrastructure, middleware, networks, communications, processing, standards, etc

Information and services interoperability

Interoperability is defined as

1. The ability to share information and services among various entities
2. The ability of two or more systems or components to exchange and use information, as needed
3. The ability of systems to provide and receive services from other systems and to use the services so interchanged to enable them to operate effectively together

There are four degrees of interoperability as follows

- **Degree 1:** Unstructured data exchange. It is the exchange of human-interpretable unstructured data. Example: the free text found in operational estimates, analysis, and papers
- **Degree 2:** Structured data exchange. This is the

exchange of human-interpretable structured data intended for manual and/or automated handling, but requires manual compilation, receipt, and/or message dispatch

- **Degree 3:** Seamless sharing of data involves the automated sharing of data amongst systems based on a commonly defined exchange model
- **Degree 4:** Seamless sharing of information is an extension of degree 3 to the universal interpretation of information through data processing based on co-operating applications

These degrees should be further refined and made technically meaningful for each of the degrees. An example refinement of degree 3 with four sub classifications follows

- 3A: Formal message exchange
- 3B: Common data exchange
- 3C: Complete data exchange
- 3D: Real-time data exchange

The intent is to specify the detailed degrees of interoperability to the requisite level of detail so that they are technically meaningful. These degrees are very useful for specifying the way that information has to be exchanged among the various systems and provide critical direction to the projects implementing the systems.

Service Oriented Architecture

Service orientation is a way of thinking in terms of services and service-based development and the outcomes of services. Service Oriented Architecture (SOA) is an architectural style that mainly supports service orientation. It has the following distinctive features

- It is based on the design of the services — which

mirror real-world business activities—comprising of the enterprise (or inter-enterprise) business processes

- Service representation utilizes business descriptions to provide context (i.e., business process, goal, rule, policy, service interface, and service component) and implements services using service orchestration
- It places unique requirements on the infrastructure —it is recommended that implementations use open standards to realize interoperability and location transparency
- Implementations are environment-specific—they are constrained or enabled by context and must be described within that context
- It requires strong governance of service representation and implementation

As the operating environment becomes more sophisticated, the challenges facing government departments are shifting away from questions of efficiency and automation towards questions of complexity management and agility. Complex webs of existing applications and interfaces create highly complex landscapes where change becomes more and more difficult and the impacts of change become harder to predict and understand. The concept of SOA provides an architectural style that is specifically intended to simplify the operations and the interconnection of different parts of that operations.

By standardizing the behavior and interoperation of services, it is possible to limit the impacts of change and also to understand, in advance, the likely chain of impacts. From a software development perspective, SOA focuses on structuring applications in a way that facilitates system flexibility and agility —a necessity in today's complex and fast-moving environment. SOA aims to break down traditional application silos into portfolios of more granular services that operate in open and interoperable ways, while extracting commodity capability into a virtualized infrastructure platform of shared re-usable utility services.

Based on the aforesaid discussions, it is only natural for the government to pursue enterprise architecture to enhance service orientation. The state of Andhra Pradesh has embarked on this journey already and the following pages describe the details of the effort from this state.

Example–How does this help in reality

In order to drive the point home, an example is presented here. This is to enhance the understanding and much more detailing may have to be done to actually implement this.

Each citizen has several interfaces with the state and central government departments. For example, an average person having a house property, a vehicle, and is residing in a city is 'represented' or 'recorded' in these departments–by way of name, address, specific number for the property or vehicle or utility meter connection by the respective departments (namely transport, electricity, water etc). There is no linking of these data bases and all these remain independently across these department. Thus a person who is a defaulter with one department of the state continues to receive all the other benefits from the other departments. For instance, if the person has not paid the property tax, but applies for a No Objection Certificate (NOC) to transfer the ownership of vehicle, he would still get this from transport department. This is because, there is no connection or interface between the revenue / local body with the transport department. While there is loss of revenue to the state department (by way of property tax for this property) and still provides services (giving NOC for ownership transfer) to a defaulting citizen.

With the introduction of state enterprise architecture and use of Aadhaar identification, the citizen is 'linked' across all the departments by the unique identification. This helps to not only verify the credentials, but also to look into such anomalies. In effect such a step would help the state and central governments to ensure the dues are collected in time and the intentional or unintentional laps are plugged to a large extent.

On the other hand, if a citizen has been paying all the dues in time and has been compliant to the statutory regulations at all times, the state government can make them as golden citizens–this is possible thru tracking the payments using Aadhaar. Such citizens may be treated with utmost dignity and care when they reach out to any department of the government for any service. This is similar to the frequent flier program of airlines or loyalty program operated by several corporates for their customers. It is time, the governments treat citizens and businesses as their customers and provide those services. This kind of steps may also motivate the so called defaulters to adhere to the norms. All these steps will increase revenue and put the resources needed for the development agenda of the Nation in the hands of the government.

In essence, the state enterprise architecture and the unique identification number of the citizen will enable the interoperability of various departments and provide seamless services to the stakeholders–mainly citizen.

Case Study–Pilot implementation of enterprise architecture in the state of Andhra Pradesh*

Enterprise architecture is a framework for conducting analysis, design, planning and implementation of the vision, goals, strategies, functions, activities and desired outcomes of an enterprise, using a holistic approach at all times, such that the IT infrastructure and IT services are always aligned

* The following information is based on the publications from the newly formed state of Andhra Pradesh on Enterprise Architecture. The information is provided here to serve as one reference and example of implementation. There may be other possible variation as the scenario evolves and the situation demands.

to the business strategies and business services, through standardization and integration. Enterprise architecture is quite relevant to government in so far as government is an 'Enterprise of Enterprises.

The benefits that are envisaged by the state by adopting a good enterprise architecture include

- Efficiency
- Productivity
- Interoperability
- Integration
- Simplicity
- Agility
- Cost-effectiveness
- Value-for-Money
- Sustainability
- Flexibility
- Industry-friendliness

The Vision of the AP State Enterprise Architecture (AP-SEA) is elaborate and addresses several aspects. However the following dimensions are relevant

Citizen-centric

- Citizens and businesses shall have a seamless and smooth interface with the government
- Departments and agencies of the government shall be able to interoperate with ease and provide integrated services to the citizens and businesses
- The medium of paper for interactions and correspondence should be reduced to the minimum in all the G2C, C2G, G2B, B2G and G2G areas

Inclusive

- Digital divide shall be adequately addressed, especially leveraging the mobile technologies
- APSEA should enhance the realization of participative and inclusive governance
- Citizen engagement should be accomplished with ease and cost-effectiveness

Technological

- Government and citizens shall be enabled to take advantage of the cutting-edge technologies like Social Media, Mobile, Analytics and Cloud (SMAC) currently and those that emerge in future
- The principles of open data, open standards and open APIs shall be ingrained in all the system development effort
- Above all, the framework should ensure the right balance between information security and privacy of personal data

The dimensions addressed by the state include the following four areas.

- The business architecture, which defines the Governance goals, organization, and key processes
- The data architecture, which describes the structure of the logical and physical data assets and data management resources
- The application architecture, which provides a blueprint for the individual applications to be deployed, their interactions, and their relationships to the core government processes
- The technology architecture, which describes the software and hardware capabilities required to realize

the eGov vision, like IT infrastructure, middleware, networks, communications and standards

Architecture principles applied

Architecture principles are a set of guidelines that reflect consensus across the enterprise. They govern the development, maintenance, and use of the enterprise architecture. A good set of architecture principles has the following five qualities:

1. Understandable
2. Robust
3. Complete
4. Consistent
5. Stable

Organization principles applied that relate to the architecture

Primacy of Principles: These principles of information management apply to all organizations within the government.

Maximize benefit to the government as a whole: All decisions relating to information management are made to provide maximum benefit to the government as a whole. Some organizations may have to concede their own preferences for the greater benefit of the entire government. Applications and components should be shared across organizational boundaries.

Information management is everybody's business: EA is an Architecture of Architectures. All organizations in the government participate in information management decisions needed to accomplish business objectives, and implement such decisions with full commitment, devoting the right and adequate resources. APSEA has a federated structure. It will focus on guidelines, mandates, standards, interoperability and integration. The option of designing

APSEA as a single, monolithic architecture is infeasible and hence rejected. Respective domain owners and managers shall develop their own sub-architectures following these principles, and federate the same to APSEA.

Common Use of Applications: Development of applications used across the government is preferred over the development of similar or duplicative applications, which are only specific to a particular department or organization.

Service Orientation: The enterprise architecture is based on a design of services which mirror real-world activities required to conduct the business of government. Service orientation places unique requirements on the infrastructure, and implementations should use open standards to realize interoperability and location transparency.

Data Principles

Data is an Asset: Data is an asset that has a specific and measurable value to the government and is to be managed accordingly.

Data is Shared: Users have access to the data necessary to perform their duties; therefore, data is shared across enterprise functions and organizations. It is less costly to maintain timely, accurate data in a single application, and then share it, than it is to maintain duplicative data in multiple applications. Shared data will result in faster and improved decisions since we will rely on fewer sources (ultimately one virtual source, i.e the single source of truth) of more accurate and timely managed data for our decision-making.

Data Trustee: Each data element has a trustee accountable for data quality. As the degree of data sharing Grows and departments rely upon common information, it becomes essential that only the data trustee makes decisions about the content of data, and authorizes its modification.

Information should be captured electronically once and immediately validated as close to the source as possible. Quality control measures must be implemented to ensure the integrity of the data.

Common Vocabulary and Data Definitions: Data is defined consistently throughout government, and the definitions are understandable and available to all users. Defining Metadata and Data Standards (MDDS) within each domain assumes great significance.

Data Security: Data is protected from unauthorized use and disclosure. In addition to the traditional aspects of national security classification, this includes, but is not limited to protection of pre-decisional, sensitive, source selection-sensitive, and proprietary information. Open sharing of information and the publication of information as per extant legislation must be balanced against the need to restrict the availability of classified, proprietary and sensitive information.

Application Principles

Technology Independence: Applications are independent of specific technology choices and therefore can operate on a variety of technology platforms.

Ease of Use: Applications are easy to use. The underlying technology is transparent to users, so they can concentrate on tasks at hand. Standards on Usability should be adhered to while developing applications. Conformance to the Guidelines on Universal Electronic Accessibility shall be ensured.

Technology Principles

Requirements-Based change: Only in response to process/ service needs are changes to applications and technology made – changes were not made just for the sake of it!

Control technical diversity: Technological diversity is controlled to minimize the non-trivial cost of maintaining expertise in and connectivity between multiple processing environments. Policies, standards and procedures that govern acquisition of technology must be tied directly to this principle.

Interoperability: Software and hardware should conform to defined standards that promote interoperability for data, applications, and technology. Standards help ensure consistency, thus improving the ability to manage systems and improve user satisfaction, and protect existing IT investments, thus maximizing return-on-investment and reducing costs. Standards for interoperability additionally help ensure support from multiple vendors for their products, and facilitate supply chain integration. A process for setting standards, reviewing and revising them periodically, and granting exceptions must be established.

Enterprise Business Architecture

Business Architecture describes the service strategy, and the organizational, functional, process, information, and geographic aspects of the business environment. In the context of e-Governance, the term business architecture can be interpreted as the collage of relationships between government and Citizens (G2C and C2G), government and Businesses (G2B and B2G), government and its Employees (G2E and E2G) and the internal processes of government itself (G2G). Given that a government is an enterprise of enterprises, these relationships and interfaces can number several hundreds.

Any government is characterized by certain quantitative and qualitative parameters that describe the nature and depth of the aforesaid relationships and interfaces. The task of the business architect is, therefore, to assess the current status of such relationships (both in quantitative and qualitative measures) and design a business architecture that seeks to transform all the relationships/ interfaces or a prioritized subset of the same.

Macro-level Business Architecture

In an enterprise of enterprises that a government is, there are several functions, activities, services and applications (together called 'artifacts' for this purpose) that are exactly identical or similar or comparable across the various enterprises. Hence a macro-view of the business architecture of the government would give us a chance to identify such artifacts and to transform them together, deploy them as common applications using the principles of cloud and shared resources, and also to optimize the effort, time and cost to develop them.

An illustrative list of such common and/or cross-cutting applications and artefacts is given below

A1 Applications/ Artefacts Common across the government

- Human Resource Management System
- Financial Management System
- e-Procurement
- Management of Logistics for governance
- Asset Management
- Litigation Management
- e-mail, video-conferencing and Calendar services
- Electronic workflow (e-Office)
- State Portal
- Right to Information
- Right to time-bound Services
- Identity Management for Employees
- Access Management Systems
- Attendance Monitoring Systems
- Employee Health Insurance

- Identity of Citizens for Delivery of Services/benefits
- e-Service Delivery Infrastructure
- Payment Gateway
- Mobile Gateway
- Information Security Management System
- Data Centre Services
- Cloud Services
- Wide Area Networks
- LAN and WiFi Services
- Cyber Security
- Knowledge Management (for public sector employees)
- Grievance Management System

A2 Applications Common across groups of departments

- Social Benefits Management System
- Enterprise Project Portfolio Management
- Urban Land Management System
- Agricultural Land Management System
- GIS-based Systems
- Location-based Services
- Name-based Systems
- Sector Promotion Services
- Educational Institutions Management System
- Content Management System

A3 Cross-cutting Applications

- House Building Permission
- e-Biz - Single-window clearances for setting up business/ industry

- Registration of Land-related deeds
- Nutrition Programs for women and children
- Agricultural loans& insurance
- Integrated Criminal Justice System
- Disaster/ Emergency Management Systems
- Government Land Management System

Micro-level Business Architecture

A number of micro-level business decisions or resolutions, illustrated below, play a critical role in developing the Business Architecture

1. Business Process Re-engineering (BPR or simply process improvements) for all the 3 categories of applications listed in the previous section shall be done in a generic/ cross-cutting manner so as to optimize the benefits to all the targeted stakeholders/ users. The BPR teams shall deal with the related departments, forms and processes simultaneously so as to normalize the processes across all the agencies. Elimination, Simplification, Optimization, Workflow Automation, Self-Service and Integration shall be the thumb rules for such a process transformation.

2. The well-established concepts like single-sign-on, digital signatures, and emerging technologies like SMAC (Social networking-Mobile-Analytics-Cloud) should be taken advantage of in all possible ways, following the practice of technology-led innovation.

3. The concept of Mobile-First shall be observed religiously while designing any service or Re-designing an existing service.

4. All processes, and more so the complex processes, shall be broken down to their elemental components. Such

Elemental Government Processes (EGPs), which may not number more than twenty across all the processes of government, shall be re-engineered and transformed to be highly efficient and transparent, so that transforming the more complex processes becomes automatic and trivial.

5. Customer-centric design, efficiency, convenience and service orientation shall dictate the way BPR is done. This is more relevant for design of online forms, workflows, service centres, payment systems, customer feedback systems etc. Citizen Services should be customized to suit the profile of different categories and classes of citizens, like Students, Farmers, Business People, Self-Helf Groups, and Pensioners.
6. Governance should be modeled around the end-to-end holistic lifecycle processes for the governed entities i.e. birth to death for citizens encompassing all the services that a citizen avails, initiation to closure for commercial establishments etc
7. A quick secondary research on the best practices in the areas identified for BPR, is recommended.
8. Service levels and performance metrics shall be recommended for each service/process, duly benchmarking against the best in the world.
9. Standard Business Modelling techniques, most suited to each domain must be adopted for documenting the re-engineered processes, each assigned an enterprise-wide Code.
10. BPR at the granular level of EGP and at the business process/service level shall be enforced uniformly and consistently in all works relating to system development and implementation.

11. Every process/service shall be delivered in multiple channels, giving a wide variety of choice to the end users. The axiom of Mobile First should guide this effort.

Enterprise Data Architecture

Data is to an information system as the blood is to the body!

- Data should be pure and shall remain pure always
- Data should circulate among the entities as freely as possible, following the principle of seamless access to all those authorized to use it.
- All data should conform to the data definition standards notified, so as to promote interoperability and to minimize the ETL efforts.
- A well-designed data governance model should be put in place, specifying the 'owners' and 'users' of each dataset.
- Above all, data should be secure from loss, corruption, unauthorized access, theft and misuse.

Data architecture is, by far, the most critical component of the Enterprise Architecture, in so far as data leads to information and to knowledge and is the basis of providing any service in the digital world. Government, seen as an enterprise of enterprises, has some unique characteristics around the data it holds:

- Large in size and Large number of datasets
- Complex and diverse
- Interdependent
- Sensitive
- Held by innumerable entities
- Most sought-after
- Requiring a long shelf-life
- Dynamic

As a result of the above unique characteristics, designing the enterprise data architecture for the government is quite involved. Therefore, the creation, storage, transportation, updation, archival protection and management of data should be founded on sound data principles.

The following additional principles shall be observed while designing the enterprise data architecture:

1. Data architecture should rest on a group of carefully identified core datasets. The core datasets are those, which contain data elements that occur most commonly used in the applications of several enterprises of the government. These are, the data elements that describe the attributes of:

a. Parcels of land–urban and agricultural

b. People

c. Establishments

d. Employees

e. Geospatial data

f. Things (as in Internet of Things)

In view of the seminal importance and critical nature of the core datasets, they need to be defined, standardized, collected, protected and maintained with utmost care and detail. The schema for the Core Databases are to be designed with equal care. Especially, it is to be noted that the Aadhaar Database has a national footprint, and is increasingly becoming the de facto standard for identification of people. The government of Andhra Pradesh had created a State Resident Data Hub (SRDH), as a mirror image of the Aadhar database. Due credence has to be given to the SRDH, while defining the Core Dataset relating to People.

2. Enterprise Master Data is next in importance. Master data is relatively invariant data, which is used to identify geographic locations, entities, and all kinds of information, which can be

represented as a standard code. The number of master datasets can be quite large for an enterprise like the government, as it relates to/emanates from the functions of various sectors or departments. A singular and integrated/joint effort has to be made across the government agencies to locate, identify and/or create master data for each domain, like health, education, infrastructure, energy and transportation. The following precautions have to be taken, while defining the master datasets

a. The master datasets already defined at the international level (like country codes, ICD Codes, etc) and the national level (Like the Census Codes, Postal Zip Codes etc) shall be adopted as they are.

b. The master datasets already notified by the Govt. of India of India, and the government of AP shall be taken cognizance of.

3. In view of the core nature and critical architectural importance of the core datasets and the master datasets, the following additional precautions need to be taken in their management.

a. The metadata relating to both should be positioned in the enterprise architecture artifact repository.

b. The ownership and management responsibilities of these datasets should be clearly defined and enforced.

c. Modifications to the datasets shall be permitted only in a fully controlled manner with appropriate audit trails.

d. Special security arrangements shall be made to protect the core and master data.

e. Disaster recovery and business continuity plans for both these datasets should be planned carefully and on a priority.

4. Domain Databases: In addition to the core and critical datasets specified above, it is necessary to identify the important databases of all domains, departments and agencies that are

essentially required to build the applications specified in section on business architecture. For each of the identified databases, a database schema needs to be prepared. A schema is the definition of a collection of database objects viz, the tables, fields, relationships, views, indices, packages, procedures, functions, queues, triggers, types, sequences, materialized views, synonyms, database links and directories. When the APSEA is being detailed, the schemas for all the core datasets, the master datasets and the domain databases need to be specified, duly considering the definitions and structures of the existing databases and schemas, and normalizing them across the domain or across the government as the case may be.

Data Models: In order that we derive the maximum benefit out of the EA effort, significant attention has to be paid to the design of a comprehensive data model that incorporates all the architecture principles stated in this document. Appropriate data models shall be designed at all the 3 levels viz, the conceptual data models, the logical data models and the Physical data models.

Other important artefacts of Database Architecture: In addition to the above architecture work, it is necessary for the Enterprise Architect to design the following artefacts in relation to the database architecture:

a. Data Access Model: This model defines the principles on which access rights shall be given to different roles in the database administration. These rights shall be defined precisely in respect of all the core datasets and master datasets.

b. Data Lifecycle Model: This model defines the standard processes for the creation, maintenance, updation, archival and deletion of data, with a special emphasis and detail in relation to the Core Datasets and the Master Datasets.

c. Data Security Model: This model defines the types of

controls (per ISO 27005) that need to be incorporated in the design of various databases, so as to ensure conformance to the highest standards of security. The ISMS should be clearly articulated in respect of all the core datasets and the master datasets.

d. Data Migration Model: When an existing application is replaced, there will be a critical need to migrate data (master, transactional, and reference) to the new application. The data architecture should identify data migration requirements and also provide indicators as to the level of transformation, weeding, and cleansing that will be required to present data in a format that meets the requirements and constraints of the target application.

Metadata: Metadata is 'data about data'. It occupies a pivotal role in the design of data architecture. A well-designed, standards-based metadata repository is an invaluable asset to application developers. To this end, the Enterprise Architect shall design metadata for the APSEA. Domain specific metadata standards and Dublin Core Standard shall be adopted for this.

Target Data Architecture: The data architecture designed keeping in view all the above principles as also the architectural vision, shall provide a holistic view of how the business objectives and vision set out in this document will be realized. Since the legacy systems, numbering hundreds across the government had been designed and implemented over a period of a decade, and as such, consist of different technologies, platforms, data models with differing levels of rigor in observing the database principles, migration to the target data architecture can be quite a complex process. Besides this, it entails a great degree of change management effort, as the organizations resist any major changes in such a fundamental thing as data structure. The enterprise architect has therefore, to create appropriate plans of data migration and change management in close coordination with the major stakeholders.

Issues in creation and maintenance of core data: Implementation of the concept of Core Data is fraught with several problems, and raises several issues, which needed to be anticipated and addressed. These are in the nature of the Source and Ownership of Core Data, Data Standards, Maintenance of the Core Data in as pure a form, Authenticity and legal status of the Core Data etc.

Enterprise Application Architecture

An application architecture describes the structure and behaviour of applications used in an enterprise, focused on how they interact with each other and with users. This involves defining the interaction between application packages, databases, and middleware systems in terms of functional coverage. Application architecture seeks to manage how multiple applications are poised to work together.

Principles of Application Architecture

- Packaged Applications shall be preferred to custom-built applications.
- Process Reform / re-engineering shall precede any custom-building effort.
- Customizations to application products should be minimum; instead the business logic of the user-agency has to be modified to align with the features of the package.
- An end-to-end-view of the business functionality has to be taken and not a fragmented/ service-level view. E.g –request to fulfilment.
- Applications shall be designed to be modular in structure and based on componentization.

- Encapsulating components shall be avoided.
- Components, modules and applications shall be reused across the enterprise. To this end, Enterprise Process Objects (EPOs) shall be developed and reused in all applications, requiring the functionality given by each EPO.
- Web-services Architecture or Service Oriented Architecture shall be adopted by default.
- Mobile Application Architecture shall be deployed by default, wherever we have large citizen interface.
- Applications shall have channel and device independence.

A Target Application Architecture shall be developed adopting the above principles. To supplement such architecture, the following matrices shall be prepared.

a. Application-Organization Matrix, to show which departments/ agencies require/use each of the applications in the portfolio.

b. Role-Application Matrix, to show what role each actor plays in each application

c. Application-Interaction Matrix, to show which applications talk to other applications and for what purpose.

d. Application-Functionality Matrix, to show the discrete services and functions that each application delivers/ performs.

Target Application Architecture

A high-level target application architecture designed for APSEA. This takes into consideration, the three categories of business applications dealing with business architecture. It also recognizes the fact that currently, the government of AP is in the process of designing a development plan for the state for the next fifteen years and that one of the strategies is to co. seven missions to produce tangible progress in the seven b. areas identified, namely, primary sector, social empowermen. skill development, services sector, manufacturing, infrastructure and urban development.

Building Blocks of Technology Architecture

The technology architecture is a collection of Technology Building Blocks (TBBs) that are designed to work in unison and seamlessly. The architecture, thereby, also becomes modular in structure and admits of easy extension, expansion, enhancement or replacement in parts, with technological advancements. The TBBs are selected keeping in view not only the current business requirements and available technologies but also the future requirements and technologies. The idea is to ensure that the technological foundation so laid should sustain and grow over a period of the next 10 years, before a need arises for it to be redesigned and re-laid.

Compute, storage and platform infrastructure: The aspirational vision of APSEA brings certain imperatives, which need to be kept in view while evaluating alternative options for the basic infrastructure like the compute power, storage capacity and platforms required. These imperatives are

a. The reorganized state of Andhra Pradesh does not have any data centre in its territory. It is currently hosting all its applications, data, websites and other soft infrastructure in the state Data Centre at Hyderabad. AP should plan for a state-of the-art data centre in its territory.

b. The realization of the aspirational vision of APSEA demands establishing a state-of the art data centre at the earliest. Any delay in establishing the basic infrastructure may delay the proper implementation of the APSEA.

c. Most of the capabilities and functionalities delineated

by the business architecture and the application architecture require the infrastructure services provided by a cloud-enabled data centre of Tier-4 level.

Considering the above, the following options emerge:

Option 1: Build a state-of-the-art cloud-enabled data centre ground-up in AP.

Option 2: Meet the requirements of APSEA by procuring the data centre services from an existing Tier-4 data centre in India.

Option 3: Promote establishment of a state-of-the-art cloud-enabled data centre of Tier-4 class in AP, adopting a PPP model, and obtain its services.

Among the three options, Option 3 appears to be the most effective, as it avoids CapEx, can secure a highly concessional rate for the various DC services through the PPP arrangement and brings the benefits of the latest technologies not only to GoAP but also to the industry in AP. Tier-4 DC assures availability of 99.995%, besides operating at a PUE (Power Usage Effectiveness) of about 1.2, among the best in the world. The establishment of the Tier-4 DC as above will meet the infrastructure requirements of APSEA in terms of compute power, storage capacity, besides bringing all the benefits of cloud computing.

Middleware: The requirements of middleware, which enables Application Integration, is achieved through the establishment of the e-Highway, as detailed in the foregoing subsection. Estonia, which is rated among the best in the world in implementing e-Governance, had established the middleware called X-Roads, several years ago. The e-Highway aims to achieve more impressive results by adopting the latest technologies like the cloud-computing, combined with the functionality of a traditional middleware product.

Security: APSEA will depend heavily on the Internet

for achieving its vision. Moreover, extensive LANs and WiFi networks are to be created in various public buildings. With the increased use of Internet as the medium for providing services, and the near-ubiquitous use of Internet by the citizens, cyber security assumes great significance. The critical information infrastructure is to be guarded more specially so as to ensure continuous availability of the critical services, like the power, transportation, water, medical services, e-Government services etc. The GOI has notified a comprehensive policy on cyber security in 2013. All the same, a complementary cyber security policy has to be designed for implementation and enforcement at the state level, in respect of the critical services provided by the state government, some of which have been mentioned earlier.

The objectives of the AP state cyber security policy are (i) to ensure the strict adoption of cyber security measures by all agencies dealing with digital assets, (ii) to provide for regular security drills and audits (iii) to create enhanced awareness among the citizens through education and publicity (iv) to facilitate the production of cyber security professionals through the educational institutions in the state and (iv) to establish robust security for the e-Governance systems in the state.

The approach to cyber security at the state level should comprise of working on several strategies like

a. Aligning with the GOI efforts on cyber security
b. Establishing organizations like State Computer Emergency Response Team (S-CERT), Centre for Security of Critical Information Infrastructure, sectoral S-CERT's for critical sectors like power, water supply, healthcare, police, treasuries, e-Governance, Transportation and Disaster Management;
c. Establishing a Security Operations Centre (SOC) and
d. Giving an increased focus on citizen awareness, security education and training.

Networks and Connectivity: The vision of the government of AP is to provide integrated services to the citizens and businesses and more significantly, to enhance the quality of education and healthcare and to increase productivity in the primary sector. All these call for a robust connectivity – connectivity of the government functionaries at all levels and connectivity of the citizens to the internet i.e connectivity within the government and connectivity with the government. The completion of the National Optical Fibre Network project of the Govt. of India assures a gigabit connectivity upto the panchayat level. From the perspective of the technology architecture of the APSEA, it is necessary to provide for the connectivity requirements within the government. The network architecture should address this.

The following points merit consideration in this regard.

a. Network architecture: This refers to the layout of the network, consisting of the hardware, software, connectivity, communication protocols and mode of transmission, such as wired or wireless. For such a complex enterprise as the government, designing an appropriate enterprise network can be quite an elaborate task. Hence it is necessary to engage a team of network specialists to design the network for APSEA.

b. Bandwidth requirements: The promotion of cloud environment leads to the logical consequence of the bandwidth requirements of various agencies varying dynamically. The traditional model of provisioning fixed bandwidth on a point-to-point basis does not hold any longer. Hence it is necessary to indicate a range for the bandwidth requirements of government agencies of different agencies. These indications may be kept in view by the network architects.

c. Software Defined Networks: The APSEA has a lofty vision. It is abundantly clear also that the enterprise architecture has to be Future-Proof. There is a compelling case for including the emerging network technology viz, the software defined network, moving away from the traditional hierarchical network architectures. The following are some of the compelling reasons in favour of SDN.

i. Software-Defined Networking (SDN) is an emerging Network Architecture, which is dynamic, manageable, cost-effective, and adaptable, suitable for the high-bandwidth, dynamic nature of cloud-based applications. 'SDN architectures decouple network control and forwarding functions, enabling network control to become directly programmable and the underlying infrastructure to be abstracted from applications and network services'.

ii. Conventional network architectures are getting increasingly complex to manage and static in terms of bandwidth provisioning.

iii. Complex policies: The complexity of today's networks makes it very difficult for IT to apply a consistent set of access, security, QoS, and other policies to increasingly mobile users, which leaves the enterprise vulnerable to security breaches, non-compliance with regulations, and other negative consequences.

iv. Changing traffic patterns: Within the enterprise data centre, traffic patterns will change significantly. In contrast to client-server applications where the bulk of the communication occurs between one client and one server, the applications of the APSEA access different databases and servers to deliver Integrated Services.

v. Consumerization of IT: Users are increasingly

employing mobile personal devices such as smartphones, tablets, and notebooks to access the enterprise network. We have to accommodate these personal devices in a fine-grained manner, while maintaining security.

vi. Big data demands more bandwidth: Handling the 'big data' needs of APSEA requires massive parallel processing on the servers, all of which need direct connections to each other. The network architects shall seriously evaluate the need to incorporate the SDN technology in part of the enterprise networks that demand dynamic provisioning, centralized management and rapid scaling.

Cloud First

Cloud computing is defined by the National Institute of Standards and Technology (NIST) as 'a model for enabling convenient, on-demand network access to a shared pool of configurable computing resources (eg, networks, servers, storage, applications, and services) that can be rapidly provisioned and released with minimal management effort or service provider interaction.'

The five essential characteristics of cloud computing are on-demand service, broad network access, resource pooling, rapid elasticity, and measured service. Cloud computing technologies are offered in 3 models, in terms of the degree of 'control' the owner of the information has on the content – Infrastructure as a Service (IaaS), Platform as a Service (PaaS) and Software as a Service (SaaS)

Increasingly, governments all over the world are adopting Cloud. In the paper 'Federal Cloud Computing Strategy' published on Feb 8, 2011, the US Chief Information Officer had spelt out the why, when and how of migrating to the Cloud environment. Several countries have published their cloud strategies as well. The government of India has published an approach paper and an implementation Roadmap for Cloud computing, in 2012. The GOI has also launched its first Cloud implementation called MeghRaj in 2013. A phased approach to adoption of cloud is recommended. The following principles apply.

a. The evaluation in terms of the deployment model should be IaaS first, followed by PaaS and SaaS.

b. The evaluation in terms of the business model should be private Cloud first, followed by hybrid Cloud. Public Cloud may be the model of last resort.

c. The adoption of Cloud/sharing can go along the following sequence:

    i. Commodity IT like websites design and hosting, Infrastructure and asset management, e-Mail, and helpdesk;

    ii. Support IT like document management, HR management and Financial Management;

    iii. Mission IT like healthcare, geospatial data and performance management.

d. The eventual state of cloud-enablement of the government will be through migration to the Cloud-enabled data centre, as already recommended in the foregoing para 1. In the interim, GoAP will do well to participate actively in the MeghRaj initiative of GOI and cloud-enable the existing SDC at Hyderabad.

e. Each major department should be asked to choose 3 applications for migrating to the Cloud by March 2015.

It is strongly recommended that the enterprise architect conducts a quick analysis of existing applications and prepares an action plan for migration to the cloud.

Platform for Integration with Social Media: Social Media has shown a meteoric rise over the last few years. The power and reach of these media can't be overemphasized. governments across the world are beginning to use social media effectively for establishing a relationship with their constituents, leading to the realization of the concept of e-Governance (distinguished from e-Government), coined over a decade ago. Social media is the foremost among the emerging technologies, namely the SMAC technologies. The blueprint for electronics, IT and e-Governance published by GoAP in July 2014, gives adequate emphasis to adoption of social media by the government agencies. While a broad framework and focused approach in a few selected departments to the use of social media might be the immediate necessity, as recommended in the blueprint, eventually managing multiple departments interacting with multiple channels of social media may pose an issue of scale and consistency. It is necessary therefore to create a social media gateway for the use of government officials in their interactions with the citizens. The social media gateway may only contain the minimum functionality like registration of Govt users, the platforms they intend to use and themes they would discuss in each channel. It may also contain an analytics engine that gives the government functionaries a clear idea of the public opinion on any current or emerging topic. The enterprise architect has to formulate the functional requirements of the social media gateway.

Design, Development and Management of Websites: Websites form a useful source of information about the government agencies. Some websites and portals enable transacting online with the government agencies. However, a majority of the websites are found to be not user-friendly or not updated with the required frequency. While guidelines do exist for the development and maintenance of web-sites, the ground realities are different. We need to put in place a framework for design and development of all important web-sites of the government satisfying the minimum criteria. The APSEA should aim to promote the following

a. Web standards notified by the standards setting bodies like W3C, IETF, ISO, Ecma International, Unicode Consortium and Internet Assigned Names Authority (IANA)

b. Development guidelines notified by Govt. of India through GIGW (Guidelines for Indian government websites) (web.guidelines.gov.in)

c. The website design principles issued by the UK government, with emphasis on user-friendliness and citizen-centricity. (https://www.gov.uk/design-principles)

d. Ease of access from mobile devices

e. Periodic audit of the web-sites from the perspective of security, quality of content, user centricity and currency of information. Content management system shown as part of the application architecture can be made use of for compliance with the requirements of consistency of information across different web-sites of the government and currency as needed/ defined in the GIGW.

Technology Standards: Standards are the bedrock on which the foundations of interoperability are to be laid. Fortuitously, AP is one of the early states to have recognized the critical role of standards. All the same, given the importance of concepts like single sign- on, smoother interface with government for availing a variety of services, and the overarching need for government to take advantage of big data analytics for policy formulation, standards become all the more important. It is, therefore, necessary to create a policy framework for development, adoption and enforcement of Standards in the eGov domain. Given the blurring boundaries between the services provided by government and the private service providers, aka telecom and Internet service providers, health and education service providers, it is necessary to establish common interoperable standards so as to add to the convenience of the citizens. The policy can also emphasize the criticality of Open Standards so as to avoid vendor lock-in and to ensure seamless integration of disparate applications, products and systems developed/ deployed by different organizations and vendors.

Interoperability, single-sign-on, future-proofing, cost-effectiveness, data portability, enhanced efficiencies, cross-sectoral mapping and analysis, ease of coordination and collation at the national level are some of the more important benefits of the policy. The work done by GOI in the area of standards viz, interoperability framework for e-Governance (IFEG), Meta Data and Data Standards (MDDS), localization standards, biometrics standards for fingerprints and iris, may be adopted. A continuous watch may be kept on the emerging standards, create self-policing mechanisms for enforcing the standards, and provide for making concerted efforts at developing integrated and joined-up services that put the standards ecosystem to test and gainful use.

It is necessary for the standards governance body to lay down the standards in the following areas:

- **Business (Domain) Standards**
  → Standard shared domain functions
  → Standard role and actor definitions
  → Security and governance standards for business activity
- **Data Standards**
  → Standard coding and values for data
  → Standard structures and formats for data
  → Standards for origin and ownership of data
  → Restrictions on replication and access

- **Application Standards**
  → Standard/shared applications supporting specific business functions

  → Standards for application communication and interoperation

  → Standards for access,presentation, and style

- **Technology Standards**
  → Standards for hardware products

  → Standards for software products

  → Standards for network products

  → Standards for software development

Summary: As can be seen from the above narration, it is clearly evident that moving to state enterprise architecture is inevitable for the benefit of all the stakeholders involved. This is purely because of the advantages it offers and the ease with which it facilitates transparent governance. It is a matter of time before every state has to necessarily embrace this model. An understanding of this and working towards building e-Governance applications in the respective departments will help the process of transition to state enterprise architecture.

5

Planning for e-Governance projects

Introduction

e-Governance projects are major initiatives of any department in the government. These have to be planned with adequate care and consideration. In order to enable appropriate planning, it is worth the while to look at past projects, learnings and challenges so that these could serve as inputs at the time of new project planning. An attempt is made in the following sections to provide a summary of these aspects.

Challenges with many e-Governance Projects

Some of the key challenges in various e-Governance projects implemented at central/state/local government level are listed below:

- Many of the projects are towards computerization, but not process improvement in the real sense. ('As-Is' computerization)
- Significant investments into projects with minimal impact/ improvement in service delivery and administration due to inadequate planning initially

- Minimal online or self-services to the stakeholders
- IT enabled processes with no improvement in the service levels
- Projects not completed in time – delayed for years
- IT systems not meeting the business requirements – common challenge
- Low return on investment (value in terms of reduction in service delivery timelines, administrative burden, improvement in SLA's, quality of service etc)
- Failure in meeting defined project objectives (if any are defined)
- Poor quality of the product and services (performance of product and vendor)
- Vendor lock-in in many cases – the initial vendor becomes the inevitable provider of service due to contractual and procedural challenges.

Key factors contributing to current environment

There may be several reasons for such a scenario. An understanding of the environment helps to work out action plan to avoid such situations in future. Following lists some key factors contributing the key challenges listed above.

- Project design incompatible with current readiness and environment
- Least time spent by the organizations in planning and design
- Lack of clear and measurable project goals, objectives and anticipated benefits
- Larger emphasis on IT enablement with minimal focus on business benefits
- Minimal focus on key project enablers (GPR, people change, capacity building)

- Minimal focus on project and systems quality assurance
- Poor communication to the stakeholders and users on objectives and benefits on objectives and benefits
- Inadequate resources for project (people and funding)
- Lack of capacities to conceptualize and manage e-Governance projects
- Senior leadership attention towards e-Governance initiatives is minimal – often regarded as a low priority
- Lack of stable project and permanent leadership with managerial powers to drive projects
- Lack of capacities to conceptualize and manage e-Governance projects

Need for a more robust approach for e-Governance

For addressing the above discussed challenges, it requires a comprehensive and robust approach for conceptualisation, implementation and maintenance of an e-Governance project. The approach shall support government or public sector organizations to:

- Get it right first time
- Orient project designs with customer focus and needs
- Achieve heightened focus on business and stakeholder benefits
- Prioritization of requirements in line with business and stakeholder needs
- Support in adoption of best practices and right approach at each phase
- Manage the private sector participation and project delivery to the results
- Phased implementation with minimal impact and maximum results to stakeholders

Essential elements of an e-Governance project

Following lists some key and essential elements of an e-Governance project.

- Vision and strategy
- Business Process Re-engineering
- Enterprise Architecture
- Software development and IT infrastructure implementation
- Business model
- Legal framework
- Change management
- Training and capacity building
- Project and program management
- Monitoring and evaluation.

e-Governance Project Lifecycle and the steps involved

The Figure 1 presents an overview of lifecycle of an e-Governance project followed by a list of key activities performed at phase of the lifecycle.

Given below are the details key activities performed at various phases of e-Governance project lifecycle and the respective deliverables from those phases. These are indicative in nature and based on the complexity of the project, some areas may vary.

Phase 1. e-Governance Strategy Development

The strategy for the project needs to be developed in line with the overall development agenda of the state and the central governments, as the case may be. The key activities performed in e-Governance strategy development phase are listed below:

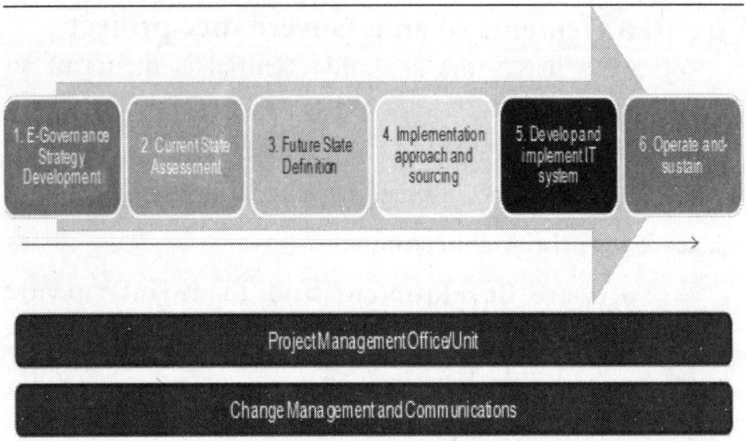

Figure 1 e-Governance Project Life cycle (Source: NISG)

- Needs Assessment – for the project.
- Define clear vision and objectives – what will be achieved and measurable objectives.
- Prioritization of services and projects – how many services will be covered under the e-Governance project.
- Incorporate domestic and global learning's – how other departments have done a similar project and what are the best practices.
- Identify institutional structures and capacities for implementation – how the services will be delivered to the stakeholders, what are the organizational and other support structure needed.
- Define funding requirements – what is the source of fund – state or central govt, world bank or any other source.
- Define monitoring and evaluation approach – how will the project be monitored during the project phase and subsequently after the roll out.

The above activities will bring in clarity and also help to

document them. Once these activities are done, it is expected to deliver

- e-Governance vision – what will be achieved
- e-Governance Objectives – Specific, Measurable, Achievable, Realistic and Time bound
- e-Governance Strategy – action plan

Phase 2. Current state assessment ("as is" assessment)

The current state assessment is 'taking stock of the situation', in other words, it is assessing the "as is" situation in the department. It involves a study and documentation of systems, processes and people related information to help plan further.

The key activities are

- To perform an in-depth assessment of the functions and services identified for coverage under e-Governance project to understand – frequency of the service, volume, time taken to perform the service etc.
- Current approach for performing the functions and service delivery.
- The key challenges and to identify improvement areas.
- List the stakeholders and record their needs and expectations.
- Review and capture of best practices and learnings from similar implementations in similar domains from other departments or states.
- Current systems (IT) implemented in the department, coverage and gaps.
- Organization structures and people capacities in terms of IT awareness and use.

The current state assessment is to be done with due diligence to capture the actual ground level scenario. Any gap in this is likely to mislead the planning process. Once these are carried out, the following deliverables are expected:

- Pain points and areas of improvement–across the services.
- Process maps – for various activities.
- List of stakeholder and their broad needs – list as many stakeholders as possible.
- IT Systems – computer applications, any other software programs.
- Scope and functionality of the program – geographical and functional.
- Strengths and gaps – things that work well and those which do not.
- IT Infrastructure (network, security, data centre).
- Organizational structures.
- Roles and responsibilities of staff – who does what and their deliverables.
- Capacities and skill sets – educational qualification, experience, IT skills.
- Change management details like barriers, possible change agents – what can work and what cannot, people with positive attitude towards change and influencers among the staff.

Phase 3. Define future state (To-be definition)

The future state assessment is 'visualizing the desired future scene', in other words, it is defining the 'To Be' situation in the department. It involves a process improvement steps and documentation of systems, processes and people related information to help plan further.

The major activities involved in this are

- To define how the identified functions and services shall be performed going forward – visualize and document it

- To define the new government processes (revised).
- To define IT solutions and services for automation of new government processes.
- To define people change management, capacity building and communication requirements for the project implementation – involves training need assessment of people, list of change agents, communication plan and who will be responsible for these activities with broad time lines.

These activities are involved ones and also need to be done diligently. These will generate the following deliverables:

- To-be business processes – process flow charts
- New process Key Performance Indicators (KPI) or other metrics – for measurement of performance.
- Changes to the legal and policy environment – through changed legislation of standard operating procedure or government order – a must as the foundation of legal and regulatory requirement.
- Functional architecture and requirements specifications for the proposed system.
- Data digitization and migration strategy – how the legacy data will be digitized, migrated to the new system.
- Service Level Agreements (SLA) the level of service provisioning and the related key performance indicators.
- Institutional structures needed for project implementation – organization chart and roles and responsibilities.
- Training and capacity building plan for the staff involved – including the content and depth of coverage.
- Change Management Plan –complete and comprehensive including people, milestones and budget.

Phase 4. Implementation approach and sourcing

This is the step in which the options and choice of approach to actual implementation will be worked out. The available options for such a project implementation are examined, their pros and cons discussed and a choice of approach for implementation is made. This is one of the crucial steps in the entire eGLC project cycle. As one can see, the approach is driven by factors like availability of funding, time lines and the people expertise.

The major activities carried out include

- Development of implementation approach and plan – various options and the choice made
- Development of business model - how the project will be funded, what revenues will be generated and how, evaluation of pros and cons of the chosen business model
- Preparation of Detailed Project Report (DPR) – the first comprehensive document on the project created to get the approval. This also contains all the high level details of the project – description, benefits envisaged, major stakeholders, funding, risks, monitoring progress, roll out plan etc
- Development of Request for Proposal (RFP)–the document used for procurement of the project. This is generated from the DPR. Consists of three parts – functional or technical specification, commercial specification and contractual specification
- Vendor evaluation and selection – how the vendors will be approached, chosen and how the process of award of contract will be done

Though the list is short and the activities appear simple, each one is an involved process and needs a deeper analysis and decision making.

Following are the deliverables from the above activities

- Implementation approach and plan document
- Implementation timelines with milestones
- List of key stakeholders and their roles and responsibilities
- Monitoring and Evaluation (M and E) plan – metrics and data points
- Project investments and costs including funding if any
- Business/implementation model – with details of who, how and how much
- Payment terms with milestones and budgets
- SLA – for the vendor to deal with
- Procurement approach document – RFP process
- Contract documents/Agreements with all conditions
- Pre-bid minutes and clarifications, vendor evaluation reports, vendor (s) identification and sign off and signed contract documents with the identified vendor – as they happen

Phase 5. Develop and Implement IT System

This is the phase in which the actual work 'happens'. The work is mostly carried out by the identified vendor or National Informatics Centre (NIC) or any other agency of the government. It is at this stage there is involvement of the staff of the concerned department to not only oversee the development and approve the outputs, but also be part of testing them as and when developed for applicability and usability. The main activities during this phase are

- Application software development – by vendor or by any nominated government agency
- IT infrastructure creation – setting up computers, network etc

- Third party acceptance testing – either by the department or by the software testing for quality assurance
- Training and capacity building – for the staff for using the application

The above activities would have created

- e-Governance solution/software
- IT Infrastructure needed to execute the application

Phase 6. Operate and Sustain

This is the phase which is continuous in nature and prolongs for long time. During this phase, the system developed through the above steps will be put to operation and use by the stakeholders. The defects will have to be rectified and any usability issues have to be addressed.

This also involves upgrading of the application to be in tune with the technology from time to time. For example, a web based application needs to be migrated to mobile and then to become a mobileapp etc.

Also to be done in this phase is a continuous monitoring of the functioning of the application based on the service levels, metrics etc so that the objectives set out initially are achieved.

All the above may be summarized as

- IT Systems operations and maintenance
- Monitoring and evaluation
- Upgradation as needed

Project Management Office/Unit

Any project of this magnitude as described needs a continuous monitoring right from the inception stage. At each stage the activities may differ, but one has to keep track of not only the scope and deliverables, but also the key milestones and the budgets. Thus the program management Office (PMO) gets involved in the following activities, and more as needed.

- Definition of programme and project implementation plans with details of milestones
- Identification of stakeholders and key responsibilities and providing the needed support
- Identification of external support needed from market (consultancy services, software development, IT infra creation, change management...)
- Definition of scope of work for the vendors and baselining them for future reference
- RFP Preparation and vendor selection
- Monitoring project implementation plans – as per approved plan
- Scope change management including changes to the scope from time to time
- Risk assessment and management along with risk response strategies
- Issue management as it arises
- Services/Systems quality assurance – by involving appropriate agencies
- SLA monitoring with respect to project management – as needed
- Project financial management – including budget control
- Change management and communications – helping and supporting as needed
- Training and capacity building – review of plans and support as needed
- Monitoring and evaluation of project objectives and benefits. Quantify and report them as needed

- Documenting the best practices and lessons learnt for use by other departments and future projects

Change Management and Communications

If at all there is a step that is most challenging in any e-Governance project implementation, and alas not paid the attention it really deserves, that would be change management and communication. As the project involves moving from current ways of doing work to new ways of doing work, it requires the people to get aligned. The change management is about changing the attitude of the people towards the new systems by getting them involved right from the beginning of the project conceptualization stage. Constantly engaging with them, taking their inputs and also communicating with them at appropriate levels and intervals are certain activities involved here.

An indicative list is given below. Additional steps may be needed based on the complexity and involvement of stake holders from project to project.

- Change management planning – to be aligned with the overall project planning itself
- Identify the impacted stakeholders – (both positively and negatively impacted) specific the change management
- Assess the readiness of stakeholders to adopt change – their skills, overall outlook and their past performance in change situations
- Identity key risks surrounding resistance to change – the risks are specific to change management initiatives (and not the project risks)
- Devise measures to address the identified risks – strategies, actions and owners for actions with time line if possible
- Develop change management strategy – overall approach

- Implement strategy – carry out the plan
- Monitoring and corrective actions – be ready to adopt and make changes to the plan, if need be and open for course correction
- Change communications – communicating with the stakeholders – can be stand up meetings, one-on-one discussions, posters, banners, email or advertisements and electronic media as the case may be
- Capacity building – understand the skill sets needed to adopt the new systems and processes and training to people as needed

In summary, though the steps have been described in detail, the actual steps may change from project to project depending on situational requirements. The point to be kept in focus is conceptualization of the project keeping the broader strategy of the department in mind while delivering value or benefit to the end stakeholders seamlessly.

6

Initiating e-Governance Projects

Introduction

e-Governance projects are very similar to other projects from a generic sense and also have some special characteristics associated with them. These pertain to their reach, roles and responsibilities of various stakeholders and their varied interests, the inherent systems and procedures that make it special in some way, and the unique need of the citizens that a particular project addresses. Thus initiating and executing an e-Governance project successfully requires not only the managerial abilities but also project management and techno-commercial skills. The following paragraphs are indicative of some of them.

Creating a Detailed Project Report

The Detailed Project Report (DPR) is an important document in the e-Governance project. This is created during the fourth phase, namely, implementation Approach and Planning phase of the eGLC. DPR is a comprehensive and complete document for investment dcision making and approval. This is the base document for planning and implementation of project.

It helps in management of scope, cost, procurement, schedule and risks. At a broad level, DPR helps identify interventions required for people, process, and technology implementation of the project.

As preparation of DPR is a critical and mandatory task in an e-Governance project, it has to be done with adequate involvement and preparation. Some of the basic needs before the DPR is prepared are

- Defining the vision for the e-gov project
- Defining the governance mechanism
- Identification and definition of problem statement
- Any relevant base line study
- Listing and analysis of stakeholders – broadly
- Overview of the scope of the project envisaged
- Anticipated benefits

Each of the above steps are taken up to delve into the details and the DPR is prepared with additional details.

The DPR is prepared using the template specific to the funding agency. If the funding is sought from the central government, the format of DPR to be followed is as given in the Meity website (www.meity.gov.in). If the funding is sought from World Bank or Asian Development Bank, then the formats specified by them will have to be followed.

For the benefit of the reader, the format suggested by Meity is given below as a sample.

The DPR as needed by Govt of India has three sections.

- Section 1 contains the background of the project and other basic introductions
- Section 2 contains project overview or summary
- Section 3 includes project details including the implementation models

The following gives a template for each chapter contents. The department which is preparing the DPR needs to simply follow the template to complete the DPR with all relevant details.

Section 1. Background of the project and other basic introductions

- Title of the project
- Whether it is part of the mission mode project or not? If so, details, thereof
- Whether pilot or rollout without pilot – if an when the project is rolled out/or no pilot planned
- Details of the project initiator – name, designation, department etc
- Details of the implementing agency
- Location of the project implementation

Section 2. Project overview or summary.

- Identification of stakeholders – list of all stakeholders impacted
- Problem statement and the issue the project is designed to address/resolve
- Cause and effect of the problems – as assessed in the initial stage
- Category of service – G2C, G2B, G2G or G2E
- Details of efficiencies aimed to be achieved through these services – in terms of service levels – estimated benefits.
- Past experience and lessons learnt (from anywhere applicable)
- Key activities and milestones
- Total estimated project cost
- Sources of funding

Section 3. Project details including the implementation models

- Goal and objectives: Identify SMART (Specific, Measurable, Achievable, Realistic and Time bound) Objectives
- Stakeholder analysis – based on the list already identified and their involvement and support
- Identification of services and services levels
  - → Services is delivered by the agency
  - → Service levels are parameters for measuring efficiency, transparency and reliability of services
  - → Service levels are defined in terms of- quality, quantity, delivery time and cost
- Implementing Strategy
  - → Horizontal or vertical functionality implementation. (geographical split or application services-wise split)
  - → Prioritization criteria of implementation
  - → Delivery channel strategy. (government offices as service centres or third party vendor in outsourced model or a public private partnership model)
- Scoping Study – across the services, geography etc
- Process Reengineering
  - → Scope and purpose of intended process change
  - → Mapping of existing processes
  - → Identification of areas of inefficiency, duplication of efforts, redundancy etc
  - → Preparation of blue print for improving efficiencies

- Change Management
  - → Conducting training need analysis for the department staff
  - → Capacity building for the department staff and others involved
  - → Awareness creation among the users
- Legal aspects
  - → Planning and ensuring communication across the employees and other stakeholders
  - → Any change of legislation and details
- Infrastructure (Including technology)
  - → Back-end server, middle ware, front-end applications and hardware
  - → Network architecture/devices
  - → Information security
- Monitoring evaluation and assessment
  - → Impact/outcome indicators, output indicators, process indicators
  - → Means of verification
- Other Activities like civil work if any
- Organization Structure: Existing and proposed, staffing and deployment – qualification, role definition etc.
- Assumptions and risk
  - → Assumptions – all assumptions to be recorded These assumptions also play a vital role because most of the planning is done keeping these in mind. In case any assumption proves to be wrong or different than assumed - the outcomes change. Thus recording assumptions helps to keep track during execution

- → Risk assessment and risk mitigation – listing the risks, assessing them based on the impact and probability of occurrence, strategy to deal with the risks and assigning action plan with owners to deal with it
- → Constraints – these are known limitations in execution of the project and subsequent roll out. Could be in areas of technical limitation or usage limitation or functionality level, but to be indicated right earnest in the beginning

- Estimated demand for growth rate of proposed services in short, Medium and long term
- Project cost and financing including milestone payments
  - → Project cost (overall)
  - → Investment costs. (any specific investments related to project in civil or infrastructure)
  - → Recurring costs. consumables, annual maintenance and annual licensing fee etc
  - → Financing – where does the fund come from and what are the proportions of fund from the sources identified
  - → Year-wise breakup of source of finance
  - → Amount of funds in form of assistance – (non-cash – can be availability of space or server etc)
- Business Model or PPP provide key Design Features
  - → Financial analysis
  - → Business model
  - → Key implementation design features
- Sustainability plan – upgradation, maintenance etc
  - → Procedural, staffing, budgetary and contractual

arrangements to ensure sustainability of project outcomes

- Implementation arrangements
  - → Management arrangements – the monitoring structure and reporting mechanisms
  - → Contracting arrangements – contract administration
  - → Accounting and audit arrangements
- Detailed Work Plan
  - → Phasing of project activities
  - → Schedule of implementation for each phase
  - → Identify critical dependencies in the project
  - → Expected timelines for completion of key milestones

Irrespective of the funding agency driven format, in any case, a typical DPR would include the following information:

- Introduction
- Clearly laid out objectives
- Target beneficiaries
- Existing e-Government services
- Newly proposed services
- Business Process Reengineering – BPR
- Technology option adopted
- Functional Requirement Specifications (FRS)
- Project management structure
- Detailed AS-IS Scenario
- Detailed TO-BE Scenario
- Change management methodology

- Capacity building
- Department e-Government group for change management /process change and
- For overall implementation of the e-Government Project
- Financials
- Means of project finance
- Cost estimates
- Evaluation of options
- Phasing of expenditure
- Options of cost sharing and cost recovery
- Models of PPP like BOO,BOT, BOOT to etc. to be considered
- Leveraging of existing core IT infrastructure (SWAN, CSC, SDC)
- Phased time frames

The DPR may also contain sections on:

- Government support sought
- Legislative changes/legal amendments,
- Infrastructure etc.
- Sustainability
- Means of sustaining the project benefits
- Means of replicating the project success
- Impact assessment
- Evaluation methodology of the Impact assessment study

In general, the DPR document is prepared by a consultant or a consulting agency. The staff and heads of the department get involved in providing all the details while the actual documentation may be carried out by a third party. However, it is important for the staff of the department to be aware of the details for review, understanding and implementation at a later stage.

Dealing with Request for proposal (Procurement related)

Once the DPR is prepared, the next step is to procure the project – namely implement the project. The project may be implemented by any government agency like National Informatics Centre (NIC) or a third party vendor. If it is a third party vendor, then the purchase procedures have to be followed to ensure transparency and integrity in the process. In order to achieve this, a Request For Proposal (RFP) is created based on the DPR.

The procurement may be a single step process or a two-step process. In the single step process, the RFP is floated and the choice of vendor is made based on defined criteria. In the two stage procurement model, initially an Expression of Interest (EoI) or Request for Information (RFI) is floated to invite interested parties to declare their credentials in executing such projects including the company's financial status. After shortlisting a few from the lot that responded to the EoI or RFI, then the RFP is sent. In this process, there is elimination of ineligible vendor right at the first stage. It eases the selection process by reducing the number of bidders for the project.

RFP is an invitation for suppliers, often through a bidding process, to submit a proposal on a specific commodity or service. The RFP process brings structure to the procurement decision and allows the risks and benefits to be identified clearly upfront.

In general, the RFP process goes through the steps as described in the Figure 1 below.

After the initial technical evaluation, the final choice of the vendor may be made based on several criteria set up by the department. Some of them are listed below

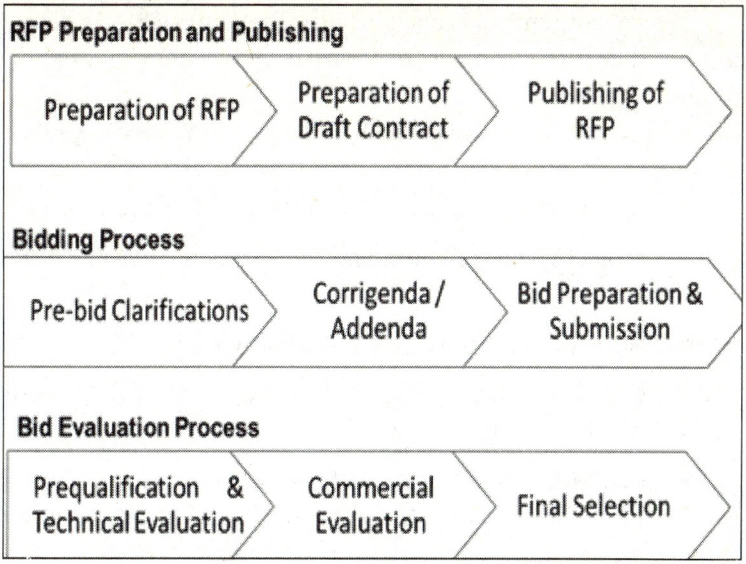

Figure 1 RFP Bidding Process Cycle and Broad Steps (Source: NISG)

- Quality and Cost Based Selection (QCBS) – Priority for quality and price is also a consideration
- Quality Based Selection (QBS) – High priority for only quality and price is not a major consideration
- Least-Cost Selection (L1) – Only the price is the consideration and nothing else is
- Fixed Budget Selection (FBS) – Based on a fixed amount for the scope defined

The RFP is usually structured in three Volumes with one Volume for each one of the above requirements.

The RFP will have to specify in great detail, the following requirements of the Buyer

- Technical and functional requirements
- Bid process and commercial specifications
- Contractual and legal specifications

Typical contents of each volume is given below for academic interest. The actual contents may vary from situation to situation in most cases.

Volume 1 – The technical and functional requirement contains

- Introduction and detailed background of the project
- Project vision, mission and objectives – taken from the DPR
- Services definition – what and how many
- Detailed scope of work for the vendor – definition of all the work proposed
- Functional architecture and requirements – as envisaged. This could change based on the solution proposed by the vendor
- Technical architecture and requirements (including security requirements)
- Other requirements (e.g. data migration, digitization etc) – migration of legacy data and conversion of paper records
- Timelines for implementation of the project – broad milestones, deliverables
- Project deliverables – what will be delivered – applications, and documents

Volume II is the bidding process and commercial specification contains

- Bidding terms and conditions (guidelines for preparing proposal)
- Pre-qualification criteria – for the vendor
- Technical evaluation criteria
- Bid opening and evaluation process

- Evaluation of commercial bids
- Negotiations, contract finalization and award – how, where and what
- Formats for providing bid response
- Pre-qualification
    - Technical
    - Commercial

Volume III is the contractual and legal specification contains

- Roles and responsibilities of stakeholders – who will do what and by when
- Service level agreement – definition, parameters and measurement methods
- Master service agreement
- Scope of services under the contract
- Breach, rectification and termination
- Intellectual property rights
- Disputes and amendments
- Change control schedule
- Exit management
- Program governance structure and schedule
- Payment terms and schedule
- Implementation schedule

Vendor Management Aspects

It is important to identify the right vendor for the project execution or operations management in any situation. In the case of e-Governance it assumes huge importance as it deals with delivery of public service and also to maintain the transparency adequately. Thus the choice of vendor plays a major role.

At a very broad level, care and diligence need to be exercised during the following phases of vendor engagement

- Before selection
- At selection
- During execution and operation of the project
- After the termination of contract

Before Selection

The choice needs to be based on the following major criteria – the list is not exhaustive but indicative

- Technical capability – ability to deal with prevalent technology, any change of technology in future and other adaptations as needed from time to time
- Financial stability – ability to invest and stay interested to continue the project through, to see the implementation and operations
- Operational capability – having the right people and organization structure to support the projects objectives

At selection

Once the above and other criteria specified from time to time have been met, the vendor is selected. On selection, the officers of the department need to engage with the vendor to ensure that the contract is understood by either parties in letter and spirit. Verification and validation of all data are completed and individual role holders (single point of contact – SPOC) from both the vendor side and the department side get to know each other and set up processes for continuous engagement. These could be by way of progress review, monitoring or any other as the case may be.

During execution or operation of the project

This is the crucial phase where the maximum attention and energy need to be spent. The project management plan becomes the reference document for the progress review.

These reviews have to be conducted objectively and the actual progress measured on a periodical basis. Any deviations have to be addressed by both parties to ensure brining the project on track. The department also needs to extend support where needed for the vendor in respect of any official clearances where the department can play an enabling role. Payments to be made based on milestone achievements from time to time.

In the case of operations, the vendor will be monitored on the basis of Service Level Agreements (SLA). It is essential that the SLA parameters are defined in such a way that they are measurable and reported as agreed. The periodical progress review meetings address the adherence to SLA, any other service matters and deviations from the normally agreed operational parameters. Any penalties as agreed in the contract or any bonus need to be exercised without fail. If any deviations to the contract they need to be documented with reasons.

After the Termination of Contract

Practically speaking, there is no major legal linkage, obviously, after the termination of the contract with a vendor. However at the time of termination there are certain activities that are crucial and need to be carried out as per contract. These are indicated below: (not an exhaustive list)

- Transfer of any assets to the department
- Transfer of any third party licenses used in the e-Governance application
- Transfer of ownership and rights of the source code of the program/application
- Handover of all documents
- Completion of knowledge transfer on the application to either the staff of the department or any other third party vendor
- Ensuring that the vendor maintains the confidentiality of the work, for the specified period as per contract

- Any other activity as specified in the contract

Summary

As the popular saying goes, 'a problem well defined is a problem half solved'. This is true and all the steps described above help one to work on defining the project clearly and plan the complete process. The attention needed at the DPR, RFP and vendor selection are critical for the success of any e-Governance project. Enough energy and attention need to be paid at this stage. Also involve the experts where possible. There is a definite need to avoid any unintentional mistakes and ill-informed decisions.

7

Administering Contracts for e-Governance Projects

Introduction to contracts and their importance in e-Governance Projects

A contract may be defined as 'an agreement concerning promises made between two or more parties with the intention of creating certain legal rights and obligations upon the parties to that agreement which shall be enforceable in a court of law.' Contract management is the final stage of procurement cycle.

It is said, generally, the reason for failure of many e-Governance projects may be traced back to lacunae in contract development or administration. It seems to be the sheer ignorance or inadequate attention being paid for the most important part of execution of e-Governance programs. The major challenges faced, in general, are

- Losing control over the supplier/ vendor who is managing the project
- Not allocating appropriate skills and resources to the management of their contracts
- Not addressing the contingency plans and risk management with clarity

- Not monitoring or addressing the service levels for the supplier / vendor properly
- Inadequate key performance indicators to measure and drive the performance of supplier

The level of contract may vary from simple to complex contract. The degree of effort put into contract management should be commensurate with the value, risk and complexity of the contract. In many e-Governance projects, the contract documents seems to have:

- Lack of clarity on specific terms and conditions of the contract during bidding processes – bids prepared based on assumptions. These assumptions may not be documented
- Dispute/disagreement on terms and conditions of the contract between selected vendor and government (as these terms are understood by vendor/government differently post award of contract)
- Significant time consumed in finalizing/agreeing on the terms – delaying the project

To avoid such issues, the best practice is to prepare a draft Master Service Agreement (MSA) and provide it to bidders as part of the bidding document (Volume III) as per the release of documents from Dept. of IT, Govt. of India.

Key Components of e-Governance Contracts

In general, for any e-Governance projects, the contract contents can be divided into the following sections: (These are indicative and it needs to be tailored for specific projects depending on the situation)

- Project specific information: Contract contents specific to the project
- General conditions of the contract: Contract clauses which are more or less common across all projects of the same or similar type

- Special conditions of the contract: Any specific changes introduced to the general conditions, based on project specific requirements
- Appendices and schedules as applicable

In the following sections, the word(s) like Vendor or Service Provider (SP) are used interchangeably. Both mean the same and the right word to be chosen based on the situation.

The project specific information will have to be drafted for each project. The components that make up the project specific information include (indicative list)

- Scope of services/work for the vendor
- Deliverables with time lines
- Project locations
- Project timelines/project schedule
- Project duration. (clear definition of start and end dates)
- Acceptance criteria for the deliverables – including acceptance tests, as applicable
- Payment schedule with milestones
- Obligations/responsibilities of the department and the vendor
- Service levels/performance indicators and service level agreement including measurement of the key indicators
- Penalties/incentive measures (as applicable and agreed mutually)
- Scope change management approach – change control board and the process etc

To make it comprehensive, it is a good practice to - inter-alia include the Request for Proposal (RFP) (all Volumes) and all its Annexures and the technical and commercial proposals of the bidder.

The general conditions/common terms of contracts include

- Definitions of terms used in the contract
- Conditions precedent to contract signing (payments, bank guarantee)
- Applicable law governing the contract – the state, country etc
- Currency of the contract (Indian Rupees, US Dollar etc)
- Language of the contract and administration
- Authorized representatives of the department and vendor with the names and designations
- Conditions on taxes and duties applicable for the contract, change in tax, duties and impact to project cost
- Approach for modifications or variations to the contract
- Breach, rectification and termination – breach of conditions, any remedial measures, termination for breach and termination for convenience
- Protections and limitations for each parties including indemnification
- Intellectual property rights – who owns it and transfer to the department at the end of the project
- Transfer of source code ownership to the department.
- Licenses – if any for third party applications used – transfer to the department
- Force majeure
- Conditions for suspension and/or termination of contract.
- Liabilities of parties
- Dispute resolution approach – mediation, arbitration and judicial approach
- Exit/transition management, as applicable

These terms remain more or less constant in the same project category, and hence can be provided in a template form. This allows for elimination of human errors, and adoption of best practices in contracts.

The special conditions of contract are different for different types of projects – as they have different priority areas. The contract clauses for a government bought out software development project may not be relevant in a Public Private Partnership (PPP) based service delivery project. The contract clauses need to be tailored based on specific project requirements, based on the type of project.

The contract considerations for the following project types are explored in the subsequent sections to provide an overview. These may not be exhaustive. Also, many e-Governance projects may have a combination of more than one of the above types and contract clauses shall be suitably tailored.

- Software development project
- IT infrastructure projects
- Service delivery projects
- Public private partnership

Some detailing is given below:

(a) Contract Aspects of Software Development Projects

Software development projects, by definition are those that have been specifically designed for a department and for the specific set of applications. These could be developed by a third party vendor or by a government agency like National Informatics Centre (NIC). The major considerations for a software development project are listed below

Source Code Ownership and Intellectual Property Rights

'Source Code' is the term for individual modules and pieces of computer programming that are compiled together to make up the software application. Ownership of source code is an ethical and legal issue. 'Bespoke Software' means the software designed, developed, tested and deployed by the service provider (vendor) for the purposes of rendering the services as part of the project, including customization components to other third party software.

As per the Indian Copyright Act, 1957, the copyright of the software developed by a third party rests with the third party, unless obtained through a written deed of assignment. Accordingly, software development project should have a clause, assigning exclusive intellectual property rights to the department:

- IPR to all the bespoke software (custom developed) developed, forms and the compilations of the project
- IPR to any logo, trademark, trade name, service mark or similar designations
- Exclusive rights to all project proprietary data
- For third party products for which the SP had IPR before the contract, IPR will continue to vest with the SP. But the department will have exclusive IPR to the project specific customisations on the product

Project Scope Change Control Management

In any software development project, it is inevitable that changes will be made, from the original specifications. For a project of any complexity, the software will rarely be implemented as originally specified. "change control" is the mechanism for parties to agree scope and cost implications of a particular change (whether amendment to the MSA/service level agreements or service change).

Some of the reasons which result in change control being necessitated

- Changes in processes/addition of a new process
- Scope expanded to include additional functionalities
- New services introduced by department

The change control procedure should be detailed in the contract and should set out the steps of suggesting, documenting, approving, pricing and implementing variations. The prices for change control should be derived from the unit prices in bid, as much as possible.

Exit Management

This clause sets out the provisions which will apply on expiry or termination of the 'contract agreement', the 'project implementation, operation and management SLA (service level agreement)' and 'SOW (scope of work/statement of work)'. Exit management ensures smooth transition at contract expiry, to a new operations and management vendor (or in some cases, internal IT team of department).

The exit management schedule details the following

- Cooperation and provision of information by the SP
- Handing over confidential information and data of the project to the department
- Imparting training to the staff for further handling of the operations
- Overlap trial execution phase as may be needed
- Transfer of project assets
- Transfer of certain agreements – connected with annual maintenance and licenses
- Transfer costs on transfer of project assets to the department
- General obligations of the SP – including financial liability till the date of termination to any third party
- Exit management plan

If exit management is not properly planned, high termination costs might arise. These costs may be due to any one or multiple of the reasons cited below

- Intellectual Property Rights (IPR) not transferred to the department
- Assistance from incumbent vendor to transition to third party not provisioned in the contract
- No provisions in the contract to calculate residual value of equipment and other assets
- Transfer of assets or any remaining payables (e.g. lease payments)

All these can be eliminated by having a well-designed exit management clause in the contract. Specific clauses should also be put in place in the contract to ensure knowledge transfer to the new vendor or the department on exit of the incumbent vendor.

Acceptance Testing, Audit and Certification of Projects

The primary goal of acceptance testing, audit and certification is to ensure that the proposed system meets the requirements, standards, and specifications as required by the client and as needed to achieve the desired outcomes. The contract clause should clearly specify the scope of acceptance testing, the testing schedule, evaluation criteria and the threshold limit for service levels.

A third party audit may be carried out to ensure compliance to the requirements set out by the department

- Concurrent audit – Audit carried out in parallel with design, development and implementation to certify deliverables at each stage
- Certification audit – Audit carried out once the software is fully developed and ready for deployment
- The scope of audit usually involves functional requirements compliance, interoperability and adherence to standards, meeting of service levels, controls review and security audit

Other considerations for Software development contracts

- Documentation: Contract to ensure that project documentation is updated by SP at specified intervals and latest documentation to be maintained with the department
- AMC for system software: In case of third party system software (database servers, operating systems), the SP should have AMC arrangements with the OEM for the contract period
- Licensing policies and Upgrades: The licenses to the system software and other licensed products should be obtained in the name of the department. Any upgrades updating of patches / service packs / fixes from product vendors should be provisioned to be provided free of cost by the SP
- Post implementation support: The contract should have special mention of the clause for duration of support from the service provider/ OEM for the implemented IT solution. This should include time duration for which the support will be required, type of support required and support required for complete solution/ particular modules

(b) Contract Aspects of IT Infrastructure Projects

Warranty Terms for IT Infrastructure

Warranty ensures sustainability and assurance or guarantee by a service provider/ OEM to the client. The Warranty clause should detail the following

- Warranty period (subject to the warranty period provided by the OEM)
- Date of commencement and commissioning
- Type of warranty (Express / Implied / Disclaiming)
- Warranty coverage
- Cost arrangements

The contract clause should clearly specify the kind of arrangements that the service provider should have with the product supplier/manufacturer (Tripartite/Back to back arrangement).

Audit and Certification of IT Infrastructure

The purpose of the audit is to ensure IT infrastructure deployed is as per the specifications provided in the Request for Proposal. The other aspects of audit include

- To audit quality as per ISO 9126 or the standard as specified or applicable from time to time
- Reliability
- Availability
- Efficiency/performance
- Usability
- To audit Security compliance as per BS 7799 / ISO 17799 (or as applicable from time to time)

Exit Management Clauses

Exit Management is applicable when the O&M contract ends and the IT Infrastructure is handed over to the department. The exit management clauses should take into account the following considerations

i. Transfer of Assets

- Project assets including hardware, software, documentation and any other infrastructure to be renewed and cured of any defects and handed over to the department
- Basis of calculation of depreciated value of project assets (IT Infrastructure) to be specified in the exit management clause
- Applicable transfer cost and stamp duty on transfer of project assets to be borne by the SP (except in case of termination due to department's default)

ii. Inventory/stock management and transfer

iii. Condition of assets

iv. Transfer of project related agreements

v. Shifting of assignments, transfers, licenses and sub-licenses related to any equipment lease, maintenance or service provision agreement between SP and any third party to department / new SP appointed by the department

vi. Documentation relating to IT infrastructure supply and installation

vii. Terms of payment/penalties, during exit.

viii. Legal terms for exit, if any as applicable

ix. Calculation of true value of assets (basis of calculation of depreciation)

Other Considerations for IT Infrastructure contracts

Other considerations specific to IT Infrastructure projects include

- Scope of consumables: Contract to specify the scope of supply and usage of consumables
- End of life and upgrades: Clauses to ensure that the IT Infrastructure components are not in the end of their product lifecycle and support is assured during contract period. The upgrades relate to the versions of licenses as prevalent and applicable and also for the hardware with applicable configurations and operating systems
- Documentation: Ensuring that up to date documentation is available with the department
- Insurance: Cost of insurance for components to be borne by SP
- Spares and Replacements SLA: SLA clauses to address quick delivery of spares and fixing of defects in the IT Infrastructure
- Hours of support: Working hours for the support staff for IT Infrastructure maintenance

(c) Contract Aspects of Public Private Partnership (PPP) and Service Delivery Projects

The model of Public Private Partnership (PPP) is resorted mainly for two strategic reasons – (a) to share the risk between the government department and the service provider (vendor) and (b) to harness the best of expertise as available from the partners, where applicable. The contract drafted for a PPP model of working should reflect these aspects amply.

The following aspects should be covered in PPP and Service Delivery projects

a. Transfer of assets: Contract to provide clarity on ownership and transfer of assets created for the project (service delivery centres, related infrastructure etc) during and after the contract termination. These have to be transferred to the department by the vendor

b. Usage of government facilities for non-government transactions: contract should specify the following terms

    - Contract to clarify whether any non-government services can be delivered through the service delivery channels (for increasing project viability e.g. payment of mobile bills for private operators through Common Service Centres - CSC)
    - If yes, approach for addition/deletion of such services.
    - Revenue sharing (if needed)
    - Avoiding conflict of priority between government and private services

c. Funds management

    - Remittance and accounting procedures for collection of payments and taxes
    - Time lines of remittance
    - Payment of transaction fees (deduction at source by

vendor or payment based on quality of services)

d. Hours of operations: Working hours for service centres or call centres, support needed for online service delivery channels

e. Liability and responsibility of service provider in case of fraudulent transactions

   - Liability to be with the SP in cases of claims / damages against the department in case of fraudulent transactions
   - SP to arrange for insurance coverage, at its expense, for cases of third party claims

f. Revenue sharing model

   - Sharing of revenues from the project between the government and the service provider
   - The safeguards in place to prevent excess payout from government, in case transactions are much higher than projected numbers (transaction fee based model with cap, sliding scale etc)
   - The measures to protect the commercial interest of the vendor in cases of projected transactions not materializing (upfront payment for certain components e.g. IT Infrastructure)

g. Addition/deletion of new services/service delivery channel

   - In case of addition/deletion of new services/service delivery channels, the modality of revenue sharing, renegotiation of transaction fee for other services etc should be addressed
   - Interests of department and the SP to be taken into account in designing the modalities (deletion may result in lower payout to SP, addition may result in higher payout)

(d) Contract aspects of Service Level Agreements and Service Level Management

Service Level Agreements are an integral part of any e-Governance contract. In any e-Governance project, government is essentially buying services, and not hardware, software and networks. Service Level Agreement (SLA) framework defines the minimum levels of service to be maintained by the Service Provider.

Some of the definitions related to Service Level Management are given below

- Service: A service is an outcome of a request and it provides an economic, social or personal benefit or right to the requestor or results in efficiency gains to an organization
- Service Level: A service level defines the quality and quantity of service, in a measurable and objective way.
- Service Level Objective (SLO): is the set of purposes or objectives sought to be achieved through defining and prescribing the service levels for an initiative or organization
- Service Level Agreement (SLA): is an agreement between the service provider and the service seeker that defines the service levels, the terms and conditions for enforcing the service levels and the remedies in case the service levels are not fulfilled
- Service Level Management (SLM): is an institutional arrangement that ensures effective implementation of the service levels and enforcement of the SLA

In government scenario, there are a lot of challenges in managing and monitoring SLA terms. Accordingly, certain design criteria should be kept in mind while designing SLAs. SLAs should be

- Be simple to apply in a field situation
- Cover ALL the services envisaged in the Project

- Lay emphasis on different services in proportion to their relative values to the stakeholders
- Be measurable through automated tools
- Be precise and unambiguous
- Be equitable as between the service provider and the service seeker
- Be cost-effective to implement
- Be legally enforceable
- Provide scope for evolution of SLA into a more mature state

The next step is the definition of services levels for each service delivered by the department. Service levels defined for those services to be delivered by the Vendor forms the basis of the service level agreements. The components of the Service Level Definition are

- Service Level Parameters: Measurable attributes of the service, which will provide a reliable and objective estimate of the quality and quantity of service
- Service Level Metrics: A set of norms prescribed against each service level parameters to provide baseline performance expected from vendor
- Service Level Measurement Method: Precise, reliable and consistent method by which the service level parameter can be measured
- Service Level Enforcement Method: Method by which the service level agreement can be enforced (deduction from payments, penalties etc)

The Service Level Parameters should fulfill the following criteria

- Alignment with service level objectives
- Coverage of complete range of services under the project

- Number of SLPs in each service area and their weightage should correspond to the priority of the service area
- The number of SLPs should not be excessively large, affecting the ease of SLA monitoring
- If required, SLPs may be defined for different phases of the project, based on the priorities of each phase (e.g. system development phase, pilot phase, operations and maintenance phase)

Service Level Metrics (range of values) are the performance metrics defined for each service level parameter

- Baseline: Acceptable level of service by the vendor
- Lower: Degraded level of service, - for some known or unknown reasons at some points in time - for which vendor may be penalized
- Higher (optional): Higher level of service for which vendor may be incentivized – carried out intentionally by the vendor by way of efficiency improvement or process improvement to get the incentives
- Breach: Highly degraded level of service / material breach, which may invite termination contract
- Service level metrics should be realistic without compromising on service level objectives

SLA can be most effectively enforced by linking the payments to the Service Provider to the degree of compliance with the SLA. The various methods of achieving this include

a. Deduction method

- Vendor gets 100% payments (monthly/quarterly/ milestone) for full compliance to the SLA
- For lower performance from SLA, specified percentage is deducted. Higher performance may be incentivized by bonus payments

b. Addition method

- A percentage of the payment (e.g. 40%) to the SP is made dependent on the fulfillment of service level Matrix
- All SLPs are assigned credits for baseline, lower, higher and breach metric. Credits will depend on the priority of the SLP
- Scores prescribed for baseline performance will add up to 100%

Automated SLA metric measurement and automated SLA calculation based on performance should form part of the functional requirements, in case of software development projects. In summary, this is an area that needs full understanding and careful execution.

Common Terms of contract

It is important for the officer concerned to be aware of the details of the contract terms. Generally, it is observed that this is an area where adequate attention is not paid due to various reasons. An attempt is made here to bring in a sense of understanding for some clauses of the contract. These are only indicative and specific terms may take a different shape based on the need and situation.

Breach, Rectification and Termination clauses

This clause specifies the terms relating to termination of the agreement by either party, in the event of material breach of obligations by the other party. The components of these clause include

c. Process of termination

- Notice provided to the other party, detailing the material breach in writing
- Within the period given for response to the notice, the breach should be set right, failing which termination proceedings will start

d. Reasons for Termination

- Material breaches (default in providing services as per the agreement, delay of a period unacceptable to the client etc)
- Change of control in service provider (merger, amalgamation etc)
- Apprehension of bankruptcy of the service provider

Upon termination of contract, all related agreements including SLAs will terminate and exit management clauses as defined in the agreement will start coming into effect.

Protections and Limitations

The protections and limitations section provides the protection available to the department and service provider, in various scenarios and provides the limitations of liability.

The clauses which are included in the protections and limitations section are

- Warranties: assurance or guarantee by a seller (vendor) promising to indemnify the buyer (Dept of the Govt) if the warranted fact proves to be untrue. Warranties may be express, implied or disclaiming warranty. In case of components manufactured by third party, the Service Provider (SP) confirms the authority to enforce the warranties on behalf of the client to the third party
- Third Party Claims: protects the department against damages to third parties arising out of reasons attributable to service provider
- Limitation of Liability: is a concept whereby a service provider's financial liability in case of losses or damages is limited to a fixed sum, most commonly the aggregate amount received by the SP for delivery of services under the contract till a defined time period
- Force Majeure: clause in contracts essentially frees both

contracting parties from liability or obligation when an extraordinary event or circumstance (force majeure) occurs. Force majeure events include acts of nature like flood, drought, lightning, fire etc or act of government or others like war, terrorist attacks, riots etc

- Data Protection: clauses to ensure that the in the course of compiling, processing and storing proprietary project data, the SP adheres to the applicable data protection laws and requirements of the project
- Audit, Access and Reporting: clause mandates the SP to provide access to all information which is in the possession or control of the SP, which relates to the provision of the Services as set out in the audit, access and reporting schedule and is reasonably required to comply with the terms of the audit, access and reporting schedule. Insurance and taxes

Insurance is a known way of risk mitigation for either parties involved in any contract. By way of this, there is a considered approach taken to protect the financial interest of the parties to some extent. The contract should address the following insurance related issues

- The type and amount of insurance coverage to be maintained by each of the parties, and party responsible for the cost of the coverage
- Commercial general liability insurance
- Insurance on software (OEM), Hardware
- Insurance for man power deployed
- Protection against any claims, suits, actions, costs, damages or expenses arising from the negligence or intentional acts or omissions of the other party

The Tax environment is driven by the prevalent economic and fiscal conditions of the government. These also change from time to time based on the evolving situations globally and nationally. In order to protect the parties involved in a contract, it is a good practice include clauses that neutralizes the changing tax regime. Typical tax related clauses should address:

- Payments as specified in payment terms will be inclusive of all statutory levies, duties, taxes and other charges whenever levied/applicable
- The SP shall bear all taxes arising out of payments received under the contract

Contract Payments

The clauses governing payments made to the service provider are included in the payment terms schedule. The schedule should address

- Total payment made under the contract and mode of payment (lump sum for project components based on milestone/man month rates/monthly transaction charges/unit prices etc)
- Prices quoted by the bidder in strong and stable currency and break down of the quoted prices
- Payment milestones and schedule
- Cost components to be covered by the SP in return of contract payment and cost components covered by Department (e.g. third party audit)
- Lead times for price changes
- How incidental costs arising in the project will be handled (e.g. change controls)

Dispute Resolution Mechanisms

Disputes arise due to the disagreements between the department and the vendor. The magnitude of dispute may be different based on the perceived breach. Disputes are addressed in accordance to the provisions of the Disputes and Amendments clause in the contract.

The first level of dispute resolution is the dispute resolution board (usually the Project Management Committee- PMC), consisting of representatives from the department and the vendor. The decision of the PMC on the dispute shall be given within a specific number of days, as mentioned in the contract.

In case of no resolution at the PMC level, the parties concerned may take up the dispute with the authorities as specified in the contract – which usually goes through an external mediator possibility, arbitration mechanism or a judicial route, as applicable.

Summary

Broad guidelines have been given above related to contracts and their administration in any e-Governance project. Sometimes, it is difficult for the person in-charge to comprehend all the details and include them or to administer them in full. It is observed that on several occasions, the department is in a fix, more due to lack of knowledge and understanding on certain aspects of the contract rather than lack of involvement or interest. Thus, the attempt above is to create awareness and use the knowledge gained to tactically deal with the vendor or the service provider/system integrator/consultant appropriately. This is also expected to help draft a better contract to benefit the department at large.

8

Legal and policy framework for e-Governance project implementations

Legal Aspects of e-Commerce and e-Governance*

Ministry of Information Technology, government of India, defines e-Governance as '…the application of Information Technology to processes of government functioning to bring about a Simple, Moral, Accountable, Responsive and Transparent (SMART) governance'. In other words, e-Governance uses technology tools in government functioning and service delivery.

Use of technology in government gives rise to many legal questions, like the validity of electronic transactions, electronic records and contracts, data protection and privacy etc. These legal aspects are in turn also relevant to the wider e-commerce landscape of the country. These aspects should be addressed in the country's legal framework, in order to provide the sufficient legal backing to e-commerce and e-Governance.

---

* The information in this Chapter is based on the prevailing clauses of the Act at the time of writing this book – May 2017. There may be possibility of amendments and changes to the Act from time to time, as it evolves. The reader is recommended to refer to the relevant publications of the Govt of India

The legal framework also includes legislations in the domain, which may need amendments as part of e-Government roll-out.

Legal and Regulatory Framework in India

The components of legal and regulatory framework in India for addressing these requirements are listed below. Each of these components is discussed in further details in subsequent sections:

1. Legislation in information technology domain:
    - IT Act, 2000
    - IT Act Amendments 2008
    - Rules under IT Act
2. Implication of existing Laws vis-à-vis IT practices
3. Indian Penal Code, Indian Evidence Act, IPR related laws (Copyright, Trademark, Patent etc)
4. Legislation in the domain in which the e-Governance project is undertaken
5. Guidelines for e-Governance under National e-Governance Plan (NeGP)
6. Specific issues like legal implications of portal based service delivery

The major legislation in the e-commerce domain in India is the IT Act, 2000, which overrides previous legislations, in providing recognition to electronic records, transactions etc at par with their manual counterparts. The details of the Act are covered in the next section.

Information Technology Act, 2000

(a) Background on IT Act, 2000

The Information Technology Act came into effect from October 17th, 2000. The Act was framed on the lines of the UNCITRAL Model Law, and India was the 12th nation in the world to adopt cyber laws. The Act contains 94 sections segregated into 13 Chapters and 4 Schedules. IT Act 2000 was amended through the Information Technology Amendment Act, 2008 which came into effect from October 27, 2009

(b) **Objectives of IT Act, 2000**

The objectives of the IT Act is summarised below

- Legal recognition for transactions carried out by means of electronic data interchange
  - → Digital signatures and regulatory regime for digital signatures
  - → Admissibility of electronic documents at par with paper documents
  - → Electronic filing of documents and e-Payments
- Define civil wrongs, offences, punishments
  - → Investigation, adjudication of cyber crimes
  - → Appellate regime
- Amend existing Acts to address IT Act provisions
  - → Indian Penal Code and Indian Evidence Act - 1872
  - → Banker's Books Evidence Act – 1891 and Reserve Bank of India Act – 1934

(c) **Applicability to the Act**

Exceptions of applicability to the Act, is extended to the following:

→ A negotiable instrument (Other than a cheque) as defined in section 13 of the Negotiable Instruments Act, 1881.

→ A power-of-attorney as defined in section 1A of the Powers-of-Attorney Act, 1882

→ A trust as defined in section 3 of the Indian Trusts Act, 1882

→ A 'Will' as defined in clause (h) of section 2 of the Indian Succession Act, 1925 including any other testamentary disposition

→ Any contract for the sale or conveyance of immovable property or any interest in such property any such class of documents or transactions as may be notified by the Central Government

The Act applies to the whole of India and also applies to any offence or contravention there under committed outside India by any person irrespective of his nationality, if such act involves a computer, computer system or network located in India. The Act has superseding effect over existing legal provisions. Section 81 of the Act states that this Act shall have effect notwithstanding anything inconsistent therewith contained in any other law for the time being in force. Only exceptions provided to the overriding effect are for the Copyright Act, 1957 or Patents Act, 1970.

(d) Major components of IT Act

The major areas addressed by the IT Act are listed below:

1. Admissibility of electronic records at par with handwritten records
2. Attribution, acknowledgement and receipt of electronic documents
3. Authentication of electronic records
4. Digital signatures and digital signature regime
5. Cyber crimes and contraventions
6. Amendments to other Acts (Indian Penal Code, Indian Evidence Act)

These areas will be discussed individually in the subsequent sections.

(e) **Recognition of electronic records**

One of the main requirements of all e-Government and

e-Commerce activities is the recognition of electronic/digital records at par with handwritten records. This recognition is extended by provisions of Chapter III of IT Act, 2000.

As per the definition provided in IT Act, 2000, 'electronic record' means date, record or date generated, image or sound stored, received or sent in an electronic form or micro film or computer generated micro fiche'. Section 4 of the IT Act provides legal recognition to electronic records "If any information is required in printed or written form under any law the information provided in electronic form, which is accessible so as to be usable for subsequent use, shall be deemed to satisfy the requirement of presenting the document in writing or printed form'.

The Act also provides for the use of electronic records in government service delivery. Section 4 of the Act specifies that in cases where:

i. the filing of any form, application or any other document with any office, authority, body or agency owned or controlled by the appropriate government in a particular manner

ii. the issue or grant of any license, permit, sanction or approval by whatever name called in a particular manner

iii. the receipt or payment of money in a particular manner

Such requirement shall be deemed to have been satisfied

If such filing, issue, grant, receipt or payment, as the case may be, is effected by means of such electronic form as may be prescribed by the appropriate government. These clauses allow for e-filing of documents, issue of certificates/licenses online and e-Payments, in government scenario. The Law also gives recognition for publication of rules, regulation etc. in electronic gazette.

In cases where the signature of the individual is required (e.g. signing of application form), such requirement can be fulfilled by using digital signatures.

The Act also provides for the conditions to be met in regard to retention of electronic records. According to Section 7 of the Act, any law provides that documents, records or information shall be retained for any specific period, then, that requirement shall be deemed to have been satisfied if such documents, records or information are retained in the electronic form, if:

i. The information contained therein remains accessible so as to be usable for a subsequent reference

ii. The electronic record is retained in the format in which it was originally generated, sent or received or in a format which can be demonstrated to represent accurately

iii. The details which will facilitate the identification of the origin, destination, date and time of dispatch or receipt of such electronic record are available in the electronic record

(f) Attribution, Acknowledgement and Receipt of Electronic Documents

In dealing with electronic records, it is essential to have clear guidelines regarding attribution to an originator of the record. An electronic record can be attributed to the originator:

1. If it was sent by the originator himself
2. By a person who had the authority to act on behalf of the originator in respect of that electronic record
3. By an information system programmed by or on behalf of the originator to operate automatically

Thus, an e-mail sent by individual can be attributed to him/her. Another important concept is the acknowledgement of receipt by the receiving party. An electronic record can be considered as received by the addressee:

1. If Originator has not specified particular method - Any communication automated or otherwise from the addressee or conduct from the addressee indicating the receipt of the record

2. If specified that the receipt is necessary, then unless acknowledgement has been received Electronic Record shall be deemed to have been never sent

Another legal aspect in electronic transaction is the date, time and place of dispatch and receipt of electronic records. Following are the provisions in IT Act, specifying the date and time of dispatch and receipt.

1. Unless otherwise agreed dispatch occurs when electronic record enters computer resource outside the control of originator
2. If addressee has a designated computer resource, receipt occurs at time electronic record enters the designated computer. If electronic record is sent to a computer resource of addressee that is not designated, receipt occurs when electronic record is retrieved by addressee
3. If no computer resource designated - when electronic record enters computer resource of addressee
4. Shall be deemed to be dispatched and received where originator has their principal place of business otherwise at his usual place of residence

(g) IT Act Amendments, 2008

The IT Act, 2000 was amended in 2008 to include additional provisions, and also to correct certain provisions. The major changes introduced in the IT Act Amendments, 2008 were to:

1. To make the Act technology neutral
2. Enabling provision added to replace Technology specific 'digital signatures' to technology neutral 'electronic signatures'. Central government to specify accepted forms of electronic signatures in the Rules
3. To enable the IT Act to be easily amendable with advances of Technology
4. Exclusion of applicability modified to allow Central government to change the list by executive orders (Rules)
5. Enabling provision for PPP in e-Governance service delivery

6. Provisions for more extensive coverage of cyber Crimes including cyber Terrorism

A number of provisions were added in the amendments, to facilitate Public Private Partnership in government service delivery. These provisions include:

i. Section 6A(1): The government may, for efficient delivery of services to the public through electronic means authorize, by order, any service provider to set up, maintain and upgrade the computerized facilities and perform such other services as it may specify, by notification in the Official Gazette

ii. Section 6A(2): The government may authorize any service provider authorized under 6A(1), to collect service charges as prescribed by government, from the person availing the service

iii. Section 6A(3): Subject to 6A(2), service charges may be collected, notwithstanding the fact that there is no express provision under the Act, rule, regulation or notification under which the service is provided to collect, retain and appropriate e-service charges by the service providers.

iv. Section 6A(4): Government shall specify the scale of service charges to be collected, by notification in the Official Gazette

v. These provisions are put in place to allow for innovative business models for PPP based service delivery.

(h) Electronic Contracts

The IT Act Amendments provide legal recognition to contracts formed electronically. Section 10A of the IT Act states that:

'Where in a contract formation, the communication of proposals, the acceptance of proposals, the revocation of proposals and acceptances, as the case may be, are expressed in electronic form or by means of an electronic record, such contract shall not be deemed to be unenforceable solely on the ground that such electronic form or means was used for that purpose'

This provision, read along with the terms of the Indian Contract Act, 1872 provides recognition to contracts arrived at by electronic means. As per the Contract Act, the pre-requisites for a Contract are the following:

1. An offer needs to be made
2. The offer needs to be accepted
3. They has to be lawful consideration
4. There has to be intention to create legal relations
5. The parties must be competent to contract
6. There must be free and genuine consent
7. The object of the contract must be lawful
8. There must be certainty and possibility of performance

Section 10A allows for all these provisions to be fulfilled electronically.

(i) Digital Signature Regime

1. Introduction to digital signatures

Digital/electronic signatures are the electronic equivalents of the handwritten signatures. Handwritten signatures fulfil the criteria that a manually signed document can be attributed to the individual, as the signature is unique to the person (authenticity, non-repudiation and integrity). There are many electronic signature technologies, which allow signing electronic records, fulfilling the required criteria.

Recognition to digital signatures is provided by Section 3 of the IT Act. According to the section:

1. Any subscriber may authenticate an electronic record by affixing his digital signature
2. The authentication to be affected by use of asymmetric crypto system and hash function which envelop and transform the initial electronic record into another electronic record

3. The private key and the public key are unique to the subscriber and constitute functioning key pair
4. Verification of electronic record possible using public key of the subscriber

Section 5 of the Act establishes equivalence of digital and handwritten signature.

The exact type of digital signature to be used is not specified in the IT Act. Section 10 of the Act confers the authority to central government to prescribe digital signature regime using rules drafted under IT Act, 2000. These powers include the powers to prescribe:

1. The type of digital signature
2. The manner and format in which the digital signature shall be affixed
3. The manner or procedure which facilitates identification of the person affixing the digital signature
4. Control processes and procedures to ensure adequate integrity, security and confidentiality of electronic records or payments
5. Any other matter which is necessary to give legal effect to digital signatures

Accordingly, the following provisions were brought about by the central government in the IT (Certifying Authorities) Rules, 2000:

1. 'Digital signature shall be created and verified by cryptography that concerns itself with transforming electronic record into seemingly unintelligible forms and back again'
2. Public key cryptography to be used for creation and verification of digital signatures
3. Prescribes ITU X.509 version 3 standard of digital signatures

4. Defines the digital signatures regime including guidelines for licensed certifying authorities

Thus, Public key infrastructure (PKI) was the recommended standard for digital signatures in India as per the IT Act, 2000. The Act also describes the Institutional structures for governing the digital signature regime.

PKI Based Digital Signature Basics

Public key cryptography is a form of cryptography in which each user has a private key and an associated public key. Distinct public / private key pairs may be used for either signing a message or for data encryption. Senders sign with their private key and encrypt with the recipient's public key. The public and private keys are 2048 bit keys (including algorithm identifier).

The Figure 1 below explains what a PKI based digital signature is:

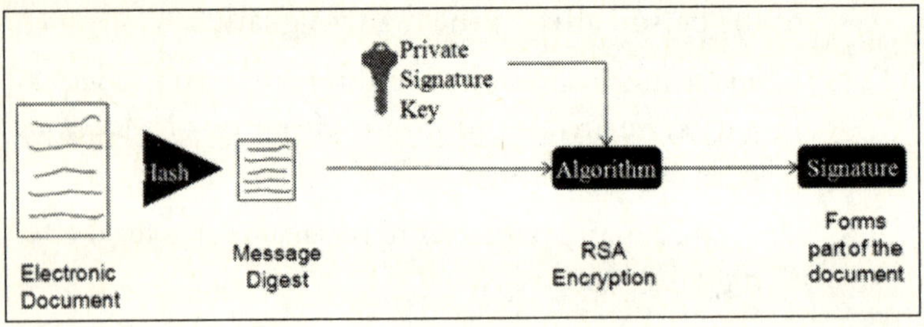

Figure 1 PKI based Digital Signature

Any message irrespective of its length can be compressed or abridged uniquely into a smaller length message called the digest or the hash. Smallest change in the message will change the hash value of the message digest. The hash value is encrypted with the private key of a person is his digital signature on that e-Document. The following aspects may be noted:

1. Digital signature of a person therefore varies from document to document thus ensuring authenticity of each word of that document.

2. As the public key of the signer is known, anybody can verify the message and the digital signature.

Figure 2 below shows how the digital signature is verified:

The electronic record with the sender's digital signature is received by the addressee. The addressee can then check the

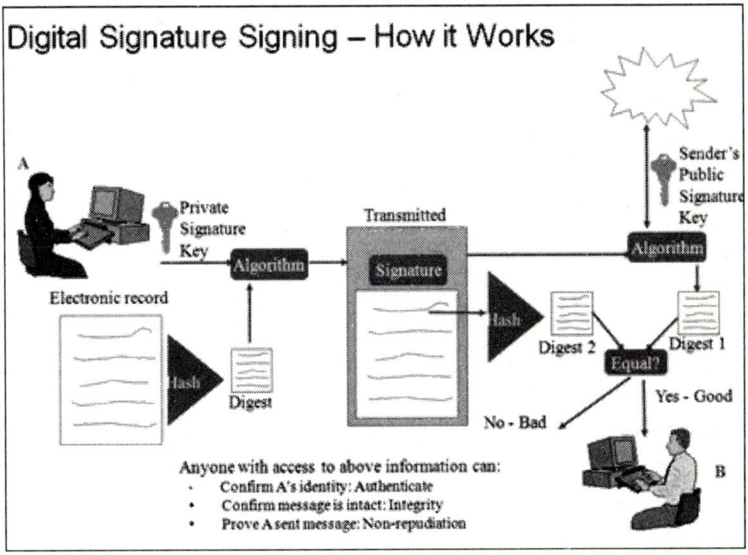

Figure 2 Digital Signature Verification

message digest with the digest obtained by using the sender's public key. If these two digests match, the addressee can be assured that the document has been sent by the sender. In case any changes have been made to the document in transit, the digests won't match ensuring integrity of the document.

(j) Electronic Signatures – IT Act Amendments

The PKI based digital signature regime specified in the IT Act, 2000 is not Technology neutral and hence is against the recommendations of the UNCITRAL Model Law on electronic signatures, 2001. According to UNCITRAL, any electronic signature technology which fulfills the criteria of equivalence between handwritten and electronic signatures should be

Service	What it means	How it is fulfilled
Privacy / Confidentiality	Protection against access by unintended recipients	By encryption using the recipient's Public Key
Authenticity	Proof that the sender is actually who he claims to be	By signing using the sender's Private Key, which can be verified by the recipient using the sender's public key
Non Repudiation	Proof that the sender has actually sent the signed message	
Integrity	Any changes in the original signed message should be detected	

admissible, without prejudice to any particular Technology.

Accordingly, the IT Act Amendments of 2008 provided recognition to other electronic signature technologies, which are identified by the central government. The conditions to be fulfilled for the reliability of electronic signatures were laid down in the Amendments

1. The signature creation data or the authentication data are, within the context in which they are used, linked to the signatory or, as the case may be, the authenticator and to no other person
2. The signature creation data or the authentication data were, at the time of signing, under the control of the signatory or, as the case may be, the authenticator and of no other person
3. Any alteration to the electronic signature made after affixing such signature is detectable
4. Any alteration to the information made after its authentication by electronic signature is detectable. and

5. It fulfils such other conditions which may be prescribed (in Rules)

The central government may, by notification in the Official Gazette, add to or omit any electronic signature or electronic authentication technique and the procedure for affixing such signature from the second schedule. The central government may prescribe the procedure for the purpose of ascertaining whether electronic signature is that of the person by whom it is purported to have been affixed or authenticated.

(k) Cyber Crime Provisions in IT Act

Introduction to Cyber Crimes

Cyber crime or computer crime refers to any crime that involves a computer and a network, where the computers may or may not have played an instrumental part in the commission of a crime.

Some examples of cyber crimes:

1. Virus attacks
2. Stealing user credentials
3. Credit card frauds
4. Cyber pornography

In cyber crime cases, computer may the role of weapon / target (credit card fraud), tool for the crime (denial of service attacks) or storage facility for the crime (pornography).

The knowledge of cyber crimes is essential for e-Governance personnel. In many e-Governance projects, contraventions to Cyber Security and cyber crime provisions are common:

1. Sharing of passwords
2. Sharing of digital signature certificates
3. Unintentional use of pirated software/making illegal copies of software
4. Using government IT facilities for download of pirated music

In most cases, the contravention is done without understanding the legal implication and magnitude of the offense. Accordingly, government personnel and operators should be educated about the legal implications of contraventions and offense.

Details of Cyber Crime provisions in the IT Act

A quick snapshot of the cybercrime provisions in the IT Act is given below. However, these may not be exhaustive and they change from time to time. One is referred to the website of Ministry of IT, Govt of India for prevailing Acts and its Amendments.

Section 43: Civil Wrongs under IT Act

Certain civil wrongs are defined in the IT Act, for which the offender shall be liable to pay damages by way of compensation not exceeding rupees one crore to the affected party. The compensation is decided through an adjudication process. These offences include:

i. Without permission of owner of the computer

- Secures access to the computer, computer system or network
- Downloads, copies, extracts any data
- Introduces or causes to be introduced any viruses or contaminant
- Damages or causes to be damaged any computer resource
- Destroy, alter, delete, add, modify or rearrange
- Change the format of a file
- Denies or causes denial of access to any authorised computer user
- Disrupts or causes disruption of any computer resource

ii. Assists any person to do anything above
   - Rogue websites, search engines, insiders providing vulnerabilities

iii. Charges the services availed by a person to the account of another person by tampering or manipulating any computer resource
   - Credit card frauds, internet time thefts

Section 43A was added with Amendments of 2008 to make it mandatory for corporate bodies handling sensitive personal data (e.g. mail services, banks, insurance companies) to put in place security practices as prescribed by the central government. Computer source code was also brought into ambit of civil wrongs by the amendments of 2008.

Section 65: Tampering with Source Code

Computer source code is the most important asset of software companies. "computer source code" means the listing of programs, computer commands, design and layout. According to Section 65, if anyone knowingly or intentionally conceals, destroys or alters computer source code, when the computer source code required to be kept or maintained by law, it is punishable by fine up to Rs 2 lakh and / or imprisonment up to three years.

Section 66: Criminal Offenses

Section 66 was amended with the IT Act Amendments of 2008 to bring more crimes in its purview. The section is applicable to all contraventions listed in Section 43, when the offense is done "dishonestly" and "fraudulently", with penalties for such contraventions increased to Rs. 5 lakh. Certain new sections were added to clarify and expand the scope of the Act:

i. Section 66A: Sending offensive messages - applies to any information that is grossly offensive or menacing or false information. Also covers cyber Stalking and Phishing

ii. Section 66B: Receiving a stolen computer resource -

applies to purchase or trading or use of stolen computers or mobiles besides information

iii. Section 66C: Identity theft - applies to password theft, theft of cryptographic key etc

iv. Section 66D: Cheating by impersonation - applies to Phishing, Job Frauds etc

v. Section 66E: Violation of privacy - applies to video voyeurism

vi. Section 66F: Defines cyber terrorism and punishment for the same. Offenses under this section punishable with imprisonment which may extend to imprisonment for life

vii. Section 66F (A): Act done with the intent to threaten the unity, integrity, security or sovereignty of India or to strike terror in the people or any section of the people by:

- Denying or cause the denial of access to any person authorized to access computer resource. or
- Attempting to penetrate or access a computer resource without authorization or exceeding authorized access. or
- Introducing or causing to introduce any computer contaminant.

viii. 66F (B): Accessing computer resources that is restricted for reasons for the security of the State or foreign relations, with reasons to believe that such resources so obtained may be used to cause or likely to cause injury to the interests of the sovereignty and integrity of India

Section 66A in conjunction with the Indian Penal Code, is used for different criminal offenses, as listed below:

Scenario	Sections violated	Liable party
The passwords to an online bank account is stolen and fraudulent transfers made	Section 43 and 66 of IT Act, Section 420 IPC	Person who has stolen and misused the account details
Victim's e-mail account is hacked and used to send malicious content	Section 43 and 66 of IT Act	Person who has stolen and misused the account details
The contents of a music CD is illegally ripped and sold online	Section 43 and 66 of IT Act, Section 63 of Copyright Act	The seller and buyer of the illegally copied music
Victim's e-mail hacked to extort money from victim threatening misuse of confidential information	Section 43 and 66 of IT Act, Section 384 of IPC	Person who has stolen and misused the account details

Section 67: Cyber Pornography

This crime involves publishing or transmitting or causing to be published obscene material in electronic form. Punishment on first conviction is imprisonment of either description up to 3 years and fine up to Rs 5 lakh. For subsequent conviction the punishment is imprisonment of either description up to 5 years and fine up to Rs 10 lakh.

Other Cyber Crime Related Provisions

The Act provides the authority to designated government agencies to intercept, monitor or decrypt any information stored in a computer resource, in the cases concerning:

1. Sovereignty or integrity of India
2. The security of the state
3. Friendly relations with foreign states
4. Public order
5. Preventing incitement for commission of a cognizable offence.

The Act also provides central government, the power to issue directions to block public access of any information to any computer resource, in cases stated in Section 69.

The Act (Section 79) provides for non-liability of intermediaries (e.g. ISPs, online auction portals like eBay) for any third party information, data or communication link made available by him, in certain cases:

1. The role of the intermediary is limited to providing a communication system (as in an online auction system).
2. Intermediary does not initiate the transmission, select the receiver, and select or modify any information in the transmission (as in the case of peer to peer sharing of pirated music).

Non liability does not apply:

1. If the intermediary conspired or abetted in the unlawful act.
2. The intermediary fails to expeditiously remove or disable access to the material on that resource (without affecting the evidence to the unlawful act), on acquiring knowledge of the unlawful act or being notified by appropriate government agency on the act.

   The Act envisages the Cyber Appellate Tribunal as the appellate body for crimes under the IT Act, 2000 and its amendments.

(l) Applicability of Other Legislations Vis-à-vis IT Practices

Indian Penal Code and Indian Evidence Act

IT Act and its amendments does not cover all possible cyber crimes. Many cyber crimes come under the Indian Penal Code – with support from relevant provisions of the IT Act. A snapshot of such crimes covered under IPC is given below:

Intellectual Property Related Laws

Intellectual Property is all about legal rights to product

Crime	IPC Section
Sending threatening messages by email	Sec 503 IPC
Sending defamatory messages by email	Sec 499, 500 IPC
Forgery of electronic records	Sec 463, 470, 471 IPC
Bogus websites, cyber frauds	Sec 420 IPC
Email spoofing	Sec 416, 417, 463 IPC
Web - Jacking	Sec. 383 IPC
Criminal breach of trust / Fraud	Sec 405, 406, 408, 409 IPC
Destruction of electronic evidence	Sec 204, 477 IPC
False electronic evidence	Sec.193 IPC
Offences by or against public servant	Sec.167,172,173,175 IPC

of thought, creativity and intellectual effort. IPR regime is put in place to incentivize innovation, creativity and research expenditure by facilitating the creator/inventor to have monopoly rights to monetize the output of his intellectual efforts. The subject matter of IPR is in many cases intangible: a logo or a trade mark, exhaust pipes for cars with a new design etc. A robust IPR regime is essential for an economy to encourage and sustain innovation. There are different types of IPR protection available. These include the different types

- Patents.
- Trademarks.
- Industrial designs.
- Copyrights.

- Trade assets.

The major IPR types having an impact in the e-Governance /IT arena are copyrights, patents and trademarks.

- Major possible IPR types

The Laws governing these IPR types are the following:

1. Copyrights Act, 1957
2. Patents Act, 1970
3. Trademarks Act, 1999

- **Copyrights**

A Copyright is an exclusive right to do or authorize others do certain acts in relation to:

1. Original literary, dramatic, musical and artistic works
2. Cinematograph film
3. Sound recording

The Rights include the rights of reproduction, communication to the public, adaptation and translation of the work. Copyright exists in expression of an idea and it is not a right in the novelty of it. Its object is to protect the writer and author from the unlawful reproduction, plagiarism, piracy, copying and imitation. Violation of the copyright is confined to the form, manner, arrangement and expression of the idea by the author.

Copyrights are the primary source of protection for computer software in India. The Copyright Act treats computer software as a special case of "literary work" extends the same protection as applies to other literary works. Copyright protection makes it illegal to make or distribute copies of copyrighted software without proper or specific authorization (Section 16 of Copyright Act).

Copyright protection assumes significance in the e-Governance context. If a third party software vendor is commissioned to develop software, the copyright for the software does not automatically vest with the commissioning authority, but with the Vendor. In case the commissioning party intends to obtain the copyright to the software, it has to be done through a formal written deed of assignment. To overcome this limitation, copyright / IPR assignment should be formally drafted into the contract between the vendor and the department.

Copyright protection is confined to only to form and expression and not to the underlying idea – thus protection is only against software piracy. In software products, the creative idea behind the software may be a more important intellectual Property than just the source code in many cases. This is necessarily true for innovations in software, for which the owner invests substantial amount of money. Such innovations are provided extra protection by patents.

- **Patents**

A patent is an exclusive right granted by a country to the owner of an invention to make, use, manufacture and market the invention, provided the invention satisfies certain conditions stipulated in the law. Patents are governed by the Indian Patents Act of 1970 and The Patents Rules 2003 and amendments thereof.

For applying for a patent, the invention should satisfy certain criteria:

1. Novelty.
2. Inventive step or non-obviousness.
3. Utility or industrial application.

During this period (20 years), the inventor is entitled to exclude anyone else from commercially exploiting his invention.

Computer software in not yet covered under the patents regime in India, except for certain sub set of computer software including embedded software (those software having industrial application).

- **Trademarks**

Trademarks are governed in India by the Trademarks Act, 1999, which is in accordance with the TRIPS (Trade Related aspects of Intellectual Property Rights) Agreement, of which India is a signatory.

'A trademark is a distinctive sign or indicator used by an individual, business organization, or other legal entity to identify that the products or services to consumers with which the trademark appears originate from a unique source, and to distinguish its products or services from those of other entities'

In the cyber world, Trademark Regulations has implications in the allotment of domain names. Domain names are website addresses (e.g. www.xyz.com) which map to a particular IP address (e.g. xx.yyy.nnn.mm). By using a domain name which is similar to the trademark of another entity, misunderstanding can be created in the minds of general public on the identity of that trademark, resulting in trademark infringement.

But a domain name is not itself a trademark, but only an 'expression of a trademark'. A domain name is a word or phrase registered in the domain name registration system. Whether a word or phrase used in a domain name qualifies for trademark protection is determined under regular trademark law.

In India, the domain names which end in '.in' are governed by the .IN Registry set up by DIT. The disputes regarding domain names in the '.in' domain are resolved in the following manner:

1. A Trademark holder (complainant) can file a complaint with the .IN Registry against a person who has registered a domain name (registrant), on any of the following grounds:
    - The Registrant's domain name is identical or confusingly similar to a name, trademark or service mark in which the Complainant has rights.
    - The Registrant has no rights or legitimate interests to the domain name.

- The Registrant's domain name has been registered or is being used in bad faith.

2. The complainant can ask for any of the following remedies:
   - Cancellation of registrant's domain name.
   - Transfer of domain name to the complainant.
3. The .IN Registry appoints an arbitrator, who gives his decision based on Arbitration and Conciliation Act 1996 and the IDRP (.IN Domain Dispute Resolution Policy) and Rules

The various types of domain name related offenses are the following

I. Cyber-squatting is the registration of a domain name by someone who lacks a legitimate claim with the intent to sell the name, or to prevent the trademark holder from gaining access to the name, or to divert traffic

II. Typo squatting is the case in which the squatter registers a variant of a famous trademark

E.g. www.facebook.com

Though many other countries have separate cyber-squatting laws, such cases are handled in India under the provisions of the Trademarks Act.

(m) Other Legal Aspects

Portals in e-Governance projects and legal implications.

Portals are used widely in e-Governance for web enablement of citizen (G2C) and business (G2B) services. Portals help achieve the following e-Governance goals:

1. Converting department services (rendered at department premises) to self- services (rendered online).
2. Anywhere / anytime delivery of government services.
3. Providing information services of the department.

Use of Portals for government service delivery gives rise to many legal considerations, which should be addressed adequately in order to build trust and confidence in the government portal. Such Legal considerations for portal based service delivery are addressed through a set of policies and terms and conditions drafted for each portal

1. Portal terms and conditions
2. Privacy policy
3. Copyright statement/policy
4. Hyper linking policy

There are certain general principles based on which these policies are prepared for each e-Government portal. These principles are discussed below:

Portal Terms and Conditions

The Portal terms and conditions[1] should have clearly defined terms and conditions addressing the following aspects related to portal use

1. Portal ownership details: Who owns the portal.
2. Usage policy of content:
    - The rules and regulations governing the usage of the content provided in the portal and the transaction services extended by the portal
    - Specific contractual clauses for system usage (e.g: Submission of false information leads to cancellation of registration or blacklisting)
3. Legal aspects: Governing law, and which court of law will have jurisdiction in case of legal disputes arising out of the portal content.

[1] 'Guidelines for Indian Government Websites' prepared by NIC, DIT available at http://web. guidelines.gov.in, provides exhaustive guidelines for e-Government Portals

4. Disclaimers: Disclaiming the contents linked from a non-government website.
5. Liability and indemnity: Limitation of liability for government.
6. Responsibility towards hyperlinked sites.

The terms and conditions should be presented to the citizen /business entity (portal user) while registering for use of portal. Only after agreeing to the portal terms and conditions, should be user be allowed access to the services rendered through the portal.

The terms and conditions presented by the portal and agreed to by the portal user, constitute a valid legal contract between the user and the government (portal owner), as per the provisions of:

1. Clauses of Indian Contract Act, 1872 (pre-requisites for a contract).
2. Section 10A of IT Act (contract formation and other pre-requisites of a contract can be fulfilled through electronic means).
3. Accordingly the terms and conditions have the validity of a legal contract in the court of law in case of legal disputes arising out of portal usage.

Privacy Policy

Most portals collect personal details / information from users, either during portal registration or during the course of delivery of services (e.g. income tax). Only that information which is absolutely essential for service delivery should be collected by the portal.

Portals should have a privacy policy, which clearly states:

1. The purpose for which the personal data is collected.
2. Whether the data shall be disclosed to anyone - to whom and for what purpose.

3. In case the portal handles high risk personal information (credit card, bank details etc), the safeguards should be mentioned (SSL, Digital Certificates etc).
4. Whether cookies (software downloads which collect user's personal data) will be transferred to visitor's system, and what is their purpose.

The privacy policy should be prominently displayed on the portal and the portal terms and conditions should refer to the privacy policy.

Content Copyright

All content provided in the portal should be backed up with proper copyright policy, explaining the terms and conditions of their usage and reference by others. The copyright policy of the department may be liberal, moderate or conservative

1. Liberal/moderate: Allows reproduction of content without prior permission. Acknowledgement of source to be provided in case of reproduction. Safeguards against derogatory use of content.
2. Conservative: Content can be reproduced only after prior permission. Specific limitations for use of content.
3. In case of content having third party copyright, all prior permissions should be obtained before publishing in the government portal.

Hyper-linking Policy

Any other website (external or government) hyperlinked at the government portal may be viewed by users as having the stamp of approval and confidence of the government. In many cases, external websites may provide links to the government portals. Therefore, all government portals should have clear-cut hyper linking policy which spells out the criteria and guidelines for providing hyperlinks to external sites.

In case of other sites providing hyperlinks to government portal:

1. The policy should clearly state whether the external site will have to take prior permission for providing hyperlinks.
2. Policy should specify that the hyperlink should open up the government portal in a new browser page (instead of in a frame within the external site).

In case of providing hyperlinks to other government / non-government sites in the portal:

1. The policy should lay down the specific guidelines / criteria for deciding which external websites can be linked from the portal.
2. If non-government websites are linked there should be a strong business rationale for the same (e.g. providing link to the site of licensed CA in e-Procurement/income tax portal).
3. Whenever the user moves to another portal through a hyperlink, an indication shall be provided to the user on the same.

Domain Legislation

In any e-Governance initiative, it is important to back it up with the required legal changes in the legislation in the domain. Processes are usually derived from the underlying legislation. Many e-Governance initiatives require changes to processes, institutional structures etc. Such changes may require change to the legal framework, to legalize the process changes, and give them enough legal backing. To understand domain legislations, consider the hierarchy of legislation given in Figure 3

At the top of the legal hierarchy is the constitution. Laws are enacted by central or state government depending on whether state/central subject. Subordinate legislation enacted by authorities identified under the law. At the lowest level are the manuals and guidelines, which have only advisory status.

While the laws need ratification by the parliament/state/

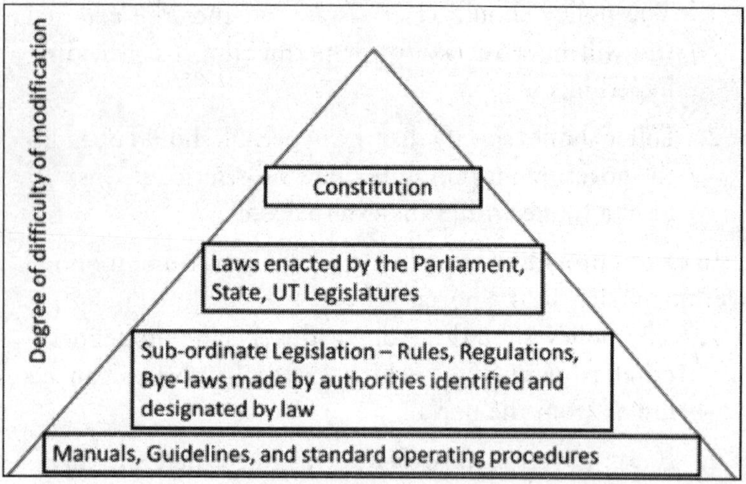

Figure 3 Hierarchy of Legislation.

UT legislatures, Subordinate legislation can be amended by executive orders. Accordingly, the practice followed in legislation is to delegate the procedural issues to subordinate legislations, while the laws provide only a high level direction.

To illustrate an example of domain legislation, the example of MCA21 may be considered. MCA21 was rolled out to enable electronic filing of compliance information by companies. The processes of company registration and compliance filing were based on the Companies Act, 1956 (and the rules made thereunder) and the Monopolies and Restrictive Trade Practices Act 1969.

In order to provide legal backing to the initiative, necessary changes were made to the Companies Act:

1. Amendments to mandate Director Identification Number(DIN).
2. Insertion of provisions 610B to 610E to mandate electronic filing.

Though most of the e-Governance projects may not require changes to domain legislation, projects with a government process re-engineering component requires legal changes. This is because some of the changes that may result from govt. process reengineering will requires legal changes:

1. Organizational structures change (e.g. change in designated agency to handle a particular task/process).
2. Jurisdictions change (anytime/anywhere services).
3. Statutory powers change (who is the authority for delivery of a certain service).

It is a good practice to conduct legal compliance audit in large e-Governance projects to ensure the following legal requirements are fulfilled:

1. The project is in compliance with the Legal and Regulatory framework (IT Act, Public Records Act, Other domain legislation etc).
2. Any changes in the domain laws necessitated by the e-Governance initiative (change in processes, institutional structures, statutory powers etc) are addressed appropriately.
3. Sufficient legal backing is available to government, in case of disputes that may arise.

(n) National Policy on Open Standards

The national policy on open standards was set out by DIT, with the following purpose:

1. Sets out guidelines for the consistent, standardized and reliable implementation of e-Governance solutions.
2. Ensure seamless interoperability of various e-Governance solutions developed by multiple agencies.
3. improve the technology choices available and avoid vendor lock-in

The policy is applicable for all systems used in e-Governance, and all standards used in e-Governance systems, including interfaces and data archival. All legacy systems should ensure external interfaces adhere to the policy.

The policy envisages selection of a single standard in each technical domain, which complies with certain mandatory and desirable characteristics. The mechanism for finalizing and implementing the standards is given below:

1. GoI identifies domains for standardization and identifies the authorized agency to select the standard.
2. The selected agency shortlists the standards and after extensive consultations, finalizes the standard.
3. Once standard is recommended, industry shall be given a definite time for progressive compliance with the standards, be it for interface or for the entire system.

Once the standard is finalized, all government IT Systems should comply with the standard recommended in the particular domain. All requests for proposals for e-Governance systems shall include the guidelines for ensuring compliance to open standards.

Summary:

Though a detailed account of various aspects of legal and regulatory framework for e-Governance project and its environment is dealt with, it is advised for the serious practitioner to look into or consult the competent person or source for the prevailing or practices.

9

Project Management, Monitoring and Control

1. Context for Project Management

A project is a temporary endeavour undertaken to create a unique product or service and is progressively elaborate[1]

A project as defined above has the following characteristics:

- Every project has a definite beginning and definite end
- End is reached if project objectives are met or project objectives will not/ cannot be met (due to technical, political functional or any other reason) and the project is terminated
- A project creates unique deliverables, products, services or results
- A project may be creating a capability to perform a service like a business function supporting production or distribution
- Progressive – proceeding in steps; continuing steadily

[1] As defined by Project Management Institute (PMI) USA

by increments. Elaborated - Worked out with care and detail; developed thoroughly

- These distinguished characteristics will be broadly defined at the early stages of the project and will become more explicit and detailed, as the team gets better and more complete understanding of the product progressively

The above characteristics and qualities fit into the framework of any e-Governance project.

Project Management: Project management is the application of knowledge, skills, tools, and techniques to project activities to meet the project requirements.

Managing the project includes Identifying requirements, addressing the needs and expectations of the stakeholders and balancing the competing project constraints including, but not limited to scope, quality, schedule, budget, resources and risk. This is shown in Figure 1 In case the scope changes, it will impact the cost and schedule. In a similar manner, when the budget is reduced, the scope or schedule had to be compromised. Quality will be a consideration for any change in the other three parameters.

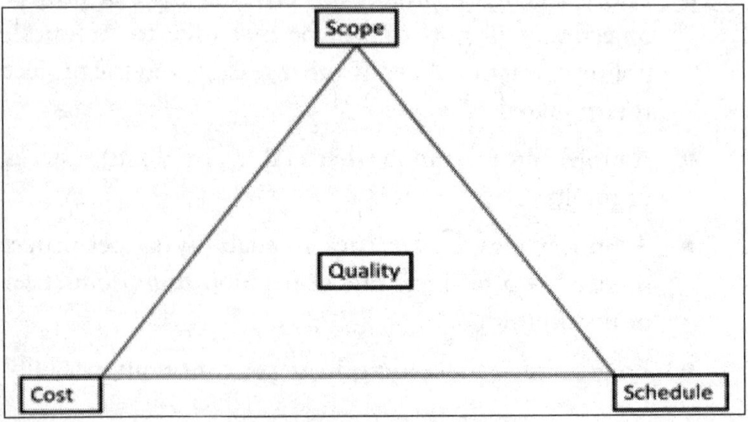

Figure 1 Triple Constraints in Projects

Projects are initiated to achieve a result, which creates an outcome /benefit. Every project uses the scarce resources like money, time and people. Due to the limited availability of the resources, varying conditions of the environment and the expectations of the beneficiary and stake holders, all projects need to be managed. The management involves dealing with various aspects and becomes essential to achieve success in creating the outcome.

Conceiving e-Governance project and defining the benefits

Conceptualization of the project is the most crucial phase of an e-Governance project. The purpose of this phase is to attain clarity on the benefits and the outcomes of the proposed initiative. The deliverables of this phase include-

- A well-articulated vision statement, a sharp mission statement and a set of specific objectives of the proposed project/initiative
- The list of customer-centric services
- The outcomes or benefits to stakeholders like improvements in speed, convenience of access, transparency, efficiency of services etc
- The mix of delivery channels appropriate to deliver the services in a convenient and affordable manner.
- An estimate of cost
- A consultation with the stakeholders to derive / validate the list of services, outcomes, delivery strategy and the transaction costs
- A high-level functional architecture showing the transformed business processes
- A high-level technology architecture that can translate the functional architecture into a reality

- A clear business model

When all the above are articulated well it results in a project proposal/document (Detailed Project Report or DPR) encompassing all the above components.

Managing Benefits

Benefits are defined as measurable improvements achieved due to the implementation of change – which is perceived as positive by one or more stakeholders. Benefits also contribute to the strategic objectives of the department. Thus it is mandatory to define the estimated benefits or the outcomes while starting to plan for any e-Governance project. In other words, no project should be undertaken, if it does not result in any benefits to the government department or its stakeholders.

The benefits thus planned or derived can be classified as (a) planned benefits and (b) emergent benefits. As the name implies, the planned benefits are the ones which were estimated and forecasted while the emergent benefits are a sort of 'by product' of certain activities that results in positive outcome for certain stakeholders or sections of the organization.

Steps to manage benefits

Managing benefits is an important activity in any e-Governance project. It requires careful planning, monitoring and control. Benefit management seeks to optimize the outcome by the following steps

- Forecast benefits are complete and realizable – benefits to be defined that have solid foundation to be realistic
- Enabling business and behavioural changes – to ensure that the forecast benefits are realized actually
- Early realization with sustenance – benefit planning and reaping the benefits to be 'timed' early enough in the project and also to keep them for long enough time, as possible
- Identify, capture and document any emergent benefits

– unplanned benefits that show up need to be captured. (any dis-benefits that come up need to be handled to reduce the negative impacts on the project)

- On the ground realization of all the above to be achieved and on continuous basis – not only on paper/reviews

It is important to note that benefits planning and realization is a serious activity and requires data and evidence on the ground. It is not to be treated like a 'tick mark' exercise just to be process compliant! Here is a model that helps to plan it systematically.

Benefit Management Model

Figure 2 Benefits Management Model

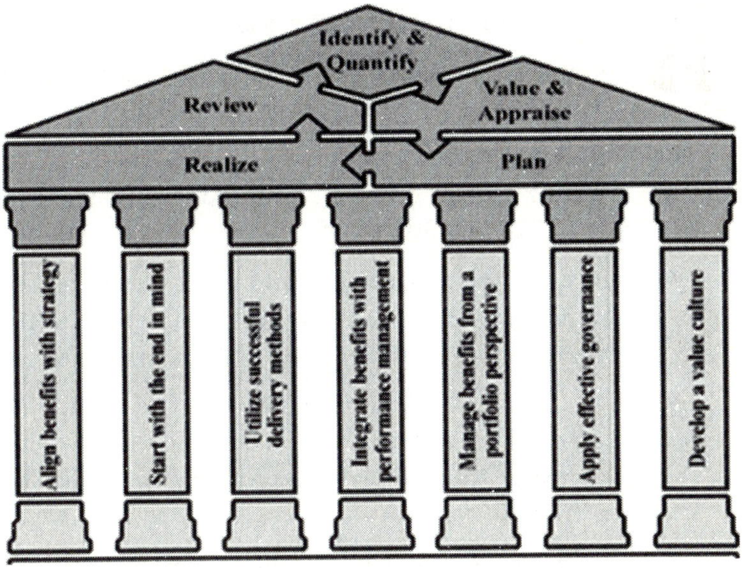

Figure 2 Depicts the benefit management model promoted by S. Jenner.

The 'roof' of the model with the specific arrows around the activities depict the flow of actions for effective benefits management. These are the processes for benefits management.

- Identify and quantify – Laying the basis for informed

options analysis, investment appraisal and portfolio/ project prioritization thus leading to benefit realization.

- Value and appraise – Ensuring the optimal allocation of resources to the relevant initiatives that contribute to the benefit realization – 'best value for money'.
- Plan – Ensuring accountability and transparency for realization of benefits, avoiding or minimizing dis-benefits and leveraging emergent benefits.
- Realize – Reaping the effects of benefits thus planned and sustaining as long as possible.
- Review – Check against the plan, modifying plans as needed and reporting to stakeholders the benefits realised, capturing the lessons learnt etc.

The following steps may be an indicative one to plan and realize the benefits in an e-Governance project.

- Align benefits with strategy – Foster economic development and demonstrate speed in actions for the country's development.
- Start with the end in mind – The overall objective is kept in mind. Thus ensuring the benefits become the outcome not the series of activities as part of modernization.
- Utilize successful delivery methods – Use of novel or distributed outsourced PPP model or any other - while the sovereign function is still maintained with the Govt department.
- Integrate benefits with performance management – The PPP participant has a service level agreement and thus on constant watch by the department for adherence to delivery standards. This not only ensures effectiveness but also transparency.
- Manage benefits from a portfolio perspective – Keeping

the overall development in mind, all actions are taken consistently from time to time.

- Apply effective governance – Regular reviews and feedback on performance.
- Develop Value culture – Delivering value to the stakeholder is utmost importance.

In summary, while planning e-Governance projects, the benefits planned for the stakeholders have to be dealt with separately for each class of them. For example, in any e-Governance project, benefits are to accrue for the end user (may be citizens, businesses etc). But the department, its staff also will get major benefits by way of ease of work, effectiveness in service delivery or ease of reporting etc. The next set of stakeholders may be the vendors or the participating agencies in the project. The benefits management project aims to list, plan and ensure the benefit realization for all the segments of stakeholders – these benefits may be tangible or intangible.

One of the main aspects of benefits management also includes managing 'dis-benefits', namely the challenges or inconveniences caused due to the e-Governance project implementation. The effort and plan should be to reduce the dis-benefits and the impact on the concerned stakeholders, for example, in the case of a road widening project, the persons who lose the land for the road need to be not only compensated financially but also communicated with regularly to ensure that their inconveniences of re-location are reduced.

Project Management Plan and documentation

The project management plan is an important document that needs to be kept as a live document through the project execution from the start. However, the project itself gets approved and funded based on a Detailed Project Report (DPR). It is to be understood that a DPR is different from Project Management Plan (PMP). The former is a document prepared to get the approval for the project and get the funds allocated. The document may contain only a broad scope of the project and summary details of the various aspects like benefits, budget and the timelines etc. Once the project is approved based on the DPR, the project management plan needs to be created by developing the detailed scope, engaging with the stakeholders, listing and planning risk mitigation, cost management and resource management etc.

The DPR is prepared using the template specific to the funding agency. If the funding is sought from the Central government, the format of DPR to be followed is as given in the meity website (www.meity.gov.in). If the funding is sought from World Bank or Asian Development Bank, then the formats specified by them will have to be followed. In any case, a typical DPR would include the following information:

- Introduction
- Clearly laid out objectives
- Target beneficiaries
- Existing e-Government services
- Newly proposed services
- Government Process Reengineering – GPR
- Technology option adopted
- Functional Requirement Specifications (FRS)
- Project management structure
- Detailed AS-IS Scenario
- Detailed TO-BE Scenario
- Change management methodology
- Capacity building
- Department e-Government group for change management/process change and

- For overall implementation of the e-Government project
- Financials
- Means of project finance
- Cost estimates
- Evaluation of options
- Phasing of expenditure
- Options of cost sharing and cost recovery
- Models of PPP like BOO, BOT, BOOT to etc. to be considered
- Leveraging of existing core IT infrastructure (SWAN, CSC, SDC)
- Phased time frames

The DPR may also contain sections on:

- Government support sought
- Legislative changes/legal amendments,
- Infrastructure etc.
- Sustainability
- Means of sustaining the project benefits
- Means of replicating the project success
- Impact assessment
- Evaluation methodology of the Impact Assessment Study

Once the project is approved based on the DPR with its content as above, the actual planning for realizing the project has to be done. That is Project Management Plan (PMP) has to be developed. At a broad level, the project management involves five different processes as given:

1. Initiating processes: Processes performed to define a new project based on the administrative/financial

authorization to start the project

2. Planning processes: Processes required to establish scope, refine objectives, and course of action required to attain the objectives of the project resulting in developing the project management plan.
3. Executing processes: Processes performed to complete the work defined in the project management plan
4. Monitoring and controlling processes: Processes required to track, review and regulate the progress and performance of the project
5. Closing processes: Processes performed to finalize all activities across all process groups to formally close the project.

The above steps in a sequential manner help to plan and execute the project. At the end of initiating and planning phase, the project management plan will be documented in detail. It shall have the defined scope, its base line, stakeholder communication, risk management plan, procurement plan scope change management approach etc. This also contains the assumptions and constraints in the project. This document is owned and maintained by the project manager.

As the project is under execution, the above is used as a reference for measuring the progress of the project. If and when any of the change to the base line, then the project plan is updated with the new details with the approval of the competent authority as defined.

Risk and its management

Risk is an uncertain event in a project that can affect the outcome of the project negatively or positively. Those that affect the outcome positively are called 'opportunities' in a project. In essence the project risk management deals with identification of risks, plan mitigation to reduce the impact of negative risks and improve the 'opportunity' for a better outcome.

- Technical, quality and performance risks.
- Relying on outdated, unproven or complex technology.
- Unrealistic performance goals/gold plated quality requirements.
- Changes to the technology used.
- Changes in the industry standards of technology.
- Newness of the technology to the organization/department.
- Project management risks.
- Poor allocation of time and resources.
- Technical team under-qualified for the job.
- Third party supplied resources.
- Inadequate quality of project plan-like bad product specification, unclear/undefined milestones, communication systems, etc.
- Crash projects.
- Poor use of project management discipline.
- Organizational risks.
- Inconsistent objectives of cost, time and scope.
- Lack of prioritization of Project.
- Inadequate or interruptions in funding.
- Unspecified payment/budget.
- Resources conflict with other projects.
- Improper working environment.
- Distributed project management.
- Over-ambitious management.

- User is unable to and has no authority to clarify doubts.
- External risks.
- Shifting legal and regulatory environment.
- Labour/union issues.
- Changing owner priority.
- Country risk.
- Force majeure risks–requires disaster recovery actions.
- Economic conditions – national and global.
- Social issues associated with the project.
- Media (electronic and print) involvement and coverage risk management plan.

The risk management plan describes how risk management will be structured and performed on the project covering the

- Methodology--approaches, tools, and data sources.
- Roles and responsibilities--lead and support.
- Budgeting for risk management.
- Timing--frequency of review.
- Risk categories.
- Definition of risk probability and impact.
- Probability and impact matrix.
- Stake-holder's tolerance.
- Reporting formats, content and distribution.
- Tracking documents all the risk management activities.

It refers to the process of determining which risks may affect the project and documenting their characteristics.

The identification starts at the time of risk planning and needs to be reviewed periodically, because some risks may appear and some other may change as the project execution progresses.

Thus the risk identification and analysis are continuous processes throughout the life cycle of the project. The identified risks are registered in a document. Following are some methods by which risks may be identified.

- Brainstorming
- Diagramming techniques
- Documentations reviews
- Expert judgment

Qualitative Risk Analysis

This refers to the process of prioritizing risks for further analysis or action by assessing and combining their probability of occurrence and impact.

Once the risks are identified, they need to be prioritized and mitigation plan worked out. In order to do this both quantitative and qualitative methods are adopted. Here the qualitative method involves defining an agreed scale for each category of the risks. Table 1 below gives a typical scale for the project objectives

Risk Evaluation on major Project Objectives					
Project Objective	Very low (0.05)	Low (0.1)	Moderate (0.2)	High (0.4)	Very High (0.8)
Cost	Insignificant cost increase	<5% Cost increase	5-10%Cost increase	10-20%Cost increase	>20%Cost increase
Schedule	Insignificant schedule slippage	Schedule slippage<5%	Overall project slippage5-10%	Overall project slippage 10-20%	Overall project slippage>20%
Scope	Scope decrease barely noticeable	Minor areas of scope are affected	Major areas of scope affected	Scope reduction unacceptable to the client	Project end item is effectively useless
Quality	Quality degradation barely noticeable	Only very demanding applications are affected	Quality reduction requires client approval	Quality reduction unacceptable to the client	Project end item is effectively unusable

of cost, quality, time schedule and scope.

Table 1 Indicative scale for IMPACT of qualitative risk on cost, schedule, quality and scope

For example if there is a risk which increases the cost of the project by 8%, it will fall under the 'moderate' risk and the impact it may have on the cost is considered as 0.2. This number multiplied by the probability gives the risk impact index. As this number increases, the risk threat increases. Table 2 below gives a typical example of a qualitative risk analysis.

Risk	Impact	Probability	Risk Index	Remarks
Cost escalation of the project	0.2	0.4	0.08	Low
Delay in purchase of software	0.4	0.6	0.24	High- to be tracked closely
Delay in identification of vendor	0.5	0.6	0.30	High- to be tracked closely
Major Change of scope midway	0.6	0.2	0.12	Medium

Table 2 Example of a qualitative risk analysis

Quantitative Risk Analysis

It is the process that is performed to numerically analyse the effects of prioritized risks on the overall project objectives.

After the risks have been prioritized by applying qualitative risk analysis, quantitative risk analysis may be performed, as needed. This can be done individually for an identified risk or a group of risks. Based on the outputs, risk responses are developed.

Tools and Techniques:

- Expected Monetary Value (EMV)
- Modelling and simulation – Monte Carlo method

As these are very involved techniques, only the names have been indicated here and not covered as part of this book. Interested persons are referred to the literature on this for further understanding.

Planning risk responses

This is the process of developing options and actions to enhance opportunities and to reduce the threats to the project objectives.

This also includes the identification and assignment of one person to take responsibility (risk-owner) for each risk. Planning for risk responses addresses the risks by their priority, inserting resources and activities into the budget schedule and project management plan as needed.

Planning for risk response involves working out strategies for negative (threats) and positive risks (opportunities).

Strategies for negative risks (threats)

- Avoid
  - → Eliminate the threat entirely by changing the project management plan.
- Transfer
  - → Shifts negative impact of threat along with ownership of the response to third party.
  - → Does not eliminate it Involves payment of premium.
- Mitigate
  - → Reduce the expected monetary value of a risk event by reducing the probability of occurrence and/or reducing the risk event value (impact of the risk)
  - → Taking early actions to reduce probability an/ or impact example designing redundancy into subsystem may reduce the impact from a failure of the original component

Strategies for positive risks (opportunities)

- Exploit
  - → Ensure that an opportunity is realized – Action : Assign most talented resource
- Share
  - → Involves allocating ownership to a third party who can best able to capture the opportunity for the benefit of the project. – Eg Special purpose companies
- Enhance
  - → Increasing probability and/or positive impacts of an opportunity.
  - → Strengthening the cause of opportunity, proactively targeting and reinforcing trigger conditions might increase probability.
    Action: Add more resources to an activity to finish early

Strategy for both positive and negative risks

- Acceptance (for threats and opportunities)

→ This is strategy adopted because it is seldom possible to eliminate all risk from the project.

→ This strategy indicates that a project team has decided not to change project management plan to deal with the risks, or unable to identify any suitable response strategy.

→ Can be passive or active, where passive acceptance requires no action

→ Active acceptance strategy is to establish a contingency reserve in time, money or resources to handle the risks

In summary, risk management plan must be

- Appropriate to the sensitivity of risk.
- Cost effective in meeting challenges.

- Timely to be successful.
- Realistic within project context.
- Agreed by all parties involved.
- Owned by a responsible person

Engaging and communicating with the stakeholders

Stake holder identification and classification

Anyone who is impacted by or can impact the project under consideration is called a stake holder.

Making a list of such stakeholders, mapping them and using it for communicating with them, help us to ensure the success of the project. It is well known that some of the stakeholders are 'powerful' while some others have a keen 'interest' in the success of the project. Based on these criteria, the stake holders may be classified and that provides for a better and focused communication with these stakeholders during the execution of the project.

A list of stake holders is created and a matrix like shown in Table 3, above is made. The power and/or interest is classified as low or high based on a consensus among the teams that are involved in making this list.

No.	Stakeholder	Power/Influence	Interest/Impact
1.	Head of the Dept	High	High
2.	Senior staff	High	Low
3.	Employees	Low	High
4.	Employee union	Low	Low
5.	Heads of other department	High	High
6.	Minister	High	High
7.	Citizen	Low	High

Table 3 Listing of Stakeholders and their power Interest mapping.

The above is translated as given in Figure 3

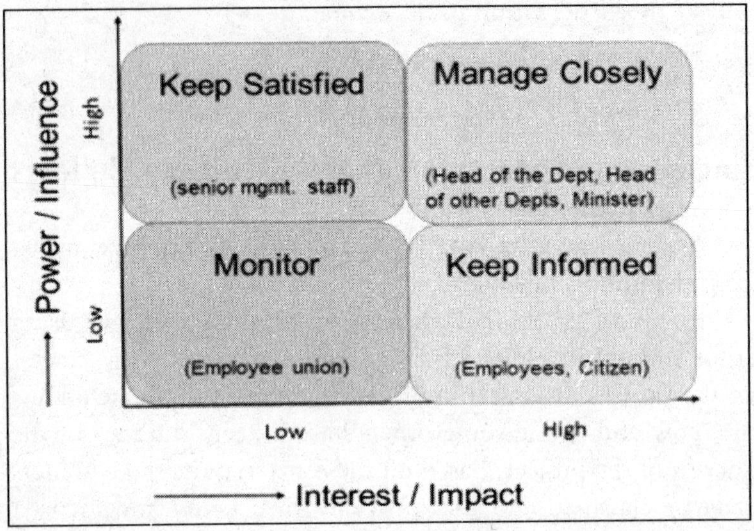

Figure 3 Stake holder mapping for planning communication

As in the Figure 3, the communication planning is done, based on the classification.

- If the stakeholders' power and interest are low, then they need to be monitored periodically.
- If the stakeholder's power and interest are both high, they need to be managed closely.
- If the stakeholder's power is high and the interest is low, they have to be kept satisfied.
- If the stakeholder's power is low and interest is high, they have to be kept informed.

The four quadrants of the figure above give enough indication for the need of communications for the stake holders. Once this is made ready, the job of meeting the specific set of stake holders and meeting their communication needs are assigned to specific persons, with details as needed.

Engaging the Stakeholder's and communicating with them

The stakeholders are key to any project in general. Especially in change projects, due to the sensitivities involved, engaging the stakeholders and constantly communicating with them will be highly beneficial to the success of the change project. Also, it helps to build a better bond with them for future as well!

Develop Stakeholder Engagement and Communication Plan

The stakeholder mapping, as discussed earlier, provides critical inputs into the key stakeholders impacted, their role and influence in the change initiative. Based on these inputs, the organization needs to evaluate/define the following for development of a communications strategy:

- Objectives of communication and engagement of each stakeholder.
- Who needs to be communicated with what information?
- Priorities and level of involvement needed from each individual or group.
- The key messages and how will they be tailored for each group.
- Appropriate modes of conveying that message (email, letter, personal briefing, notices etc).
- Ways to maintain stakeholder interest in the project / initiative throughout its duration.
- Ways to listen to the stakeholder response and measurement approach to evaluate response.

Table 4 gives a typical communication matrix. It is not only important to design the communication specific to the needs of the stakeholder group, but also equally important to gather feedback on the communication, progress etc from them. Thus the Organization needs to define the feedback mechanisms

Stakeholder	Category/Strategy	What to communicate	When (Frequency)	How (mail, letter, briefing)	Who will communicat	Remarks
Minister	Manage Closely	Progress of work	Monthly	Note and personal briefing	Head of the Dept	Fix meeting with Minister's PA one week in advance
Citizen	Keep informed	Milestone of work completed	Quarterly	Paper ad, TV / radio announcement and meeting with citizen groups if needed	Officer in charge of the project	

Table 4 Typical Communication Matrix: (Example only for illustration purposes)

needed, including communication evaluation survey, running periodic focus groups, working with the local change agents within the change network etc, for updating/refining the communications management plan.

Implementation of Engagement and Communication Plan

In this phase, organization will need to launch the engagement and communications activities based on agreed upon stakeholder engagement and communications plan. The specific activities performed in this stage include:

- Distributing materials via the appropriate channels, including populating the website and/or portal, as applicable.
- Managing communication activities, workshops, town hall type meetings and focus groups to deliver or facilitate face to face communication.
- Implementing feedback and discussion channels and opportunities.
- Coaching and supporting the change network and senior and local line management on their on-going communications and engagement role.

Key points in communication

In the context of aforesaid points, the following need to be remembered.

There are five key principles of effective communication:

1. Organisational change (Moving to e-Governance) cannot occur without communication.
2. Communication is not a single step or component of a change process - it must occur in parallel, fully integrated with the change process.
3. Strategic planning for communication entails more than selecting ingredients or tactics according to a cookbook or recipe.

4. Communication is not something done to a target audience, in a unidirectional way. Effective communication is a two-way process, focused on dialog.
5. Communication professionals apply the rigorous planning process, including assessing stakeholder needs, creating and coaching message delivery, and building feedback loops.

It is mandatory to keep these principles in mind while designing and implementing communication to the stake holders during a change process.

Monitoring and Evaluation Framework

e-Governance project should be aimed at achieving benefits to the government and specific stakeholder. As discussed in the earlier sections, the first and foremost activity in undertaking an e-Governance project is to establish a clear vision, objectives and benefits expected to be delivered by the project to the target stakeholders. It is imperative for the organizations to monitor and track achievement of stated objectives and benefits throughout the Lifecycle of the project. Hence, definition of a Monitoring and Evaluation (M&E) framework for the project is a crucial element in e-Governance project design and implementation.

Outputs and Outcomes

Outputs of e-Governance project are the deliverables generated by the government, consultants, implementation partners and associated stakeholders at various phases of an e-Governance initiative. These outputs, for e.g., include e-Governance vision and strategy, reengineered business processes, IT system, IT applications, IT infrastructure, training etc. These outputs should be clearly stated in the scope of the project and based on the responsibilities allocated to various stakeholders.

Outcomes refer to the desired result of an initiative undertaken to meet a need or solve a particular problem. Outcomes, for e.g., may include areas such as reduction of passport delivery time to three days, improvement in literacy rate by 15%, to minimize leprosy from 15% to 5% etc.

The outcomes relate to the objectives and benefits defined for the project and are final results supported by intermediate outcomes (benefits milestones). Outputs are defined to measure project performance. Outcomes focus on business performance.

Monitoring and Evaluation

Monitoring and evaluation refers to tracking the outputs and outcomes, respectively, as defined for the project. Monitoring relates to tracking the project progress, outputs and deliverables as per the defined project plan whereas evaluation refers to assessment on achievement of business objectives and benefits defined for the project. The details below provides overview and difference between monitoring and evaluation.

Monitoring:

- Regular observation and recording of activities taking place in a project.
- Process of routinely gathering information on all aspects of the project progress.
- Involves giving feedback about the progress of the project to the sponsor, implementers and beneficiaries of the project.
- Tracks inputs and outputs and compares them to plan.
- Identifies and addresses problems.
- Ensures effective use of resources.
- Ensures quality and learning to improve activities and services.
- Strengthens accountability.

Evaluation:

- Is a selective exercise that attempts to systematically and objectively assess progress towards the achievement of an outcome.

- An assessment of a planned, ongoing, or completed project to determine its relevance, efficiency, effectiveness, impact and sustainability.
- The intent is to incorporate lessons learned into the decision-making process.
- Determines project effectiveness.
- Shows impact.
- Strengthens financial responses and accountability.
- Promotes a learning culture focused on service improvement.
- Promotes replication of successful interventions To make resource decisions.
- Decision-making on best alternatives.
- Support of public sector reform / innovation.

Understanding Evaluation Types

There are two types of evaluation in general i.e. outcome evaluation and impact evaluation/assessment. Table 5 below summarises outcome and impact assessment followed by few examples.

Do's and Don'ts in project management

Following are some tips based on experience in managing projects of various types and sizes. The list may not be exhaustive and only provides an indicative guidance on important aspects.

Type	Purpose
Oulcome	1. Examines specific program outcome and accomplishments. 2. what changes were observed, what does it mean, and if change are result of the interventions?
Impact	1. Gauges the program's overall impact and effiectiveness. 2. Aims to strengthen design and replication of effective programs and strategies

Table 5 Evaluation Types

DO's

1. Define the scope of the project as unambiguously and as clearly as possible.
2. List and record what is not covered in scope of the project explicitly.
3. Record all assumptions related to the project.
4. Identify and enlist the support of all stake holders.
5. Identify and define the communication needs of all stake holders.
6. Develop a detailed project management plan.
7. Understand and use appropriate tools or techniques for estimation, scheduling etc.
8. Understand and devise appropriate procurement model for the project.
9. Make the vendors / suppliers understand the need and importance of the project for enlisting their commitment
10. List the risks and plan mitigation strategies as needed. Track the risks throughout the project and revise as the scenario emerges.
11. Assign competent persons for the project team, as much as possible.
12. Nominate and train the members of the project team to equip them with suitable skills.
13. Motivate the team by giving as much detail and importance of the project and enlist their commitment.
14. Plan and stick to the communication of project progress to stake holders.
15. Monitor the progress of the project with respect to defined plan.

16. Hold people accountable for their responsibility areas.
17. Indicate exceptions (potential crisis) and seek clarity as and when needed from appropriate authorities.
18. Ensure quality assurance in the project.
19. Track the costs closely and indicate exceptions to the authorities in advance.
20. Reward / recognize the members of the team for their good performance and provide development inputs to those that fall below expectations.
21. Take appropriate decisions as and when needed to avoid project delays.
22. Assess the stakeholders and risks periodically during the execution of the project.
23. Record lessons learnt and best practices as and when it happens.
24. Provide advance information on any challenges and prepare the stakeholders for any surprises.
25. Close the contracts and all project related activities on completion of the project.

Don'ts

1. Assume anything related to project, unless stated explicitly and recorded by the concerned stake holder.
2. Crash the schedule of the project (time duration for completion) without proper planning of resources.
3. Commit to deliver what is not possible, technically or otherwise.
4. Avoid or postpone project reviews.
5. Communicate partial or improper information on the progress of the project to any stake holder.

6. Include a person or persons in the project without matching skills / competency for the role in the project. (If so, plan for training them in the skills needed).
7. Postpone decision making unless otherwise it is required due to exigencies.
8. Enlist vendors or suppliers who are not capable to deliver as per the needs of the project.
9. Bye-pass any process in project management without adequate back-up or better process.
10. Change or transfer persons in the project unless otherwise it is absolutely necessary.

Summary

It can be seen from the above, managing projects is an involved activity. It is an art, science and craft. It requires dexterous and robust management skills to execute and complete the project successfully. One needs to be balanced in approach, have high energy and focus to deliver successfully.

PART 2

e-Governance

Managing Change and Case Studies

10

Change management during e-Governance Project implementation

The way change management is perceived and enacted

'You cannot step into the same river twice' said Heraclitus, the ancient Greek philosopher best known for his doctrine that change is a fundamental truth applicable to the entire universe. Thinkers, scientists, philosophers and academicians through ages have dealt with the concept and reality of 'change' in different contexts, for different purposes and in different perspectives. The single thread that unites these myriad intellectual endeavours is the indomitable fact that change is ubiquitous. What is distinctive about change in the modern era is the 'rapidity' of change and the diversity of change 'drivers.'

In the context of e- governance which is essentially driven by a plethora of ICTs, and with reference to organizations responsible for the same, change ironically takes a rather philosophic contour in that their very 'existence' depends on the ability to understand, leverage, initiate and deal with change.

In his book 'Only The paranoid Survive', Andy Grove writes

about the distress of the top leadership in dealing with change, providing inputs to important organizationally relevant aspects of change management and change leadership. We quote the following from his book that sums up their pro-active strategy of dealing constructively with organizational change that is worthy of emulation..

'I remember a time in the middle of 1985,' writes Andy Grove, "after this aimless wandering had been going on for almost a year. I was in my office with Intel's chairman and CEO, Gordon Moore, and we were discussing our quandary. Our mood was downbeat. I looked out the window at the Ferris wheel of the Great America amusement park revolving in the distance, then I turned back to Gordon and I asked, "If we got kicked out and the board brought in a new CEO, what do you think he would do?' Gordon answered without hesitation, "He would get us out of memories". I stared at him, numb, then said, "Why shouldn't you and I walk out the door, come back and do it ourselves?'. The key message is that change and its management are the responsibilities of the leaders, irrespective of anything else.

Just as it was with Andy Grove and Intel in the mid 1980's, it is even more so today with a vast majority of nations, governments and organizations that find themselves in the vortex of unprecedented change. Leaders in any calling in life and livelihood who respond to change and act swiftly with clear purpose and focus are often successful. There are also those organizational leaders who anticipate change and invent the future who are even more successful. They take a holistic and inter-disciplinary approach to change and do not see it as a mere rule based management process. To them change operates in the matrix of socio- cultural dynamics of the organization, be it in public or the private sectors. They set examples which other organizations follow and emulate with varying degree of success. However, many organizations do not reap the overt and latent benefits of change or survive the waves of change, especially in the present IT era. There are many models that can be used for successful organizational change. It is important for organizational leaders to identify and use a model for transformation that will help their organizations survive and flourish.

The Figure 1 gives the varied dimensions of change.

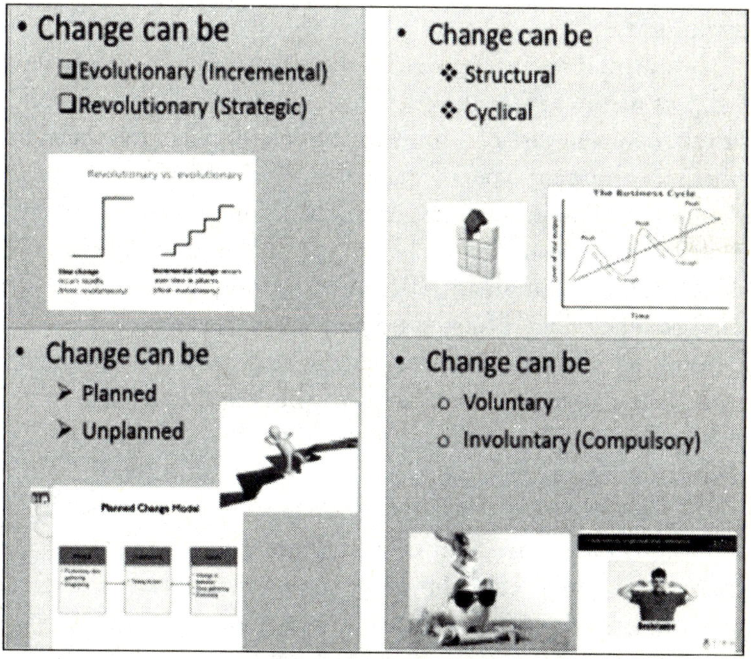

Figure 1 Dimensions of Change

Change can be evolutionary or revolutionary. Radical organizational change involves a break with the past, a break from an existing 'orientation'. This involves transforming the organization to another orientation.

Change can be structural or cyclical. An example of a structural change is, at the time of writing this book, the country was getting ready to change the tax structure to Goods and Services Tax (GST), which is a structural change. The cyclical change is that it happens over and over again with some periodicity – like the changes that are brought about during the annual budget/ fiscal policy in a country.

Change can also be voluntary or involuntary. Change can also be planned or unplanned.

As it is well known, a planned voluntary change helps one to deal with it much more dexterously than the unplanned and involuntary.

Some major differences in the phenomenon of change today as distinct from the previous eras are as follows. (1) The simultaneous nature of a multitude of changes (2) the speed at which the different types of changes occur (3) The complexity of changes (4) The immediate communication and impact of the changes throughout the world and (5) The need for individuals as well as leaders of organizations and for that matter nations at a larger societal level to step up and make quick decisions and earnestly address problems associated with change. The problems and challenges facing organizational thinkers and leaders relate to the speed and complexity of change 'drivers' and change required today.

While discussing change leadership, which will be done in more detail in the following pages, it is necessary to define change and organizational transformation in terms of the degree to which organizational change occurs as well as how rapidly the change occurs. Change is the movement, no matter the degree of its rapidity, of an organization from the existing plateau toward a desired future state in order to increase organizational efficiency and effectiveness. Such changes may be sporadic or as on-going, continuous improvement initiatives as a result of organizations reacting to external forces for change. Changes like these may be a part of improvement initiatives such as Total Quality Management (TQM) and Six Sigma or Organizational Development (OD) initiatives based on various change models.

Today, organizational leaders are increasingly facing the phenomenon of change that is hitherto unprecedented or unmatched in terms of type, quantity, speed, span, reach, the time available to address change issues and expectations for performance results. Leaders must also simultaneously think clearly and make the right decisions about future change, some of which is long term and some of which is immediate. This requirement of simultaneously planning for the long term and the short term is not unique. They must also simultaneously plan for the very short term which often means immediate responses in a matter of minutes or hours instead of weeks or months. This also requires ready information availability and much more planning for contingencies. Otherwise, change 'happens to and overpowers' organizations instead of organizations being on the forefront of change.

The research and literature on the topic of organizational change is rich with diversity, although relatively much less work has been done in the area of change management in the public sector and the government set up. Change factors can emanate from both the external and internal environments. As organizations face the dynamic, changing environment, they are required to adapt, change and in some cases, totally transform themselves into almost new entities. Organizations often change in response to external environmental threats and opportunities and such other environmental factors that may motivate organizations to change. The most widely-stated causes come from macro-environmental factors such as major economic and political changes, technological advances, rapid expansion in the global marketplace and altering demographic and social structures. A set of representative factors that impact change are depicted in Figure 2

Organizations go through various internal change processes throughout their normal life cycle where organizational leaders may create change-driving forces within the organization. For

Figure 2 Typical Factors that influence change

instance, some organizations initiate radical change that results in structural transformation through which organizations attempt to revitalize business orientations through changing the organizational and reporting structure. Other changes such as mergers and acquisition, new top management teams and changing company dynamics because of reorganization and restructuring require organizations to make significant changes not only in strategy and structure, but also organizational culture and processes.

Often, the radical and revolutionary types of change that results from restructuring and reengineering are necessary only because an organization and its leaders and change managers ignored or were unaware of changes in the environment and did not make incremental changes as needed. Such 'knee-jerk' reactions, so to say, are bound to end in problems. Regardless of which forces cause organizations to see the need for change, organizational leaders continue to struggle to maintain or increase their companies' competitive advantage as rapid changes occur both in the external and internal environments. The driving forces for organizational change are the result of the need to constantly improve productivity and efficiency.

Once organizational leaders realize the need for change, they also face challenges in terms of successfully implementing initiatives that will lead to change. The focus of change leaders and champions must be on the process of implementing organizational change, with issues such as how change occurs, who initiates the change, reactions to the fairness of the change implementation, and whether the implementation process was managedjudiciously. When an organization is going through change, it is time for management to exercise effective and efficient leadership. This they must also do in the ethical sense with all honesty and fairness. They should become the role models for the rest of the staff and exhibit behaviours that demonstrate what is expected from employees in relation to the change. This would be consistent with social learning theory and the concept that people learn through observation of others. Also during a time of organizational change, management needs to send positive messages about the change itself.

On one level, positive verbal reinforcement from management that the organizational change is desirable and beneficial will expedite employees' willingness to learn to accept the change and to be part of the change process. On another level, this will motivate employees in a direction of change. This is a vital motivational approach for management to employ during organizational change phases as a means of laying the groundwork for new learning and changes in behaviour to take place.

Change management in the public sector–A 'different' paradigm:

Implementing or managing organizational change in public sector organizations is a uniquely challenging task. When it comes to ICT backed or related change, the challenge is rendered more formidable. Change in the public sector often involves resolving conflicting interests and conflict situations that are both intra and inter-group in a largely bureaucratic set up.

It has been said that changes in the public sector are not just more 'difficult' than those in the private sector, but they are 'different' as well. Change is not simply an exercise in convincing the various stakeholders to get on side but also becomes an exercise in negotiations and compromise. Doing what is ' right' in the public sector is a matter of responding to conflicts and negotiating with various interests much more than it is for a corporate executive trying to implement a change strategy in the business sector.

In 1970, Stan Herman came up with the idea of the 'Organizational Iceberg' to depict the strength of the informal and hidden elements in organization life. The strength of the iceberg analogy lies in the fact that it rightly illustrates the relative importance and size of the informal part of an organization. The influence and power of such informal structures is quite formidable in a public sector set up.

Changes which are aligned with the organizational culture are often embraced with enthusiasm and implemented faster. Indeed, it is the strength of the culture that makes this type of rapid change possible. Changes that threaten the underlying culture are extremely difficult to implement.

Change leaders must recognize and respond to people who might be resistant to the change. Resistance to a change is a force, like inertia that prevents the disruption of the organizational equilibrium that tends to be in favour of the status-quo. According to the laws of physics, a body will remain at rest when the sum of all the forces operating upon it is zero. As changes are introduced, forces create stresses and strains to disrupt the normal equilibrium. Much of the change literature has highlighted the importance of establishing a need for change and to create a consensus around this need.

Articulating envisioned outcomes is another important challenge in change management in the public sector. This must stem from the well-articulated vision of the organization. A vision statement describes the core values and purpose guiding an organization as well as an envisioned future which entails dynamism, resilience and change. It must be a verbal picture of the future that clearly communicates a valued direction for designing, implementing, and assessing organizational change. It should also appeal to the core values of all stakeholders in the e-Governance projects.

A well thought out blueprint of a plan is the beginning of any e-government project. The following roadmap is important in this context for initiating change as a prelude to initiating e-government project.

The working group on e-government of the Pacific Council on International Policy presents roadmap for e-government in the developing world in the year 2002.The roadmap presents 10 questions those e-Government practitioners from around the world believe are crucial to successfully conceiving, planning, managing and measuring e-government. The Roadmap working group suggests that e-government officials and change champions ask themselves these ten questions before they embark on the e-government path. The 10 questions are as follows:

1. Why are we pursuing e-government?
2. Do we have a clear vision and priorities for e-government?
3. What kind of e-government are we ready for?
4. Is there enough political will to lead the e-government effort?

5. Are we selecting e-government projects in the best way?
6. How should we plan and manage e-government projects?
7. How will we overcome resistance from within the government?
8. How will we measure and communicate progress? How will we know if we arefailing?
9. What should our relationship be with the private sector?
10. How can e-government improve citizen participation in public affairs?

The relevance of the above will be and have been touched upon in various chapters of this book both explicitly and implicitly.

Change management models:

There are several change management models in vogue – which have been devised based on extensive research. The choice is so vast one can choose to pick from them as applicable to the organizational situation. In this book, the authors present a few models that are more appropriate in e-Governance project situations. Interested reader is urged to see the literature for more detailed treatise on this interesting topic.

ADKAR (Awareness, Desire, Knowledge, Ability and Reinforcement) model

When an organization undertakes a change initiative, then change only happens when the employees who have to do their jobs differently can say with confidence, I have the Awareness, Desire, Knowledge, Ability and Reinforcement to make this change happen. This is the ADKAR Model of change management. It is also known as the Prosci Model, developed by Prosci Institute, USA. The Prosci's model consists of three main phases: (1) Preparing for change, (2) Managing change, and (3) Reinforcing change.

The first phase in Prosci's methodology is aimed at

getting ready. It answers the question as to how much change management is needed for this specific project. The first phase provides the situational awareness that is vital for effective change management. The second phase of Prosci's process is focused on creating the plans that are integrated into the project activities - what people typically think of when they talk about change management. Based on Prosci's research, there are five plans that could be created to help individuals move through the ADKAR Model. Finally, the third phase of Prosci's process helps project teams create specific action plans for ensuring that the change is sustained. In this phase, project teams develop measures and mechanisms to see if the change has taken hold, to see if employees are actually doing their jobs the new way and to celebrate success.

Readiness for change strategy plays a crucial role in mitigating resistance to change and thus in reducing the failure rate. A push for change from top management is likely to produce positive perception. When employees are in a positive frame of mind about and ready for organizational change, they appear to be more receptive and willing to try out a system.

Building people's understanding of and commitment to changes associated with the implementation is very important. It helps build positive attitudes toward the system. Training provides hands-on experience for the users whereby they can appreciate the qualitative attributes of the system and its potential benefits. Onsite training and on-site support for staff as well as managers during implementation is vital here. A support organization (e.g. helpdesk, online user manual) is also critical to meet users' needs after installation.

ADKAR has become one of the most popular change management models from Prosci Institute. This simple acronym has helped thousands more effectively manage change around them- be it changes at work, at home or in the community.

The moot question that confronts most theorists of change and change leaders is why some change management measures succeed almost effortlessly while others similar in intent fail despite best efforts? One possible answer to this paradox is the ADKAR Model. It is a unique goal oriented and task based change management model. This model, accordingto its proponents, facilitates and empowers change management teams to focus on specific and intended change management results. This model developed by Prosci Institute has its roots in the movement to align traditional change management activities with a project's goals or intended results. A diagrammatic representation of the five elements of ADKAR model is at Figure 3.

The ADKAR module of change management thus rightly emphasized the following:

1. Awareness phase: One must look into whether the employees are aware of the need to change. Awareness on part of both leadership and employees is a precondition to successful organizational change initiatives. In terms of Lewin's model this falls under the Unfreezing phase of change process.

The fundamental question facing almost all organizations involved in e –government projects is this - how can you overcome the hurdles facing any organization struggling to change addiction to the status quo, limited resources, demotivated employees, and opposition from powerful vested interests? Awareness of the need for change and the consequence of not changing is important in this leadership context. In a bureaucratic set up where salaries, tenure of service and career is more assured and stable, the awareness to change does not set in that easily. The structures, systems and attitudes are more oriented towards the status-quo.

Building awareness as defined within ADKAR requires sharing both the nature of the change and answering why this change is necessary. It means clearly explaining the business drivers or opportunities that have resulted in the need for change.

It also means driving home the point as to why a change is needed now, and explaining the risk of not changing. Lack of awareness has been cited as the number one reason for employee resistance in Prosci's latest benchmarking study.

The results of a decision depend on the nature and quality of force with which it is translated into action. You may have the power, but do you have the force inherent in it to enable it to achieve your ends? Newton's second law has a precise answer to this question. Power is of many sources. It may arise out of your position, what you possess in general or a particular situation and so on. But power in itself is at best a decorative appendage in life. Force must be innate in power for acts of power to be forceful. Forceful power propels or accelerates an event or individual to act at a pace that is desirable to achieve your intended objective.

2. Desire creation phase: The employees must know that adopting a particular ICT or a set of them is beneficial to them. They must feel this in their mind. Change leaders must tap into the primordial instinct of self interest in each employee. Desire answers the question of 'why' change is desirable by each employee.

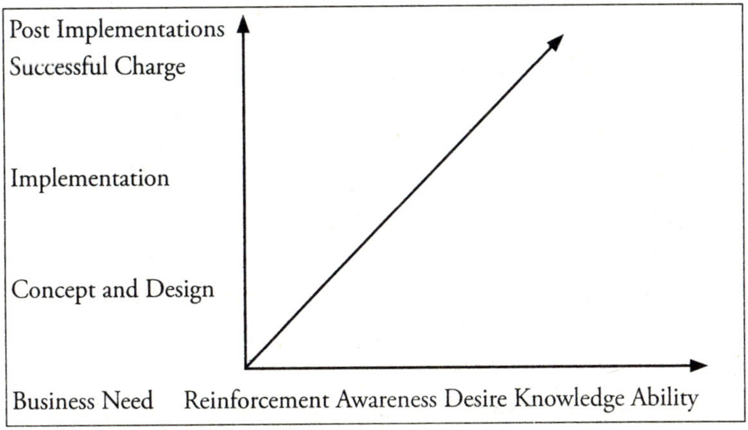

Figure 3 ADKAR Model of Change Management:
The Five Elements or Objectives

Not creating the desire for change will lead to conflict situations and the individual and the group levels. This could result in resistance to change at those levels. It is true that lack of awareness does create conflict, but lack of desire to adapt the appropriate means or technology will lead to even more acute conflict and resistance to change.

Negative attitudes towards change can very adversely affect all change management initiatives. When employees are not willing to change their attitude and behaviour, it presents a formidable problem. But when the hard working, skilled and smart ones resist change it becomes an aggravated ironical problem.

These otherwise valued employees aren't purposefully subversive or resistant. They may be unwittingly caught in 'competing commitment'- a subconscious, hidden goal that conflicts with their stated commitments. Competing commitments make people personally immune to change. At extreme negative spectrum, they can undermine best employees' and a company's success in change initiatives.

To initiate and drive change managers and leaders must tailor their strategies to the types of resistance they will encounter. For instance, with employees who fear change, skills training must be provided. Situational factors must be considered. For example, to avert an imminent crisis, change must be quick even if that intensifies resistance for a brief period. It will subside subsequently. To lead change successfully, situational variables and factors must be analyzed and understood. Leaders and change masters must determine how much and what kind of resistance to expect. Leaders must assess their own explicit and implicit advantages or otherwise relative to that of the resisters.

Parochial self-interest is one major reason why employees resist organizational change. They will resist change if they think and come to believe that they will lose something of value as a result of change. People also resist change when they do not fully and clearly understand its implications and perceive that it might cost them much more than they will gain. Such situations often occur when trust is lacking between the person initiating the change and the employees who are affected by the change initiative.

To make those who resist change initiative more open and committed to the change, leaders must encourage their participation in its design or implementation. This method increases grassroots support for change but can cause problems if people lack the expertise to develop effective plans. If people fear they can't make needed adjustments, they must be provided skills training and emotional support. No other approach works as well with adjustment problems, but it can be time consuming and expensive. If powerful people or groups are resisting because they'll lose out as a result of the change, negotiations can be used.

Some individuals have a low tolerance for change. Some People also resist change because they fear they will not be able to develop the new skills and behaviour that will be required of them. All human beings are limited in their ability to change, with some people much more limited than others

If the initiators of the change involve the potential resisters in some aspect of the design and change implementation of the change, they can often forestall resistance. With a participative change effort, the initiators listen to the people the change involves and use their advice. What is needed are the right initiatives and right motivations. Three steps are recommended to deal with resistance to change. Change leaders must:

i. Mobilize commitment to change through joint diagnosis of problems

ii. Develop a shared vision of how to organize for competitiveness

iii. Spread revitalization to all departments- without pushing overtly

3. Knowledge phase: This phase is coterminous with the creating of correct communication channels under the 'changing' stage of Lewin's model of change. All doubts and fears of change among employees must be set to rest.

In the 'Digital' civilization today, information is more important than physical capital to any business. Intellectual capital is embedded more deeply in the ethos of organizations. Knowledge is not discovered like oil or gold is constructed through concepts. Knowledge is created through the reconstruction of older concept as well as invention of new ones. It becomes knowledge only when a particular group or society validates at the concept. Knowledge is therefore a social and organizational construct.

The most meticulously planned knowledge management strategies would fail if the knowledge gaps exist. There must be a commitment at all levels to creating a culture that supports client oriented structures and processed. End-user resistance, interpersonal rivalry, inter-divisional apathy, and faulty aligning of the citizens' needs would be some of the results of inappropriate cultural practices and attitudes. Training in ICT technologies and techniques related to e- governance at different levels is a continuous process.

Some organizations put so much weight on procedures and process that they confuse ends and means, form and content. Managers design detailed presentations meticulously and devote large amounts of time to obtaining sign-offs. Despite the appearance of progress, there's little real headway. It is like running two steps forward and three steps back.

Change leaders must do a delicate balancing act of striking the right chord between 'task orientation' and 'people orientation'. The neglected leadership role from the roll-set bouquet is that of the leader as the designer of a ship apart from being its navigator and captain.

4. Ability building phase: The knowledge gained above

must be put into practice on a continuous basis. Ability also implies identifying knowledge gaps in implementing ERP and filling the same.

Ability phase of ADKAR is coterminous with the 'change' phase, or corresponding to the second phase in Lewin's three Stage model. It implies implementation, empowered action and team effort. Action is putting ideas and concepts to work. Action is tangible and so are its results. Leadership involves both building a future and a break with the past. The role of a leader here can be likened to the captain of a ship who determines its speed and direction. He or she may speed up, slow down, change direction and take a detour or surge straight or full stream depending on the weather, intervening obstacles and contingencies. The decisions of a leader likewise determine the movement of the organization itself, and such decisions are at times unconventional.

The 'ability' phase of ADKAR module of change management heavily depends upon employee attitudes. These attitudes can be favourable or negative or unfavourable to change. The root cause of failure of change management measures and initiatives is not just communication gaps, lack of training or poor project management. Organization Design (OD) measures of change management tend to fail despite all the above being excellent. It is in the individual employee who is the most fundamental unit, the DNA so to say, of any change management intervention. Overcoming these hurdles is a continuous process because the innovation of today soon becomes the conventional norm of tomorrow. Reflective openness is a very important leadership trait needed in this context. For reflective openness, there must be freedom to air and share ideas.

Ability building is very crucial to organizations in the public sector given the fact that these organizations faced so many internal restrictions and hurdles. Change management in the government or public sector organization is therefore a bigger challenge In a bureaucratic structure, the following are generally evident:

i. Employees don't understand how their jobs contribute to important execution outcomes in the context of change management.

ii. Time and money are avoidably expended because of inefficiency or bureaucracy in the execution process.

iii. Execution decisions take too long to make or are too complicated.

The importance of team work cannot be understated in this context. Individuals may work extraordinarily hard, but their efforts do not efficiently translate to team effort. By contrast, when a team becomes more aligned, a commonality of direction emerges, and individuals' energies harmonize. There is less wasted energy. In fact, a resonance or synergy develops, like the 'coherent' light of a laser rather than the incoherent and scattered light of a light bulb.

Building shared vision is vital. If any one idea about leadership has inspired organizations for thousands of years, it's the capacity to hold a shared picture of the future we seek to create. One is hard pressed to think of any organization that has sustained some measure of greatness in the absence of goals, values, and missions that become deeply shared throughout the organization.

5. Reinforcement phase: Reinforcement ensures that after the change has been adopted and implemented, individual employees do not revert back to the old ways of doing things.

Within an organization, a leader must institutionalize a feedback mechanism. The feedback can be both positive and negative. The former must be accepted but must not result in complacency. The latter must not be snuffed out nor must it result in fatalism or compromise.

An organization must be responsive to such feedback in

order to be resilient to its own future. Negative feedback too has the power to initiate an introspective process both within an individual and an organization alike. Sharing ideas, exploring attitudes between individuals and divisions will enhance both individual and organizational performance. Though positive and negative feedback have different meanings and usage, they could be made to serve a common purpose- your personal and professional excellence and success.

Reinforcing feedback and discovering how small changes can grow is important. Pygmalion effects have been shown to operate in countless situations. A small action snowballs, with more and more and still more of the same, resembling compounding interest. Some reinforcing (amplifying) processes are 'vicious cycles ', in which things start off badly and grow worse.

The reference to 'feedback' simply means that some portion of the output is returned to the input to form part of the systems excitation. Negative feedback was given utmost importance.

Reinforcement phase is complemented by pre and post implementation training during change driven by ICTs. The importance of continued training at the end user level in particular is highly important. This will be explicated in the analysis of case studies in the sections that follow in this book.

Lewin's Model

There are three distinct steps recommended in change management if it is to be effective. Those are unfreezing the present, moving from the present and re-freezing. If this model is not followed, then changes will be unsuccessful or at best short-lived. In other words, one can cause needed change to occur. However, in order for change to be permanent, one must dismantle the present (and the capability to move back to the present), move from the present to the future and put in place the people and processes to ensure permanency. This model is still relevant in terms of what to do. However, the speed at which it must be done has increased dramatically.

The three stages with the salient activities in each stage are as follows:

1. Unfreezing–This involves determining what needs to change. This can be arrived at by surveying the organization to understand correct strategy and understanding why change must take place. This calls for (a) Ensuring strong support from across the hierarchy (b) Creating an urgency or need to change (c) Correct communication to set doubts at rest and remove fear of change

2. Changing–This involves (a) Further communication and implementation of change strategy, (b) Empowered action and (c) Involvement of employees.

3. Refreezing– This involves (a) Making change environment a part of organizational culture (b) Reward system (c) Feedback system (d) Training and support and (e) Showcasing success.

Lewin's Model is best suited for planned change and not for responses to unplanned change. Yet, it is applicable when unplanned change occurs, particularly if leaders and change managers know in advance that there is some probability that the change will occur.

Kotter's Model

John Kotter developed a model which should be used at the strategic level of an organization to change its vision and subsequently transform the organization. Studies using this model have shown that the change process goes through a set of phases. Each phase lasts a certain amount of time and mistakes at any phase can impact the success of the change. Kotter's eight step model is depicted in the figure 4 below:

i. Create urgency- People typically prefer the status-quo. Change means uncertainty about the future. Uncertainty makes people uncomfortable. Further more, it is human nature to mistrust things about which people are uncertain. That is why people avoid change. To encourage people to assist with the change, leaders must

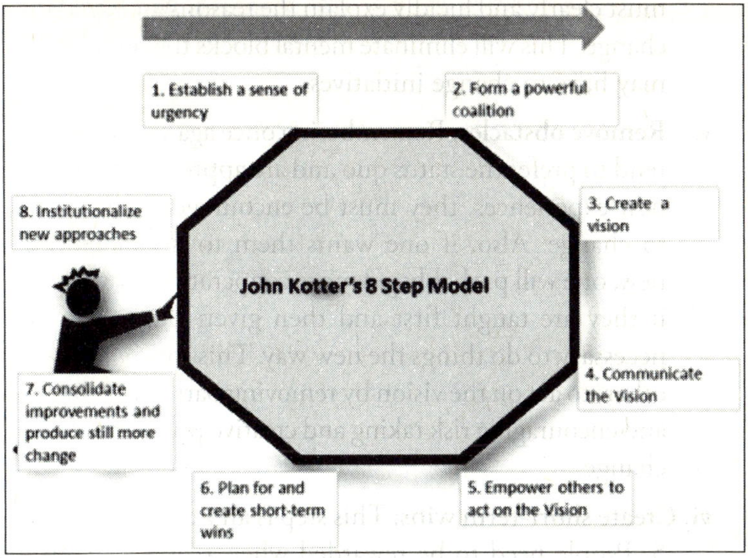

Figure 4 John Jotter's Model of Change

create a sense of urgency and also remove uncertainty.

ii. **Form a powerful coalition:**This step is similar to interventions in drug treatment. To counteract resistance, one option is to form a powerful coalition of managers to work with the most resistant people.

iii. **Create a vision for change:** While it is not impossible to get things done without a definite plan of action, it is much simpler if there is a clear plan in place. Since the status quo is more comfortable for most people, they are likely to revert to a complacent attitude and not flow with changes without a plan in place. Creating a vision and the strategies for achieving the vision will help expedite the change.

iv. **Communicate the vision:** If people do not know that change is coming or has occurred, they are more likely to resist the change. Top management and leadership must clearly and lucidly explain the reasons and need for change. This will eliminate mental blocks that employees may have to change initiatives.

v. **Remove obstacles:** Remembering once again that people tend to prefer the status quo and are apprehensive about new experiences, they must be encouraged or inspired to change. Also, if one wants them to do something new, one will probably get more cooperation from them if they are taught first and then given the new tools necessary to do things the new way. This step empowers others to act on the vision by removing barriers to change and encouraging risk taking and creative problem solving change.

vi. **Create short-term wins:** This step is an extension of step 5. People need to be rewarded when they break away from old behaviours and do something that is new and desirable. Basically it is positive reinforcement. This is the step where you plan for, create and reward short-term 'wins' that move the organization toward the new vision change.

vii. **Build on the change:** Change must be nurtured and necessary adjustments and adaptations are to be made to facilitate change.

viii. **Anchor the changes in corporate culture:** When it comes to work, one can never tell someone enough about all the good reasons why the things they do make them – and the company – a success. Otherwise, some people will tend to behave as if they have no reason to do anything differently than they did before. So, to make the changes more permanent, one should reinforce them by demonstrating the relationship between new behaviours and organizational success change.

Implementation of e-Government projects may prefer one

model over the other depending on situational variables. These variables include the nature and scope of the project, the state of development of the organization, the nature of the intended beneficiaries of the projects etc. It is also possible to skillfully choose a hybrid module taking out the best and the most situated elements from different models.

Critical Success Factors (CSFs):

Organizational leaders who are considering or contemplating change should clearly understand which strategies they want to change and define CSFs so that they will know the extent to which the desired change is possible. These must be equally well communicated to all those who will be impacted by the change. Some of the change models do not address this phase of change. Organizations must communicate the strategic objectives to the work force. If this is not done, the transformation effort will be reduced to a series of unrelated change initiatives.

The preconditions of accepting change within an organization are broadly classified as following:

(a) Leadership and sponsorship

(b) Skills, skill sets and competencies

(c) Organizational alignment

(d) Communications – vertical and horizontal.

(e) Performance management system and performance appraisal.

(f) Organizational change management strategies.

Managing change involves several acts of balancing and counter-balancing. Among others, it involves striking a balance between individual and collective actions, focusing on content and procedures, and harmonizing short-term and long-term goals. Change is difficult to bring about through the efforts of just one individual, howsoever powerful or charismatic he or she may be. It is necessary that groups and teams of people are made to collaborate in articulating the nuances of the change process

It is also a fact that change is always and not necessarily a painful process in whichever sphere it is introduced. Any organization seeking to effect change has to grapple with forces both within and outside the organization that may hinder, slow down or be inimical to change efforts. Often managers and change leaders undermine or do not sufficiently take care of the external forces which come in the way of promoting it. Managing change almost invariably involves a certain degree of 'shock treatment' followed by a 'healing therapy', depending upon the power and role-relationships of various actors in the change system and change process.

With exponential technological development and advances, a growing knowledge workforce and the shifting of hitherto accepted work practices, change is becoming an everyday and constant feature of organizational life. While many organisations acknowledge the need for change and even take initiatives in this regard as many as 70% of the change programmes do not achieve their intended outcomes.

Comprehensive behavioural change models indicate that there are a range of factors that influence the ability of an individual to change that go beyond their rational, conscious thought processes. These include unconscious desires and fears as well as conditioned behaviour and thinking.

The way in which staff are enabled to positively adapt to change in their work practices and work environment and culture has been identified as one of the leading critical success factors in successful change strategy implementations.

Change management also refers to all activities associated with the interaction of technology, processes, and people. A report by Deloitte states that, implementing an ICT based processes and systems may force the reengineering of key business processes and/or developing new business processes to support the organizations goals. The resulting changes may significantly affect organizational structures, policies, processes, and employees. Therefore, change management can be considered as a special case of risk management.

The Change Impact Assessment (CIA) works across a multitude of segments: changes in business processes, policies and procedures, employee knowledge and skills, IT and technology, corporate culture.

Change implementation planning logically follows the change impact assessment. The lack of impact assessment activities may lead to problems and hurdles with planning and confirming the steps of change implementation in business divisions.

Implementation of change in any organization is inseparably and intricately connected with its organizational culture, its structures and processes and its leadership competence. It is also common knowledge that people in organizations pay most attention to behaviour demonstrated by their leadership. Thus a culture of the appropriate leadership initiatives and styles are important.

Managing change or driving it will be tougher and complex in organizations involved in services provision and services delivery as distinct for manufacturing. This is all the more applicable to organisations in the Government and the PSUs in the services sector, where the citizen and / or customer facing front office is as important as the back-end operations. The so called 'line' and 'staff' are crucial for services delivery.

While CSFs are important so are Critical Failure Factors (CFFs).The Vedanta school of philosophy of ancient India talks of a method called on 'Neti-Neti' to reach the ultimate truth. This is the path of negation which roughly translates as 'Not this-Not this'. The case studies that would follow in this book and the lessons that can be learnt from them will shed light on what not to do to avoid failure of e-government projects using this path of negation.

Kotter points out six errors that are often committed by change managers and leaders in change management initiatives. These are acutely relevant to digitalization and e- governance projects and initiatives.

Error 1: Not establishing a great enough sense of urgency. Compared with other steps in the change process, phase one can sound easy. It is not. Kotter says that well over 50% of the companies he has watched fail in this first phase. What are the reasons for that failure? Sometimes executives underestimate how hard it can be to drive people out of their comfort zones' says Kotter.

Error 2: Not creating a powerful enough guiding coalition. This implies creating a leadership team with a unified vision and a clear sense of direction. This involves examining market and competitive business realities and environmental analysis which in turn requires Identifying and discussing crises, potential crises, and major opportunities as well.

Planning for and creating short-term wins will inspire and motivate employees. A very important step in institutionalizing new approaches is by articulating the connections between the new behaviour and successful results in a visible and tangible manner. It also involves developing the means to ensure leadership development and succession.

Error 3: Lacking a vision- Without a sensible and clear vision, a transformation effort can easily turn into a list of confusing and incompatible projects that can take the organization in the wrong direction or nowhere at all. A useful rule of thumb: "If you can't communicate the vision to someone in five minutes or less and get a reaction that signifies both understanding and interest, you are not yet done with this phase of the transformation process" says Kotter.

Error 4: Under communicating the vision: In more successful transformation efforts, executives use all existing communication channels to broadcast the vision.

Error 5: Not removing obstacles to the 'new' vision that entails change management.

Error 6: Not systematically planning for, and not creating, 'short-term wins'.

Mechanistic and Organic changes:People make up the internal social system of the organization. They consist of individuals and groups, large groups as well as small ones. People are the living, thinking, feeling beings who created the organizations. They are sentient beings who have feelings and attitudes. Organizations exist to serve people. People do not exist to serve organizations. The work force is one of the critical resources that need to be managed. In managing human resources, managers and leaders have to deal with many issues, some of the vital ones being the following.

1. Individual employees who are expected to perform the tasks allotted to them.

2. Dyadic relationships such as superior-subordinate interactions.

3. Groups who work as teams and have the responsibility for getting the job done.

4. People outside the organization system such as customers, vendors, strategic partners, channel partners, investors and government officials.

Thus the stakeholders of an organization include both internal and external ones. An overview of 'structure' and 'system' is relevant here. Structure defines the official relationships of people in organizations. Different jobs are required to accomplish all of an organization's activities. There are managers and employees, accountants and assemblers. These people have to be related in some structural way so that their work can be effective.

Organizations can be structured as relatively rigid, formalized systems or as relatively loose, flexible systems. Thus the structure of the organizations can range on a continuum of high rigidity to high flexibility. There are two broad categories of organization: 1. Mechanistic form of organization 2) Organic form of organization

The mechanistic form of organization is characterized by high levels of complexity, formalization and centralization. A highly mechanistic system is characterized by centralized decision making at the top, a rigid hierarchy of authority, well but narrowly defined job responsibilities especially at lower levels, and extensive rules and regulations which are explicitly made known to employees through written documents. In mechanistic organization, labour is divided and subdivided into many highly specialized tasks (high complexity), workers are granted limited discretion in performing their clearly designated tasks and rules and procedures are carefully defined (high formalization). There is limited participation in decision making which tends to be conducted at the highest levels of management and leadership.

A highly organic system is characterized by decentralized decision-making which allows people directly involved with the job to make their own decisions, very few levels in the hierarchy with flexible authority and reporting patterns, loosely defined job responsibilities for members, and very few written rules and regulations. It is relatively simple, informal and decentralized. Compared with mechanistic organizations, employees in organic organizations, such as design firms or research labs, tend to be more generalistic in their orientation. But some organizations can display both types of structures. For instance, in a mining company there can be organic structure inside the mine while mechanistic will be above ground at administrative level.

The implementation of e-government projects in evidently bureaucratic and mechanistic structures must take into account the organically predisposed preconditions to change. These include

1. **Respect for people:** Individuals are perceived as being responsible, conscientious and caring. They should be treated with dignity and respect - trust and support: Effective and healthy organizations are characterized by trust, authenticity, openness and supportive climate
2. **Power equalization:** Effective organizations de-emphasize hierarchical authority and control
3. **Confrontation:** Problems should not be swept under the carpet. They should be openly confronted
4. **Participation:** The more the people who will be affected by a change are involved in the decisions surrounding that change, the more they will be committed to implementing those decisions

The importance of leadership at different levels in the hierarchy is important in this context. Effective leadership is needed to use the right channels and content to communicate with the employees during the pre and post ICT driven change implementation phase.

As stated elsewhere earlier, implementation of e-government initiatives is a highly humane activity over and above the technology involved in the same. However, technology does form a part of the process.

The 'soft-side' of e-Government project implementation:

The subtle but sure role of organizational culture:

In the context of organizational change, change management consists of two sides - the hard side and the soft side. The hard side refers to the processes, systems, strategies, and technologies that will assist in implementing change. This hard side is relatively not 'hard' at all compared to the soft side. The soft side involves behavioral and attitudinal changes. The soft side change includes persuading, reassuring, institutionalizing confidence building measures, communicating correctly, establishing a resilient feedback mechanism, motivation strategies etc. This soft side permeates the underlying organizational culture.

Organizational culture is one of the most important human elements in change management and any ICT driven project. It is ultimately organizational culture that determines and influences individual commitment to change initiatives. This in turn is directly related to the achievement of the organization's vision and the very objectives of the change initiatives.

Organizational culture, organizational leadership and most importantly the perspective of the end-user of ICTs are central to any successful ICT driven project efforts, and for that matter, any OD initiative or change management initiative. Intricately linked to this are the issues of knowledge management and the communication process. There are some interesting studies in this area. The components of organizational culture are represented diagrammatically at Figure 4

Organizational culture is known to be important for the success of projects involving organizational changes. Organizational culture has a deep impact on attitudes of individual employees. These attitudes as a collective entity are very powerful in making or braking change initiatives.

There are two extreme types of organizational culture which not only are different in structural characteristics but also differ in the underlying attitudes and beliefs of the people working in them. The first is a 'segmentalist' culture and the second is an 'integrative' culture. Segmentalist culture stress on 'weak coordination', 'compartmentalization' and 'stressing precedent and procedures' in. Integrative culture more emphasize are on 'encouraging cooperation', 'combination' and 'looking for novel solutions to problems'. Different forms of organizational culture could lead to be supportive of, or against organizational change in different situations.

Another aspect related to this is the organizational

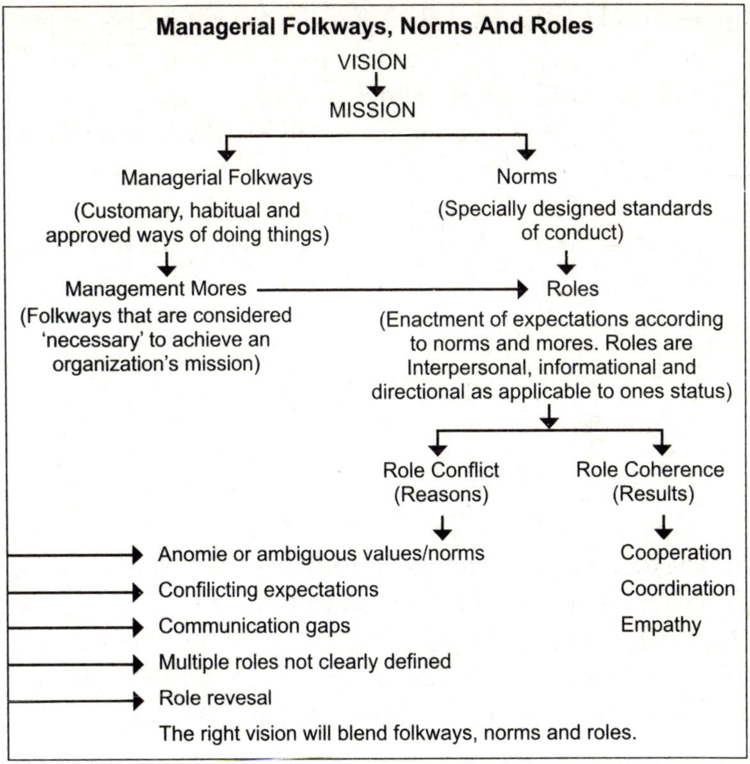

Figure 4 Components of organizational culture

'structure.' While 'systems' are more process oriented, organizational structure is essentially hierarchy of roles and role relationships within an organization. Job descriptions and functional interdependencies come into play here. The vital question here is the power or strength of inertial forces on organizational structure. Organizational culture acquires importance when the systems and structures need to be changed. This brings into focus the individual and group attitudes to change. Culture becomes a weakness when important shared beliefs and values interfere with the needs of the business, its strategy, and the people. This condition is usually a significant weakness because it is hard to change a culture's content. An organization's culture could be strong and cohesive when it conducts its business according to action and explicit set of principles and values, which the management devotes considerable time to communicating to employees and which values are shared widely across the organization.

Culture influences organizational life through five basic processes that lie at the heart of any organization. These include the following.

1. Cooperation
2. Decision-making
3. Control
4. Communication
5. Commitment

The importance of end-user attitude to ICT backed change:

The attitude toward change generally consists of a person's affective reactions to change, cognitions about change, and behavioural tendency towards change. The individual responses to organizational change are classified into three types. First, affective responses are a greater or lesser feeling of being linked to, satisfied with, or anxious about change. Next, cognitive responses are the opinions one has about the advantages and disadvantages, usefulness, and necessity, and about the knowledge required to handle the change. Then, behavioural responses are the actions already taken or which will be taken in the future for or against the change. This is especially true for the case of ICT systems since they require learning to overcome knowledge barriers, and unlearning of what is already known.

Based on the existing conceptualizations of organizational commitment, it can be seen as having three components reflecting a desire (affective commitment), a need (continuance commitment) and an obligation (normative commitment) to maintain employment in an organization. Affective commitment refers to the employees' emotional attachment to, identification with, and involvement in the organization. Continuance commitment refers to an awareness of the costs associated with leaving the organization. Formally, normative commitment reflects a feeling of obligation to continue employment.

It can be argued that individuals with strong organizational commitment would be more willing to accept organizational change if such a change does not alter the basic values and goals of the organization and is seen as beneficial to the organization. Organizational commitment is more often than not, next most important determinant of attitude toward organizational change. An individual's commitment to an organization affects how she or he evaluates organizational change. Perceived personal competence has also been found to be strongly related to organizational commitment.

There is a growing body of empirical and theoretical evidence supporting the positive relationship of perceived personal competence to employees' attitude toward change. The change oriented action is a function of employee motivation; and thus employees with strong perceived personal competence are likely to pursue further change initiatives.

Employee attitudes are clearly important to organizations. When attitudes are negative, they are both a symptom of underlying problems and a contributing cause of forthcoming difficulties in an organization. Declining attitudes may result in wildcat strikes, work slowdowns, absences and employee turnover. They may also be a part of grievances, low performance, poor product quality and shabby customer service and disciplinary problems. The organizational costs associated with poor employee attitudes may severely reduce an organization's competitiveness.

Favourable attitudes, on the other hand, are desired by management and leadership because they tend to be connected with some of the positive outcomes. Employee satisfaction, along with high productivity, is a hallmark of well-managed organizations.

Sometimes even highly skilled and competent people resist change. This is because they perceive that change will make them less competent. A key challenge for managers and leaders is therefore dealing with employees who increasingly expect to have concern shown for their attitudes and feelings as well as to receive rewards. They have an attitude of entitlement – believing they deserve things because society owes it to them. However, these expectations can at times be unrealistic. Effective behavioural management that continuously works to build a supportive human climate in an organization can help produce favourable attitudes.

The root cause for resistance to change could be one, or as it usually is, more than one of the following reasons given the specific characteristics of each organization. This is even more so in the government organizations and the public sector.

Uncertainty: Perhaps the biggest cause of employee resistance to change is uncertainty. In the face of impending change, employees may become anxious and nervous. They may worry about their ability to meet new job demands, they may think that their job security is threatened, or they may simply dislike ambiguity.

Threatened self-interests: Many impending changes threaten the self-interests of employees at different levels within the organization. A change might potentially diminish their power or influence within the company, so they resist and oppose it in different ways.

Different perceptions: A third reason that people resist change is due to different perceptions. A manager may make a decision and recommend a plan for change on the basis of her own assessment of a situation. Others in the organization may resist the change because they do not agree with the manager's assessment or perceive the situation differently.

Feelings of loss: Many organizational changes involve altering work arrangements in ways that disrupt existing social networks. Because both formal and informal social relationships are important, most people resist any change that might adversely affect those relationships. Other intangibles threatened by change include power, status, security, familiarity with existing procedures and self-confidence.

Resistance to change and dealing with it

It is said that resistance to change is as natural as change itself. No resistance from the people involved should be taken light and it should be addressed, as much as possible. Here are some ways to deal with resistance:

1. **Participation:** Participation is often the most effective technique for overcoming resistance to change. Employees who participate in planning and implementing a change are better able to understand the reasons for the change. Uncertainty is reduced, and self-interests and social relationships are less threatened. Having had an opportunity to express their ideas and assume the perspectives of others, employees are more likely to accept the change gracefully.

2. **Education, training and communication:** Educating and training the employees and communicating the positive aspects of change helps very much in reducing their resistance. If open communication is established and maintained during the change process, uncertainty can be minimized.

3. **Facilitation:** Several facilitation procedures are also advisable. For instance, making only necessary changes, announcing those changes well in advance, and allowing time for people to adjust to new ways of doing things can help reduce resistance to change.

4. **Force-Field analysis:** Force-field analysis can help overcome resistance to change. In almost any change situation, forces are acting for and against the change. To facilitate the change, change managers start by listing each set of forces and then trying to tip the balance so that the forces facilitating the change outweigh those hindering the change. It is especially

important to try remove or at least minimize some of the forces acting against the change.

Change management and role of leadership Alchemy:

Alchemy is the legendary medieval European science of transmuting ordinary metal to gold. The Alchemists were an exclusive group of people privileged to know this secret. In terms of dealing with change driven by ICTs and in e-Governance projects, the leader must verily be an Alchemist of sorts. He must be not just a transformational but also a 'trans-mutative' leader. He or she must make something extraordinary out of the given.

Change management is essentially about leadership. This is of highest relevance when such change is systematically driven from within. This would be in the context of communication process, conflict resolution and CSFs.

From organizational leadership perspective, four types of reinforcement methods available to manage or modify an individual's behaviour. These are (1) Positive Reinforcement (2) Punishment (3) Avoidance Learning (4) Extinction.

The application of positive reinforcement to a given response or behaviour increases the likelihood that the particular behaviour by the individual will be repeated. For example, an engineer is given the task of designing a new piece of equipment (stimulus). The engineer exerts a high level of effort and completes the project in time (response). The supervisor reviews the work and not only praises the engineer for his or her work, but recommends, for example, a pay increase or paid holiday for the excellent work (positive reinforcement).

Negative reinforcement increases the frequency and strength of a desired behaviour by making it contingent upon the avoidance of undesirable consequences for the employees. In order to avoid a pay-cut or being marked absent employees come on time to punch their identity cards in the electronic attendance system at the entrance of the office. Just to avoid the unpleasantness in the future, the person will try to exhibit the desired work behaviour. Thus the negative reinforcement implies the mere anticipation of noxious stimuli from the environment by the employees will reinforce the desired behaviours.

The application of punishment is used to decrease the likelihood that the undesirable behaviour or response by the individual will be repeated. Just as positive reinforcement strengthens a particular behaviour, punishment weakens it. The use of this punishment is in the hope that it will change an employee's response back from deviance to acceptable behaviour. The difference between punishment and negative reinforcement is that in the former case, noxious consequences is applied to decrease the frequency or strength of an undesired behaviour, where as in the latter, a noxious consequences is withheld when a behaviour is exhibited.

Just as with positive reinforcement, this type of reinforcement is a method used by managers to strengthen desired behaviour. When a particular reinforcement can prevent the occurrence of an undesired stimulus, it is termed avoidance learning. In order to avoid reprimand and criticism, the employee makes a special effort to comply with accepted behaviour. With the avoidance learning, the individual works hard to avoid the undesired consequences of the stimulus.

Extinction is the withholding of positive reinforcement for a previously acceptable response. With continued non-reinforcement over time, the response or behaviour will eventually disappear or be eliminated. Extinction involves three steps: (i) Identifying the behaviour that needs to be eliminated (ii) Identifying the 'reinforcers' which encourage the behaviour that is desired to be eliminated and (iii) Stopping the reinforcers after sometime (it becomes the 'new habit'). Shaping behaviour is a process of changing an undesirable behaviour to a desirable behaviour by following a successive approximation of desirable targeted behaviour with proper reinforcement.

Leadership processes refer to superiors' trust and confidence in their subordinates. The superiors behave in the manner that encourage subordinates to feel free to discuss important matters about their jobs and the superiors try to get ideas and opinions from subordinates and use them constructively.

The cultural nurturing process is a very important and indispensable aspect of leadership. This includes organizational 'climate' that leaders help develop. Other aspects of climate are also interrelated to develop an information organization that supports or opposes formal goals. A corporate culture might be defined as the overriding ideology and established patterns of behaviour and norms that influence actions and decisions. Culture, be it corporate or government, is a set of important assumptions, often unstated, that members of an organization share in common. These shared understandings consist of norms, values, attitudes and beliefs. Every organization has a culture that exerts powerful influences on the behaviour of its employees. Organizational culture provides meaning, direction and the basis for action. Shared assumptions, beliefs and values among members of an organization set a pattern for activities, opinions, and actions with that firm.

Thus, a leader in ICT oriented change projects must play the unenviable role of an Alchemist in efficiently managing the organizational culture, commitment, communication processes and internal systems and orient them to the intended objectives of change management.

Role of communication and feedback processes

Organizational communication process is a systemic and structural element that has direct impact on any ICT based change initiatives or the implementation of any e-Governance project. A good communication system is one of the most important critical success factors in organizational change. If not handled well or structured properly, it can become a critical failure factor. The history of failed cases in change management is repeat instances where noble and visionary intentions have failed because of gaps in the communication process.

It is generally agreed that communication involves the

sharing of ideas, knowledge, feelings and perceptions. Within the workplace, communication takes place for a number of direct and indirect reasons, and explicit and implicit reasons. Primarily it is necessary for passing information between people working in different divisions or departments of the same organization and between the organization and other entities and stakeholders. Communication-written, spoken or even nonverbal-is also used by leaders and managers for evaluating performance, directing or instructing staff and motivating others.

Communication process contains seven main elements, namely (i) Sender, (ii) Message, (iii) Receiver, (iv) Feedback, (v) Channel, (vi) Context or setting and (vii) Noise or interference. As communication occurs, sender and receiver interact by encoding/sending and decoding/receiving messages. Encoding means putting the message into words or diagram or nonverbal signals so that it can be transmitted. The receiver hears, reads or looks in order to decode or interpret the message. We will not go into the pedagogy of communications here but out only its practicality and practicability in ICT driven change management initiatives. The feedback systems and mechanisms are highly significant in this context.

Feedback is an essential part of successful interpersonal communication. It is the receiver's response to the sender's message. It tells the sender how their message is being received and helps the receiver confirm whether their perception of the message is correct. It can be intentional or unintentional. Feedback thus provides continuity in the communication and Indicates effective understanding or misunderstanding of the message. It stimulates further communication and discussion.

A communication channel is the means or the techniques as stand-alone or together used to signal or convey a message. These channels are internal to the organization as well as outside the organization and are thus external channels. An appropriate channel suits the communication purpose, the need of the sender, the message and the needs of the receiver. Different channels of communication are used inside an organization. Horizontal channels operate between colleagues at the same level of hierarchy or status within the organization's structures, while vertical channels move communication up and down between different levels in the organization.

Hence, formal communication channels represent a major structural means of control within organizations. Informal channels and grapevine also plays an important role in this control process.

The other side of the control aspect of communications is the 'conflict' aspect. This is rooted in various problems such as the following. Many failed e-Governance projects across the globe have suffered some of these problems and hitches.

(a) Semantic problems: The use of inappropriate language, symbols, and words may affect the understanding capacity of the receiver. The sender must ensure that proper words and language are chosen to communicate the intended message so that there is no room for misinterpretation or confusion and the receiver decodes the message exactly as it was encoded. Many words commonly used in communication carry quite different meanings for different people.

(b) Status effects: Status effect also often hinders communication in as much as people occupying higher positions in the organization have a tendency to tell a lot to the subordinates but not to listen. If a two-way communication is blocked, there is scope for friction and conflict.

(c) Physical distraction: When people communicate with each other, various types of distraction can hinder the communication process. Distractions may occur because of situational factors such as constant telephone interruptions, people walking in and out of the room, or loud noises in the background.

(d) Information overload: This refers to the sheer volume of information which is beyond the level of a person to grasp or comprehend. Communication may be ineffective when too much information is transmitted at one time or when complex and complicated information is presented within a short time frame. The problem is compounded if the individual also has limited attention span and poor memory retention. Often, top and middle level employees are flooded in communications, in terms of volumes, complexity and multiple sources. This includes variety of information received from different modes such as e-mail, memos, official letters, reports, instructions, circular, telephone, meetings etc. All those have different levels of urgency and importance.

(e) **Time pressures:** Time is always in short supply in the world of business in particular,, and this fact often leads to distortion in communication. A major temptation when pressed for time is to short-circuit formal communication channels. Because of time pressures, many messages are hastily, incompletely and inadequately communicated by managers, leaving the listener with much ambiguity and confusion as to what has been said and what action should be taken.

(f) **Cultural differences:** Words, colours and symbols have different meanings in different cultures and sometimes even between sub-cultures within a national boundary. The same is applicable to organizations, especially large ones like the Pan-India's BSNL.

(g) **Trust level:** When there is lack of sufficient trust between the communicating parties, selective listening takes place, resulting in ineffective communication.

(h) **Absence of two-way Communication:** If communication is only one way–from top to bottom or from superior to subordinate–without any feedback, this would hinder communication from taking place in an effective and efficient manner. For instance, the receiver might decode the message in a way that was not intended. Neither the receiver nor the sender will then realize that the message was misinterpreted until it becomes too late. This may lead to desperate rectification measures or at time the situation may be beyond repair.

There are some tried and tested ways to overcome barriers to communication. The process of feedback and follow up makes communication a two-way process. In face-to-face situations, the sender should try to become sensitive to facial expressions and other signs that indicate how the message is being received. It is often important to solicit questions of clarification from the receiver. When more formal communication is involved, the writer may specify specific forms and times for responding to ensure feedback.

Parallel channels and repetition: is an effective means to overcome communication barriers. A major principle of communication technology is to provide parallel channels of communication that reinforce each other.

Since feedback involves both receiver and sender, it is important to understand the conditions under which feedback session will be more effective both from the sender's and receiver's perspective. For feedback to be most effective, the person giving the feedback must give specific and not general or vague feedback. This must be done immediately or soon after the event has taken place rather than long after the event has occurred. The feedback must include only those aspects that the receiver can rectify rather than on aspects over which the individual has no control. This can be both descriptive and evaluative.

The feedback must be focused and on a few critical issues where improvement is most urgently expected rather than on a wide range of problem areas. The latter would lead to a dilution of core issues. The giver of feedback must examine his or her own motivation in giving the feedback. The giver of feedback must in turn be sure that the receiver is ready to receive feedback. Be non-threatening and disregard your superior status while offering feedback.

It is universally accepted that communication can be in the following directions – (1) Downward (2) Upward and (3) Lateral. A proper and skilful deployment of each of these in the situational matrix unique to each organization is crucial to manage internal changes in e-government initiatives driven by ICTs.

Downward Communication refers to the flow of communication from supervisor to the subordinate. To improve downward communication, managers can present job instructions clearly to subordinates, explain lucidly why things need to be done in a particular way so that people who perform the jobs understand the same better. For example, clear staff regulations, rules, handbooks, procedures manual etc. are the good examples of downward communication.

Upward communications refers to the flow from the subordinate to the superiors. To improve upward communication, it is generally recommended that one must screen upward messages so that the more relevant aspects of the information are received by top management, provide the climate in which members can communicate both positive and negative messages, detect biases when they occur, reduce status difference and wherever possible, require quantified data to be submitted rather than provide subjective information for decision making.

Lateral communication takes place between or among members who are at the same level in the organization. For example, two supervisors of the same department or different departments discussing work matters with each other. To improve lateral communication, it is desirable to establish openness and trust among members of various departments, develop reward systems that facilitate inter-departmental cooperation, learn that what the other departments are doing by getting involved in interdepartmental meetings and, if possible design the organization structure in such a way so that greater opportunities of interdepartmental contacts exist. This will facilitate the creative and constructive use of negative feedback too. The elements of negative feedback is presented at Figure 5.

Another apparently trivial, but in reality not so, aspect of the communication process is the role of informal communications and 'grapevine'. This is more so true in the government and the public sectors. Informal communication system is the

Type of response	Negative feedback is correct	Negative feedback is incorrect
Confirmatory	Check veracity and accept it	Check veracity and clarify if it's correct
Corrective	Take steps to amend the situation	Set right misconceptions. Eliminate the 'courses' that let one to form the feedback.
Explanatory	Explain to the team and make them understand the need to change.	Explain why it is incorrect to ensure it does not repeat.
Diagnostic	Analyze the situation and understand it.	Understand the reasons and circumstances that led to such a feedback. These may be hidden and chronic in nature.

Figure 5 Negative feedback and responses

diametrically opposite system of formal communication. In this system the communication is made without following any predetermined rules of policy. Informal communication plays a vital role to operate the organization's activities.

It will be seen in the case studies that many well intended e-Government projects across the world have failed because of the lack of proper communication channels before and during the implementation of such projects.

Organizational conflict and change management

Conflict is a natural and at times an inevitable organizational reality. This is particularly true in times of large scale organizational change in the context of ICT driven e- Government projects with the unions, interest and pressure groups at play. Conflict has both negative and positive functions. In organizations, conflicts can be interpersonal, intra-group, inter-group or intra-organizational in nature. Intra-organizational conflict encompasses vertical, horizontal, Line-staff and role conflict.

Vertical conflict refers to conflicts that occur between

individuals at different levels. Conflict between the superior and subordinate is an example of vertical conflict. Such conflicts could happen because of perceived transgression of psychological contract, inadequate or ineffective communication, selective perception, misperception, incongruence in goals, values, cognition, affect and behaviour etc.

Horizontal conflict refers to tensions between employees or groups at the same hierarchical level. Horizontal conflict occurs because of interdependence among the parties concerned in the work situation or the common pooled resources shared. For example, sharing of common resources such as computer lab etc. among the various departments is likely to produce tensions among the departments. Incompatibility of goal and time orientations often results in horizontal conflicts. Conflicts will take place between the units due to misunderstanding distrust and frustration experienced by both parties. Horizontal conflict generally tends to increase as: (a) functional interdependence increase among people or groups at the same level (b) More units depend on common resources that have to be shared such as raw materials and (c) The fewer the buffers or inventories for the resources shared.

'Line' and 'staff' Conflict refers to the conflicts that arise between those who assist or act in an functional capacity (staff) and those who have direct authority to create the products, process, and services of the organization (line). Staff managers and line managers usually have different personality predispositions and goals and come from different backgrounds. Staff managers have specialized skills and expertise acquired through training and education and have greater technical knowledge which is intended to help the line manager. Staff personnel serve as advisors for the line personnel in as much as they have the expertise to streamline methods and help in productivity enhancing and cost-cutting mechanisms. Line managers may feel that the staff people are unnecessarily interfering in their work by always telling them how to do their job and thrusting their ideas and methods. Staff personnel often get frustrated that the line personnel do not consider all the ideas put forth by them and thereby fail to benefit.

Role Conflict arises because different people in the organization are expected to perform different tasks and pressures build up when the expectation of the members clash in several ways. There are two types of role conflict. They are as follows.

1. **Inter-sender role conflict:** This occurs when different role senders (bosses) expect the individual to perform different things and these expectations and the messages conflict with each other.

2. **Inter-Group Role conflict:** This occurs when role requires associated with members in one group conflicts with role requirements stemming from members in another group.

There are three basic sources of inter-group conflict: 1) Goal incompatibility, 2) Decision making requirements and 3) Performance expectations.

Goal incompatibility is defined as the lack of agreement concerning the direction of group activity and the criteria for evaluating task accomplishment. This is considered the most frequently identified source for inter-group conflict. The critical elements which contribute to goal incompatibility are: 1) time and goal orientation and 2) barriers to goal accomplishment. Different time (short versus long term) and goal (techno-economic, financial, operational market and scientific) orientations create a state of differentiation between two or more interacting groups. When two widely differing groups, such as manufacturing (short-term and techno-economic orientation) and finance (cost cutting, revenue and audit orientation) interact, this state of time and goals orientation differentiating can act as a source of conflict. If goal attainment by one group is seen as preventing other groups from achieving their goals or contrary to perceived vision and organizational goals, barriers to goal accomplishment arise.

Decision-making requirement can address if it takes care of specific requirements of decision-making used by each of the interacting groups. Two aspects that are related to decision-making requirements are 1) degree of task uncertainty and 2) the availability of resources. The nature of the particular task being performed by each of the interacting groups may require different amounts of information flow before a decision can be reached. The greater the task uncertainty inherent in each task, the greater the need for additional information.

The third source of inter-group conflict is performance expectation and is concerned with the situation in which the activities or performance of one group affects the subsequent performance of other groups.

There are many proven conflict management techniques. These include (1) Avoidance (2) Accommodation (3) Competition (4) Compromising and (5) Collaboration.

Avoidance involves a general disregard for the causes of the conflict and the person or group might diplomatically sidestep a conflicting issue, postpone addressing it till later, or withdraw physically or psychologically from a conflict situation.

Accommodation is a negotiation style method of conflict management where one party is willing to oblige or adapt to meet the needs of the other party. That party that accommodates loses and the other party wins. Accommodation is useful for negotiation on minor issues. Competition occurs when one party negotiates to maximize its results at the expense of the other party's needs. Competition leads to one party gaining the advantage over the other. One party wins while the other party loses, in an absolute or relative sense. It is a Win-Lose scenario.

Compromise is the settlement of differences through concessions on part of one or both parties. In compromising, the party tries to find some expedient, mutually acceptable solutions which partially satisfy both the parties, though neither is fully satisfied. A compromising stance addresses the issue without avoiding it, but does not explore the alternative in a way that would be completely satisfying to both parties as in the case of collaboration.

Collaboration occurs when people cooperate to produce a solution satisfactory to both. This is a win-win scenario. Collaborating involves an attempt to work with the other person or groups to find solutions that would be satisfying to both parties. Here, the underlying concerns of both parties are acknowledged, explored in depth, the disagreements examined in detail and resolutions arrived at by combining the insights of both the parties.

A creative solution usually emerges because of the joint efforts of both the parties who are keen on both gaining from the situation without hurting the other. Collaboration is useful in the following situations.

(1) When the goals of the two parties are both too important to be compromised. (2) When the commitment of both parties is essential for important projects to succeed. (3) When the objectives of the parties are to learn and to merge insights that different people or groups bring to a problem because of their diversity. It involves accepting and working through hard feelings which are interfering with a desired interpersonal relationship.

Thus, in collaborating, the intention of the parties is to solve the problem by clarifying differences rather than by accommodating various points of view.

During the analysis of case studies in digitalization and e- governance in the following chapters, the different types of conflicts, their sources and how they were addressed by the leadership would be critically yet constructively examined.

11

Case Studies in e-Governance project implementation and lessons that can be learnt

This chapter is devoted to case studies and the learnings from them. It is said that people who learn from their mistakes are smart while those who learn from mistakes of others are smarter! There is so much to learn from others through case studies – both the best practices and those that should be avoided.

CASE STUDY-1

GPR in ERP at BSNL

Government Process Reengineering (Also called Business Process Reengineering in the present case) and digitalization of end-to-end organizational processes by successful implementing of Enterprise Resource Planning (ERP) in BSNL (Bharat Sanchar Nigam Limited).

Note to the reader: This project was in line with government of India's e-Governance initiatives and BSNL's vision of leveraging technology to provide affordable and innovative telecom services/ products across customer segments, thereby also providing vital communication infrastructure for nation building. This achievement and success story was recognized and cited in Indian PSU IT Casebook-2016.

Background

BSNL was incorporated on 15th September 2000. It took over the business of providing of telecom services and network management from the erstwhile Central Government Departments of Telecom Services (DTS) and Telecom Operations (DTO), with effect from 1st October 2000. It is one of the largest and leading public sector units providing comprehensive range of telecom services in India.

BSNL has installed a massive network in the country and is now focusing on improving it, expanding the network, introducing new telecom services with ICT applications in villages and winning customer's confidence. As on date (April, 2017) it has about 43.74 million line basic telephone capacity, 8.83 million WLL capacity, 72.60 million GSM capacity, 37,885 fixed exchanges, 68,162 GSM BTSs, 12,071 CDMA Towers, 197 Satellite Stations, 6,86,644 RKm (Route Kilometre) of OFC, 50,430 RKm. of microwave network connecting 623 districts, 7330 cities/towns and 5.8 lakhs villages.

For purposes of revenues and operations, BSNL is divided into 'circles' that are further divided into Secondary Switching Areas (SSAs). Each SSA is considered as an independent profit Centre and therefore conducts its business independent of the other SSAs. Therefore, 334 SSAs across 26 independent entities represent a significant challenge for people and change management.

The above details are depicted in Figure 1.

Introduction

The case of Business Process Reengineering (BPR) and ERP roll out in BSNL, a wholly owned Public Sector Unit under the ministry of telecommunications can be a quintessential example representative of the challenges faced by government departments and PSUs in initiating ICT based organizational change initiatives.

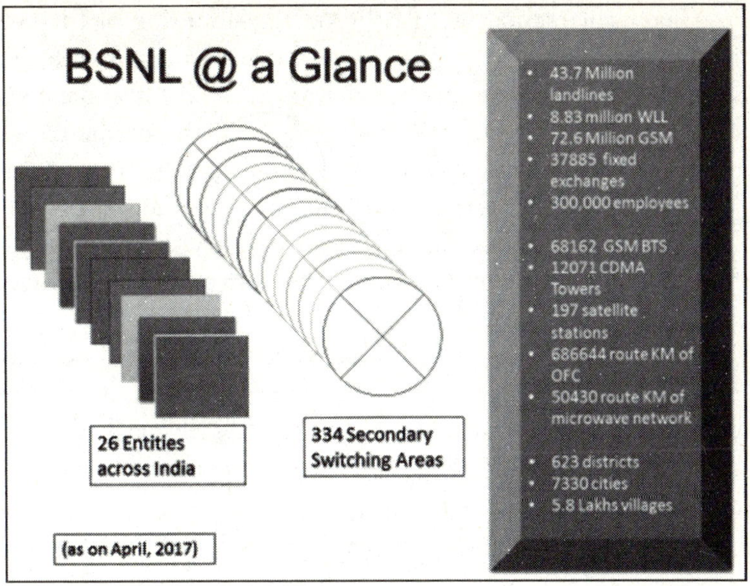

Figure 1. BSNL at a Glance.

It may appear that ERP implementation in BSNL is a technically oriented strategy with only technology as the focus. This however is not and ought not to be the case for any such strategy to be successful. It is an intensely sociological phenomenon which involves aspects such as organizational behaviour, organizational development, change management, leadership, power, communication processes and conflict management. These are integral and indispensable processes in ERP implementation, which is essentially an organizational change initiative thus involving change management strategies.

Since the company did not have consolidated IT or ICT systems, it resulted in a slew of customized and localized applications, different databases and internal processes over the years. Added to this, the company was facing tremendous pressure in the market with the private players eating into its customer base.

The implementation of BPR and the adoption of ERP in BSNL was one of its biggest digital initiative aligned with the vision of the government of India to use ICT for enhancing operational efficiencies and reaching out to the public by all government departments and PSUs. It is arguably one of the largest ERP roll outs in the world in terms of scope and span. The ERP roll out is sync with BSNL's vision of leveraging technology to provide affordable and innovative telecom services / products across customer segments.

The ERP project at BSNL required 65,000 SAP licenses and 315,000 ESS (employee self-service) licenses for all the employees. The biggest challenge that BSNL faced was the heterogeneity of its systems. Next to it was its huge employee base totalling around 300,000.

Relevant Organizational Theories:

It is necessary to have an overview of the theories and concepts about bureaucracy. BSNL is a quintessential ideal-type of a public sector organization. It is one of the largest public sector units in India and its systems and processes can be seen as predominantly representative of those in any other government organization or public sector organization not just in India but across the world in general. It therefore forms an ideal representative sample of ICT supported change initiatives in the public domain.

There is a theory in Jainism known as 'Syadvada' which states that by understanding 'all aspects' of one thing one can understand all aspects of 'all the things'. We may venture to say that by understanding the process of digitalization in the context of the public sector behemoth BSNL, one can reasonably understand the most subtle of nuances, issues, pain-points etc. of change management in any public sector organization. This is important because the government and the public sector are the main drivers of e-Governance initiatives.

Max Weber's view of bureaucracy fits BSNL and any

government organization agency or department perfectly. BSNL too has both the benefits and disadvantages of bureaucracy. This is important in the context of change management because bureaucratic structures and systems tend to offer more resistance to change.

Typical Challenges:

For its financial accounting and in other operational areas, BSNL had manual processes at the circle and SSA level. As a result, the finance department had to consolidate over 750 trial-balance accounts. For example, while HRMS (the HR and payroll package) was functional, it was not integrated with the financial system. As there were standalone systems, an integrated view across functions and organizational hierarchy was not available. Cross-functional reconciliation too required huge effort and took time. In addition, there were issues with auditing of results at the SSA, circle, and head-office level. Furthermore, tracking of taxation pay-out in context of changing tax regulations was a continued challenge for the company. This was resulting in a loss of INR 200 crore (US$44 million) annually in pay-out toward taxation. The same is indicated in Figure 2.

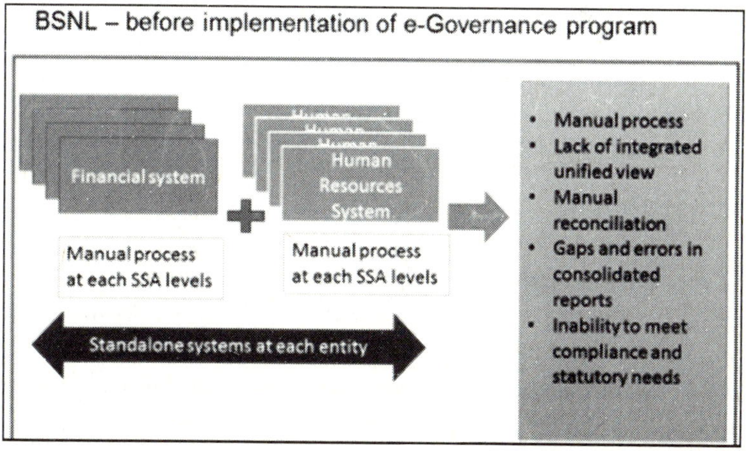

Figure 2 Scenario before implementation of ERP (e-Governance program)

Proposed Approach and Solution:

BPR and ERP introduction was therefore aimed to make the telecom giant more resilient and perform its mandate of providing vital infrastructure for nation building.

BSNL choose the Indian born multinational company HCL Technologies Private Limited (HCL) for the roll-out of ERP. HCL collaborated with SAP for BSNL's ERP project. As a member of the consortium, HCL partnered with HCL Info systems, which was the lead consortium bidder, and with Ernst and Young (E&Y) for business process reengineering (BPR).

The first phase of the implementation was to get started the business process reengineering (BPR) exercise. This basically studied the existing systems and gaps that BSNL had compared to some of the other leading players in the market. After this exercise that took about three months, HCL and E&Y came out with a detailed business blueprint of organizational transformation.

The problems, challenges and pain-points faced before deployment of the ICTs were many and these were addressed very effectively by BSNL. These included:

(a) Technology and integration issues

(b) Revamping business process

(c) Work culture issues

(d) Attitude problems of individuals and groups

(e) Communication and inter/intra group conflict

(f) Issues pertaining to roles and authorization

Change Management Strategies and actions:

The challenges were dealt with effectively by using innovative and creative methods and strategies. Three innovative tools and methods were used to create a sense of ownership of the project among employees, make it participative during roll-out and resolve pain-points and communication gaps.

The first and foremost challenge in implementing ERP is studying the existing legacy processes and to adopt the same in the SAP environment with necessary modifications if needed. This was followed by 5 other processes, as tabulated below:

Process of Implementation		
Process 1	As Is	Study of the existing system
Process 2	BPR	BPR was done which explored the possibility of doing things in different ways to Improve efficiency in the operation. It involved re-thinking, re-designing some of the existing processes and practices. BPR brought out many deficiencies of the existing setup. Enterprise best practices were studied and adopted
Process 3	BBP (Business Blue Print)	The existing processes and the newly adopted processes were documented.
Process 4	Realization	The BBP (design) was implemented in the ERP system
Process 5	Cut over	Declare Black out period [Stop business Transactions]to migrate the Legacy data
Process 6	Go Live	The new system is adopted

In the initial stages data collection was a very major challenge and then cleaning the data for the preparation of various templates for migration to SAP with respect to master data and transactional data. BSNL process owners approved migration success criteria. BSNL data owners were required to validate that the migrations have worked according to an agreed migration plan.

BSNL Data Migration Team (DMT) was responsible for the managing the extraction of legacy data from systems transforming the data as required and loading that data into SAP. For systems that are controlled by other third parties, BSNL was responsible for organising the data extract which was then passed to BSNL Data owners for analysis and all further downstream stages of the process. HCL data migration managers did monitor and report on BSNL DMT's progress.

Second part of challenge was providing user training to all executives of BSNL who were involved in the legacy process so that they can effectively utilize the ERP processes created equivalent and in replacement of the legacy processes.

BSNL's ERP system had the following modules:

1. Finance and Management Accounting (FICO)
2. Materials and Inventory Management including e-procurement (MM)
3. Plant/Equipment Maintenance (PM)
4. Human Resources Management and Administration (HRM)
5. Sales and Distribution (S and D)
6. Project Systems (PS)
7. Real Estate and Telecom Infrastructure Management (REM)
8. Production Planning (PP)
9. Supply Chain Management (SCM)
10. Business Information System (BIS)
11. Business Intelligence and Analytics (BIA)
12. Strategy Enterprise Management (SEM)
13. Quality Control (QC)
14. Enterprise Portal (EP)

From a larger perspective, the challenges that stared squarely at the face of BSNL were two-fold.

- Externally, the market was rapidly evolving with changing consumer behavior, rapid inclusion of private sector players, and intensified price wars.

- Internally, BSNL faced strong employee resistance to change and continued to operate on legacy systems and processes that were decentralized. The internal challenges were analyzed clearly and taken in the overall spirit of effective change management. BSNL has a huge employee base of over 210,000.

BSNL evolved a unique and organically sustainable methodology for successful Business Process Re-engineering / Government Process Re-engineering and digitalization. It delved within itself and discovered the power of 'We'.

Three unique tools and methods were used by BSNL's leadership to manage organization transition driven by ICT in select Proof of Concept (PoC) circles. These have successfully tackled issues and problems pertaining to the 'human' side of change management. Three kinds of groups were formed for implementing the project. (1) Quality Circles (2) Focus Groups and (3) In-groups.

The communication technology used in the interaction by the Focus Groups, In-Groups and Quality Circles were (1) Face-to-face interaction (2) Audio-conferencing (3) BSNL Intranet discussion groups (4) Video-conferencing.

Quality Circles

A quality circle is a participatory management technique that involves and takes the help of employees in solving problems related to their own jobs. Circles are formed of employees working together in an operation who meet at regular and pre-determined intervals to discuss problems and to devise solutions for improvements. Quality circles have an autonomous character, are usually small, and are led by a supervisor. Employees who participate in quality circles usually receive training in formal problem-solving methods—such as brain-storming, Pareto analysis, and cause-and-effect diagrams—and are then encouraged to apply these methods either to specific or general organizational problems. After completing an analysis, they often present their findings to management and then handle implementation of approved solutions.

On certain issues that are highly localized, employees implement the solutions themselves even without orders from the management in order to improve the performance of the organization and motivate employees. Quality circles were at their most popular during the 1980s, but continue to exist in the form of Kaizen groups and similar worker participation schemes.

Quality circles in many organizations, especially in countries like Japan, were part of a system of relatively cooperative labour-management relations involving company unions and lifetime employment guarantees for many full-time permanent employees. Quality circles provided a means by which production workers were encouraged to participate in company matters and by which management could benefit from production workers' intimate knowledge of the production process.

Focus Group

A focus group is a set of a small number of people, (usually between 4 and 15 who although maybe relatively unfamiliar with each other, are selected because they have certain characteristics in common that relate to the topic of the focus group. The moderator or interviewer creates a permissive and nurturing environment that encourages different perceptions and points of view without pressuring participants to vote, plan or reach consensus. The group discussion is conducted several times with similar types of participants to identify trends and patterns in perceptions. Careful and systematic analysis of the discussions provides clues and insights as to how a new system or process is perceived by the group. Focus groups aim at an open discussion instead of on individual responses to formal questions and produce qualitative data.

Focus groups have a long and interesting history and were used during the second world war to examine the effectiveness of propaganda. The Sociologist Robert K Merton who was associate director, set up such groups at the bureau of applied social research in the USA prior to coining of the term itself by the marketing psychologist Ernest Dichter.

There are many variants of focus groups. These include the following:

1. Two-way focus group-one focus group watches another focus group and discusses the observed interactions and conclusion
2. Dual moderator focus group-one moderator ensures the session progresses smoothly, while another ensures that all the topics are covered
3. Duelling moderator focus group (fencing-moderator) - two moderators purposefully and deliberately take opposite sides on the issue under discussion
4. Respondent moderator focus group-one and only one of the respondents is asked to act as the moderator temporarily
5. Client participant focus groups-one or more client representatives participate in the discussion, either covertly or overtly
6. Mini focus groups-groups are composed of 4 or 5 members only
7. Teleconference focus groups-telephone network is used and often video-conferencing too
8. Online focus groups-computers connected via the internet are used

In BSNL, a combination of respondent focus groups and mini focus groups were created. Face to face interaction, teleconferencing and on-line discussions were used the means of interaction by the groups.

Such focus groups can give valuable information about how groups of people think or feel about a particular topic and thus greater insight into why certain opinions are held. This helps in fine-tuning existing and on-going programmes and in improving the planning and design of new programs. Reliable means of evaluating existing programs is also provided.

Focus groups method takes advantage of the fact that people naturally interact and are influenced by others. In such groups the project leader or change champion can interact directly with respondents. This allows for clarifications, follow-up questions and probing. The focus groups also generate data arising from respondents' own words. Thus the project leader or change champion can obtain deeper levels of meaning, make important connections and identify subtle nuances. The results are easy to understand and more accessible to decision-makers.

In BSNL, the members of focus groups consisted of officials from different functional areas and different departments. They had different administrative heads too. The thread that united them was that they were all inter - related and inter-dependent on each other due to the very nature of workflow in the new ERP environment.

Both quality circles and focus groups used brainstorming to inspire ideas and action oriented debate. Brainstorming is a group creativity technique by which efforts are made to find a conclusion for a specific problem by gathering a list of ideas spontaneously contributed by its members. The term was popularized by Alex Faickney Osborn in his book 'Applied Imagination'.

In-Group

An In-group is a social group to which a person psychologically identifies as being a member. By contrast, an out-group is a social group with which an individual does not identify. The terminology was made popular by Henri Tajfel and colleagues during his work in formulating social identity theory.

In-groups are powerful entities in the organizational change process. The element of informality gives them enormous power to influence individual and group attitudes. In-groups consist of cohorts with a strong similarity that binds them. This can be a position in the organizational hierarchy, a particular function or similar role profiles. Leadership must encourage such In-groups and bring out positive energy. Thus, organizational In-groups can be equated to peer groups in schools or colleges. Anyone with kids or teenagers in the house can understand the impact of peer groups. Once an opinion is formed by the influence of the peer group, it is extremely difficult to change the same. The same principle works out in In-groups. Leaders can manipulate In-groups systematically to imbibe, reinforce and disseminate attitudes that are favorable to change among employees.

These soft-interventions went a long way in making the BPR effort and ERP roll-out a success.

Looking around to gather lessons

Otto Von Bismarck is quoted to have famously said - 'Only a fool learns from his own mistakes. The wise man learns from the mistakes of others'. It may be worthwhile to look at some spectacularly failed attempts at BPR and ERP implementation and learn from them - what not to do. This is akin to the famous 'negation' principle enumerated in the Upanishads – 'Neti-Neti', meaning 'not this, not this.' At times, in both personal and organizational life, 'what we must not to do' or avoid doing is as important as 'what to do' to be successful. To have a comprehensive grasp of the complex issues, and in all fairness, to the spirit of seeking knowledge and truth, we will discuss both phenomenal success stories and stupendous failures in the private sector.

Some cases of not-so-successful and the lessons learnt

1. Let us first take the classic case of BPR and ERP that was intended to usher in massive change in the systems and structures of HP (Hewlett-Packard), the multi national hardware giant. ERP is business process management software that allows organizations to use a system of integrated applications

to manage the business end–to-end seamlessly and automate many back office functions related to technology, services and human resources. It is used both to manage change and to be a catalyst to drive change in organizations. SAP ERP is enterprise resource planning software developed by the German company SAP SAP ERP incorporates all the key business functions of an organization.

HP had close partnership with SAP since 1989 when SAP began developing SAP R/3 product. It was offering consulting services for implementation of SAP's 'supply chain' and ERP software. First SAP R/3 was deployed on an HP 9000 Enterprise server in 1992 at Wuerth. More than 50% of SAP's customers used HP's infrastructure to run ERP software taking consultancy from HP for faster and accurate implementation.

In the year 2000 HP had become keen to make web-based activities more simple, direct, efficient and effective. At this stage, HP had over 20 SAP R/3 implementations representing FI, PP, MM, SD, CO, Business Intelligence (BW), Advanced Planning and Optimization (APO) and Warehouse Management (WM). These implementations were based on different versions and had multiple SAP Graphic user Interfaces (GUIs). The user base for these applications was around 10,000. Since HP was already using SAP R/3 software, it considered SAP's internet-enabled technology product- MySAP9 as a good fit for its business.

In December 2003, HP adopted a business-process-based approach that combined IT with business objectives. HP had cherished the ambition to implement a single order management system for quite some time. HP executives expected that the new SAP system would enable customers to receive exact product build and delivery dates without placing multiple orders. Contrary to all expectations the IT intervention initiative at HP was a massive failure.

Lessons: The internal investigation team that was constituted found the following causes for the legacy system to ERP migration failure: (1) Communication problems (2) Data integration problems (3) Poor planning and improper testing (4) Inadequate implementation support/training. The total financial impact of the failure including backlogs and lost revenue was pegged at 160 million US dollars, more than 5 times the cost of implementing the project.

ERP implementation failure at HP was a demonstration of how human and socio-cultural factors could affect technology based organization design initiatives in the context of change management. Thus, every implementation of an ERP or for that matter any digitalization project warrants a fresh approach and if it's not mapped out in detail, it might miss its objectives. ERP essentially involved a business change and change management strategies in many divisions of an organization and therefore there could be no standard approach to its implementation. This is precisely the reason why the success of an ERP implementation depends upon how a coherent paradigm of change management is put into place. HP's project failure because it ignored such factors.

2. Select Comfort is a U.S. based company that manufactures the Sleep Number and Comfortaire beds as well as foundations and bedding accessories. Within a few months of sincere effort to migrate to the ERP environment, the fairy-tale beginning came to an end. In 2009, Select Comfort's ERP initiative was abandoned rather than actually failed. The entire project was improperly conceived from the beginning because there was no pressing business need to change the existing systems. A new CIO who had joined initiated the project without studying the system on 'AS IS' basis. The scope was massive (ERP, CRM, SCM, APO, etc.,) and the project was executed only by internal employees.

Lesson: When there is no business need, ERP implementation should not be force-fitted.

3. Levi Strauss also experimented with ERP and failed. After 'go-live' shipping was prevented for one week as there were legacy system integration issues. Levi is an interesting case study because

many industry experts believe the SAP implementation was used as an excuse for bypassing or avoiding broader economic issues affecting Levi. The company did not ensure that all legacy system interfaces were carefully tested before going live.

Lessons: (a) An integrated approach is needed to understand the entire business context and the economic situation of the organization's performance. (b) Integrating the legacy systems and testing them out thoroughly is a must for smooth roll out of the new system.

4. Hershey foods went live with their SAP implementation just before Halloween in 1999. For the candy company this was the beginning of their peak season and the 'go-live' created a major business disruption at the worst time from a revenue and operations standpoint.

Lessons: (1) Insufficient training and user preparation. (2) Unrealistic implementation timeline. (3) Improper 'go-live' schedule – The company went 'live' at peak sales season and did not allow enough time to 'set right' data integrity and process issues.

5. A similar case was with Whirlpool Corporation's SAP ERP projects failure in 1999. Just before a Labour Day 'go-live' several warning signs of serious problems appeared. Interfaces and batch jobs that fed external systems indicated serious performance problems but Whirlpool management and their SAP implementation vendor, a reputed global consultant, decided to go ahead and migrate to SAP anyway.

Red flags with enterprise applications should be carefully evaluated for a 'go or no go' decision by change leaders as 'go-live' date approaches. Testing of interfaces cannot be ignored and serious performance problems or known interface problems should not be pushed beneath the carpet.

Lessons: (a) Resolve performance problems of interface and all systems connected with it (b) Not to ignore any problem without a thorough investigation.

6. Many large government ERP initiatives too have failed

across the world. In 2011, UK Government scrapped what is considered to be the largest public IT project of all time, an attempt to provide electronic health records for all of the country's citizens. The Herculean and audacious effort begun in 2002 but failed to produce a workable system, despite massive spending outlays that have been estimated at about US$18.7 billion. The medical and paramedical personnel in Nova Scotia hospital reportedly suffered for at least 6 months because of faulty pay-checks due to problems with an SAP system project led by a large vendor. This was a much published case in the media.

Lessons: (a) GPR is an endeavour that must be taken right earnest and not as a routine. (b) Contingency plans must be in place before launching any e- governance initiative.

7. Let's take the example of Nestle, the Swiss transnational food and drink company headquartered in Switzerland which can be cited as another typical case of ERP failure due to non-technological reasons. Nestle is the largest food company in the world measured by revenues and other metrics, for 2014, 2015 and 2016. Nestle SA is the parent company of the chocolate making global giant. In 2000 Nestle SA decided that it wanted to leverage its size and begin acting like the giant it is. To do so, it signed a 200 million US dollars contract with SAP to roll out an ERP system to its 2.30 lakh employees in 80 countries around the world. In addition to this, Nestle SA also committed to an additional 80 million US dollars to be spent on consulting, maintenance, and upgrades. The top leadership at Nestle SA realized that the company needed to standardize its business processes if it wanted to be competitive. The roll out was scheduled to take three years for Nestle SA's largest sites with the others to follow. Apart from the top management, the employees down the line were unaware of the importance of this change. They did not adapt to the new work environment. The project ultimately fell flat on its face.

Lessons: (a) Organizational wide plans must be backed by meticulous groundwork (b) Taking the entire team along is important.

The human side of e- governance project implementation is vital to the success of any such initiative.

Some cases of success and the lessons learnt:

In all fairness, now let us also look at some success stories of BPR and ERP in the corporate sector too. A spectacularly successful attempt at implementing BPR and ERP in the case of a large global company is that of Vodafone.

1. London based Vodafone's business has seen incredible growth since its avant-garde beginnings nearly 3 decades ago. By revenue, it is the largest mobile service provider in the world, and it caters to almost 400 million customers across Europe, the US, Africa and Asia. Vodafone grew quickly in its various markets by successfully establishing local operating companies that catered products and services to the local market's needs.

In 2006, a group of Vodafone executives approached the company's board with a plan for a business transformation aimed at creating a centralized shared services organization and a set of common processes in finance, human resources, and the supply chain for all of its operating companies. From the start of the initiative, Vodafone management wanted to instil the idea that the project was a business transformation underpinned by an ERP implementation and not an ERP implementation that would change local business processes.

Almost a year before the ERP implementation began, all the operating companies' department heads of finance, supply chain, and human resources were made to participate in a series of workshops in London to map out common, global processes in their respective key areas. The goals of those workshops were to arrive at a consensus and agree on core concepts and gain buy-in from the business for proposed changes. The blue print for BPR was put firmly in place.

Once the processes were firmly established, Vodafone took

another innovative step to ensure that they would be implemented as designed, and that the business leaders maintained control over the processes after the ERP implementation began. The step included creating the Vodafone Global Design Authority, a committee made up of key senior business leaders across the organization responsible for owing the processes. Any time a person or group suggested a change to one of the processes (which include the IT organization during the ERP implementation), the Global Design Authority had to approve the change.

With a year of process design and the fine-tuning completed, Vodafone targeted procurement as the first business process for transformation using the new SAP ERP System. But rather than establish a centralized procurement department, Vodafone created a procurement company that was based in Luxembourg and operated on the centralized SAP platform. The Vodafone Procurement Company was empowered to sign contracts with suppliers and buy goods or services on behalf of the individual Vodafone business. The unique structure ensured the majority of the company's spending went through the central organization. This also ensured that the suppliers could better see and plan their volumes with Vodafone because they're selling to one company instead of to many.

With the new procurement company up and running on the SAP system, Vodafone took on its next major transformation step. It created a centralized shared services organization and brought it onto the SAP ERP system. Vodafone selected Budapest, Hungary as the location and built an entire shared services organization from scratch – including purchasing a new office building and hiring staff – while simultaneously implementing SAP ERP.

After the pilot implementation in Hungary, Vodafone chose to introduce the operating company in Germany to the new processes and brought it onto the SAP platform.

In addition to which legacy systems were currently in place, there were two major personnel factors that determined how successful a rollout would be, namely - the skills of the local project team and the willingness of the local organization to accept change.

Vodafone's primary systems integration partner, Accenture, filled in skills gaps when needed and assisted with change management in the local markets. Gradually, the project team – including Vodafone internal staffers and the Accenture experts – learned to assess early on how to best allocate resources in a specific project. For example, if members of an operating company weren't present for the project kick-off meeting, or they were there but disinterested, the project team knew that company would require more attention.

The project team had to be sensitive to local trends occurring during the rollouts. For example, if an operating company resided in a country experiencing a downturned economy, the technology change could be embraced by some as a way to improve their situation, but eyed by others as an additional distraction during a very stressful time.

Vodafone's business transformation project has produced significant results both in terms of cost savings and business efficiency. At a strategic level, the benefits of getting the various operating companies to think more uniformly has produced less tangible, but equally important benefits. Vodafone is demonstrating to its customers how the business itself is working internally with speed, simplicity and trust.

Lessons: (a) Engagement of stakeholders early in the game and getting their buy-in for the change (b) Evolving a working plan involving all those stakeholders (c) Establishing a governance mechanism for the overall program (global design authority) including changes to the planned program (d) integrated procurement process (e) running a pilot to test the implementation plan and validate the overall approach and (f) managing the people side by filling gaps of competency with appropriate steps.

2. The case of implementation of ERP in Rolls Royce Company is yet another success story. The change initiative was a success because the leadership saw the implementation as a humane process rather than a 'plug and play' solution, so to say, the change management and organizational development.

The main problem that Rolls Royce encountered had been with the accuracy of data. The new ERP system required the retrieval of old data from the legacy systems that has to be normalized, screened and stored in a sensible data format within the new systems data repository. The duplication of data was a major concern that Rolls-Royce had to address. In some special areas the old systems were kept running until such time as they could be phased out by the new systems, and to do this Electronic Data Systems (EDS) built interfaces between the systems.

The ERP Project at Rolls-Royce covered many different departments and many different topic areas, all of which have associated risks. Some of the risks were: (1) The possible failure or inability to align goals through conflicting directions within the organization. (2) The possible failure of providing inadequate and ongoing support after implementation, from both Rolls-Royce and EDS. (3) The resistance of change to new process methods by management and supervision. (4) Management and supervision may treat the project as merely an IT implementation, rather than change in process methods. (5) Inadequately educating and training of the workforce to operate the new system properly.

The core implementation teams of Rolls Royce had taken into account the needs of both the managerial level officers and end-users. This included matching the process to the software configuration, training people to accept change, and getting them to do business in a totally new way and data clean-up of legacy systems have been involved.

It also included training senior management, particularly the executive group, who are responsible for the overall direction of the company and are not technically orientated, managing effective relationships and leading teams in both technical and non-computer based environments and simulation exercises. Shop-floor communication with line workers was also an exercise that required line workers to attend workshops.

Lessons: (a) Effective engagement of stakeholders (b) Listing and managing the risks of the program (c) Involving the people across the organization in the entire initiative (d) Focusing on the people side of the problem much more than the pure technology change initiative.

Conclusion

At BSNL, the task was not easy, given the large and distributed scale of ERP system implementation. The roll-out spanned over five years and in five planned phases with clearly set objectives.

To sum up, it can be seen in the case of BSNL and other MNC giants that the critical success factors of any change management or organizational transformation initiative backed by ICT has intensely inescapable people and process issues.

With this successful digitalization project, BSNL can thus aspire to achieve the following in the future, as evident in the acronym itself;

1. Brand management and re-branding
2. Service quality enhancement
3. Network management efficiency
4. Leveraging its assets and material resources optimally

CASE STUDY–2

GIS application in Bharat Net

GIS based Web and Mobile application for monitoring the progress of Bharat Net project.

Note to the reader: An innovative system comprising Geographical Information System (GIS), Web application and

Mobile application have been designed and implemented to monitor the complex BharatNet project spread over the entire country reaching out to remote and rural areas.

Background

Bharat Broadband Network Limited (BBNL) was incorporated on February 25, 2012 as a Special Purpose Vehicle for the establishment, management and operations of NOFN (presently BharatNet).

BharatNet (is the largest rural connectivity project of its kind in the world. It aspires to link each of the 2.5 lakh Gram Panchayats of India through broadband optical fibre network. On its completion, Bharat Net is expected to facilitate broadband connectivity to over 600 million rural citizens of the country. It is expected that the establishment of BharatNet would not only have a transformational impact on the lives of citizens, but it would also open up new avenues for Access service providers such as Telecom Service Providers (TSP), Internet Service Providers(ISP), Cable TV Operators, content providers etc. to launch next generation services. This is also expected to create local employment opportunities encompassing e-commerce, IT outsourcing, rural BPOs etc. as well as services such as e-banking, e-health and e-education for inclusive national growth. This will additionally enable delivery of various services such as local planning, management, monitoring and payments under government schemes at panchayat level.

It is universally accepted that access to broadband significantly boosts economic growth. A World Bank study conducted in 2009 shows that for every 10 percentage points of broadband penetration, developing economies grew by 1.38 percent whereas developed countries' economies grew by 1.21 percent. A study conducted by Indian Council for Research and International Economic Relations (ICRIER) in 2012 reports that Indian States can be expected to grow by 1.08% points for every 10% increase in the number of internet subscribers. Taking the findings of this report as the base, it is estimated that BharatNet will provide economic benefits of around INR 66,500 Crores.

Alignment with Digital India

The provision of broadband connectivity to every citizen is one of the key objectives of Digital India, and the commissioning of the BharatNet is expected to mark a significant step towards realization of this ambitious vision.

In so far as the funding arrangements were concerned, net cost for establishing and maintaining NOFN was to be funded by the Universal Service Obligation Fund (USOF) based upon bids received by an EA (Executive Agent). As the precise estimate was difficult to chalk out at that time, an indicative requirement of funds was approved. The EA was to prepare the estimates of the funds required for the project under supervision of USOF and the funds were to be allocated based on actual bid amount and after necessary approval by the competent authority. A Detailed Project Report (DPR) prepared by TCIL. The administrative expense of the EA was to form part of OPEX of the project. The absolute amount of the expense was subject to approval. USOF funds entire CAPEX and OPEX net of revenue streams for a period of five years. Suitable incentives were provided to the EA for maximizing revenues. The funds were allocated by the ministry of finance to USOF within the amounts accrued/ accruing to the USOF and there is no additional liability on the state exchequer outside of USOF was envisaged. For the purpose of accountability, the expenditure on the incremental infrastructure so created and the resultant revenue is clearly demarcated and kept separate from any other revenue or expenditure to be earned or incurred by the EA.

Before embarking on nation-wide implementation, it was thought prudent to carry out pilot projects at different geographical locations. BBNL embarked upon pilot projects in three blocks covering 59 GPs in three different states - Arain in Ajmer District of Rajasthan, Parvada in Vishakhapatnam District of Andhra Pradesh and Panisagar in North Tripura District of Tripura. The pilot projects were completed on October 15, 2012 and the Department of Electronics and I.T (DeITY) enabled the delivery of G2C services through a counter funding program in these GPs. BSNL, RailTel and PGCIL were entrusted with the physical implementation on behalf of BBNL. Accordingly, the work was split State-wise between BSNL, RailTel and PGCIL in the ratio of 70:15:15. Incremental fibre approach was adopted by leveraging the existing fibre of BSNL and the other PSUs for reducing cost of the project.

Appropriate technology

On the technology adopted for the project, a Technical Advisory Committee (TAC) recommended in March 2012 that the technology choice depends on striking a balance between BharaNet objectives and ground realities. The lack of availability of power supply in rural areas in general, availability of space in GPs, lack of skilled manpower to maintain advanced technology equipment (Gram Panchayat) in GPs and sustainability were identified as factors influencing technology choice. Two scenarios were indicated.

- One scenario described was poor power availability with less fibre and closely spaced GPs for which passive electronics i.e Passive Optical Network (PON) was recommended.
- The other scenario spoke of good power availability, fibre availability and GPs located at distances for which hybrid or active technology was recommended. It was decided to use Gigabit Passive Optical Network (GPON) as the technology of choice considering the architecture and ground conditions of power availability etc.

An innovative system comprising Geographical Information System (GIS), web application and mobile application has been designed and implemented to monitor the complex BharatNet project spread out over the entire country reaching out to remote and rural areas. Use of GIS is intuitive because the main activity of the project is laying of communication network that can be easily mapped on a GIS. Web application enables all the field data to be collected to a central location for analysis and projection on the GIS. The Mobile application serves as a tool to collect field data. It eliminates the need for manual data entry and works as a remote sensor. A dashboard presents a snapshot and comparative progress of the entire project.

The main activities in the project are procurement and transportation of material that includes OFC and accessories, duct and terminal equipment; laying OFC that includes trenching, ducting, cabling and acceptance testing (AT) of the depth of cable laid; and setting up equipment that includes installation of terminal equipment, AT of end-to-end connectivity and lighting up the GP. Management of such a complex and widely distributed project was a daunting task.

An innovative system (hereinafter called the system) comprising Geographical Information System (GIS), web application and mobile application has been designed and the activities that impact the project the most and measuring in a timely manner with a tool that is simple to operate.

Activities covered

The activities that impact the project the most are the field activities of trenching, ducting, cabling, equipment installation and testing. These activities are carried out in far flung and remote areas where there may be no communication networks whether mobile or land line. Measuring these activities in a timely manner for effective management of the project is a difficult task. The difficulty is further compounded by the constraint that the tools used to measure the works must be simple so that a worker on the site can operate the tool.

GIS is a natural choice to represent routes and points over the large geographic expanse of the project. The availability of Global Positioning System (GPS) locator in smartphones makes it possible to record the coordinates of the routes and points. Development and use of mobile applications has become easy with a conducive application development ecosystem and availability of low priced smartphones. Data can be easily transported over the internet to a centralized computer system. All users can access the system from their locations using a web application that makes the system very simple to access. Well known formulae such as Vincenty's 4 can be used to calculate distance between two coordinates with good accuracy even when the points on the ground are close. All these technologies have been integrated in an innovative way to build an effective project management system.

Web application enables all the field data to be collected to a central location for analysis and projection on the GIS. The mobile application serves as a tool to collect field data. It eliminates the need for manual data entry and worked as a remote sensor.

A dashboard presents a snapshot and comparative progress of the entire project. An outline of the system is in Figure 3. Operation and Implementation aspects envisaged are as follows:

Mobile phone application forms the bottom layer of the system. It uses the GPS facility in the mobile phone to capture the latitude and longitude of the point on the ground where the activity is happening. There are mainly two types of activities: point activity and route activity. Point activity includes an activity occurring at a point. For instance, installation of terminal equipment is a point activity because it involves setting up the equipment at a Gram Panchayat (GP) which is a point on the map. Route activity includes an activity on a route. For example, trenching is a route activity because it happens along a route from one point to another. The application stores the captured information into the local phone memory. It keeps checking for availability of internet connection and uploads the data to the central database whenever the internet connection is available.

The application also has a facility to check all route or point data captured on a map that can be used in case internet connection is available.

The mobile application works in two modes – offline and online. In offline mode, the application records the coordinates and the accuracy as provided by the mobile phone GPS locator. It does not use any underlying map to show the current location. This is necessary because in remote areas where the project is being implemented, there is often no mobile network for internet connection which is required to access map services. In such cases, the accuracy is shown on the screen to the user with the coordinates of the point. The accuracy of the coordinates is seen to improve as the device is kept still at one point and the accuracy level shown on the screen guides the user in recording coordinates. The recorded coordinates and the concomitant accuracy are refreshed every five seconds to help record the coordinates with the best accuracy.

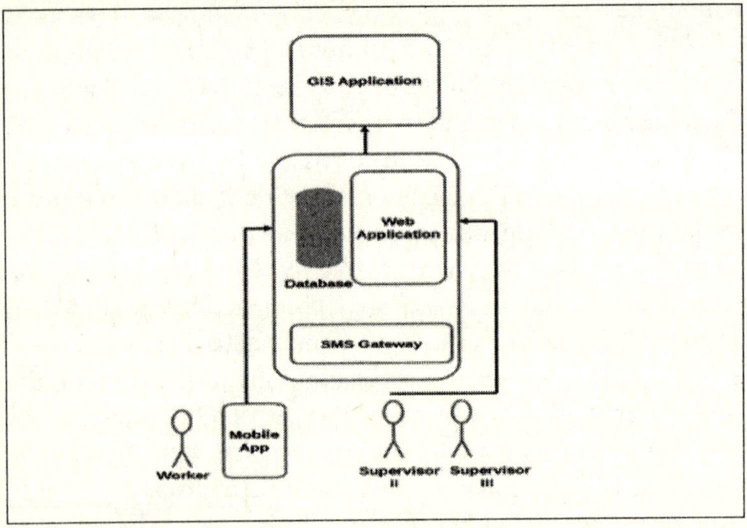

Figure- 3 BharatNet GIS Dashboard

In online mode, the application is able to record the exact

location of the activity. In this mode, the application uses map services to display the full imagery of the location along with guiding arrow and a dot. The guiding arrow represents the coordinates the application has recorded from the GPS locator. Once the coordinates of the point of activity have been recorded, the application prompts the user to take a picture of the location. In case of open trenching, the user takes a picture of the trench where the digging or ducting is being carried out. In case of Horizontal Directional Drilling (HDD), the equipment used to sync with the beacon shows the current position of the drilling process.

A picture of the equipment with its screen showing the current beacon position is taken. This also captures the depth of the tunnel where the duct and the OFC would lie. The picture of each point of activity provides a real view of the path or point and helps in verification of the data as discussed later. The recorded routes and points are uploaded to the web application whenever there is internet connectivity.

The worker in the field where activity is being carried out uses the mobile application running on his phone. When he starts the day's work, he selects the gram panchayat where he is working and the type of work. He then the records the coordinates and picture of the starting point. Every twenty meters or so, he/she records the coordinates and pictures of the points of activity. When he completes the day's work, he records the last point data and ends the route. He may record data for several sections on various routes during the course of the day's work. He can use the dashboard to view the various routes or points recorded and upload or delete data.

The web application has a user hierarchy of supervisors and workers. There are three types of supervisors – supervisors I, II, and III. Supervisors I and II belong to BBNL whereas Supervisor III belongs to the implementing agency. Supervisors use the Web application to review the data uploaded by the Workers.

The web application maintains a database of all the recorded routes and points along with accuracy. The route and point activities recorded by the field workers must be authenticated by their supervisors and verified by BBNL supervisors before they can be accepted as representative of actual work done. This is to ensure correctness of data and to enable supervisors to monitor the progress of work. Since supervisor III is the direct supervisor of the workers, he/she first examines the uploaded coordinates and pictures.

Each coordinate and its accuracy is listed as a line item in a table on the supervisor screen. A summary of points is shown in a separate table. The point data that are verified, rejected or pending can be separately selected in the line item table. Each line item has a link to a map with satellite imagery, roads and landmarks. The map has several layers – one for each type of activity. It shows the planned route for the GP along which the OFC was planned to be laid; all the points recorded for a Gram Panchayat; a table with a list of activities carried out in the GP and check boxes; and pictures corresponding to each point. Each picture presents to the supervisor a view of the ground activity. A trenching, ducting or cabling activity can be easily identified by the picture of a trench, a duct being laid or fiber being pulled through duct.

A point for trenching activity without the corresponding picture of a trench or an HDD equipment showing the presence of a beacon and depth will be meaningless. Similarly for other activities. Though the supervisor may not be present on the ground in the field, he gets a real view of the ground activity to help him make a decision on the authenticity of the data. Terminal equipment installation picture will clearly show the view of the equipment being installed. The accuracy level helps determine how close the point is to the actual location of the activity. If the planned route is close to the route of execution activity, this reinforces correctness of the point's data.

Often the planned route may be old and circumstances on the ground may force the work to be carried out on a different route. The occurrence of several simultaneous factors also presents the opportunity to assess the correctness of the planned route. Each layer can be separately viewed by checking the corresponding check box. A point too far away from the general path described by the points collectively suggests an erroneous point. Taking into account the various factors presented to the Supervisor III, he/she may accept or reject a point. Once points have been accepted by supervisor III, a line is drawn through them to complete the route along which the route activity took place. At this point of time, this route drawing is only provisional and is shown in grey colour. Now, supervisor II is presented with all the details on the map as already listed earlier along with the route drawn in grey. He/she can again accept or reject the points data taking into account all the corresponding details. Verification by supervisor II who belongs to BBNL confirms the route or point activity and shows the route according to a predefined colour scheme.

It is possible to configure new activities in the system on the fly up to a predetermined total number of layers. A new activity has to be configured in the web application. The new activity then automatically appears in the mobile application on fresh login. This makes the system flexible and it is possible to adapt the system to new requirements and new types of networks. In case arial OFC is to be laid, terrestrial wireless systems are deployed or satellite based systems are implemented, new activities corresponding to these types of network can be configured in the system.

Each activity can be mapped on to a new layer on the GIS. The system sends SMS alerts to supervisors and their controlling officers. Since supervisors need to access the web application whenever there are points data for authentication, a system of alerts has been configured. The system lists all those supervisors who have points waiting for their authentication twice a day, once in the afternoon and once in the evening.

An SMS is sent to them on each occasion alerting that there is data awaiting their authentication. After waiting for a predefined period, if point data remain unattended, the system escalates the alerts to the controlling officers of the supervisors. SMS alerts are also sent when a new user is created intimating the username and password to the user. This ensures that all users of the system are kept well informed about the progress of work in the system.

The system has a dashboard that shows the progress of the entire project all over the country. For each route activity i.e. trenching, ducting, OFC laying and depth AT, the total length of the work completed is shown in kilometres. For each point of activity i.e installation of terminal equipment, lighting of GP and end-to-end AT, the number GPs for which the work has been completed is shown. To look at progress made in each state, district and block, one can drill down with drop down lists of states, districts and blocks. It is also possible to look at progress on a daily weekly, monthly, quarterly and yearly basis. A comparative chart is also provided to compare progress made in a period vis-a-vis the corresponding previous period.

The system is now operational in the field and has been found to be effective in monitoring execution of the project in real time. The activity points are available on the map as soon as the work is carried out and the coordinates of the activity are recorded with the mobile application. Routes are clearly marked on the map and available for view as soon as they are authenticated by the Supervisors.

Conclusion

Thus, it can be concluded with reasonable certainty that the BharatNet project monitoring system is an example of e-Governance applied to restructure business processes. It has eliminated manual preparation of reports that are prone to error and do not reflect real time status of work. The wide spread of the project and its complexity are elegantly handled by the system making it possible for management to closely monitor the project.

It is also an example of how sophisticated technologies can be utilized to reach out to the remote and unconnected areas of a large country such as India. Workers with little education can operate such technologies and contribute to an overall improvement of the system. Government schemes that often need to reach out to far flung areas can benefit greatly from the opportunities presented by innovative and elegant technological solutions.

Lessons

1. It is possible and important to devise applications that can be used for monitoring the project execution itself
2. Such a system helped not only in detailed planning but also quick decision making
3. Innovative in-house solutions can be designed for ICT backed changes
4. Necessity for change and innovation can be felt only when problems are faced head–on and not brushed aside or avoided
5. Skill–set development in usage of IT tools is vital for practical utility of IT tools
6. Constant monitoring of the project during field level usage is important to ensure the 'best-fit' solution to needs

CASE STUDY–3

Digital Denmark 2016-2020

Advantages of consistency and coherence in formulating and implementing e-Governance projects

Note to the reader: The Digital Strategy 2016-2020 of Denmark sets the course for public sector digitization efforts and their interaction with business of Denmark and the industry. Jointly with the business and public institutions at local, regional and central-government levels, this strategy is aimed to help build the basis for a strong and secure digital Denmark. While some initiatives have already been launched, others will be defined or adjusted until 2020 in response to the opportunities and challenges ahead. This strategy is envisioned to fully equip citizens, public employees and businesses for the digital Denmark of the future.

It is also pointed to the reader to keep in mind and draw parallels between Digital India and the digital strategy of Denmark, not only for academic comparison but also for application and results on the ground.

Background

Denmark is in an advantageous position to embrace the digital future. It is a small country with a population that has great trust and confidence in each other and in the public sector. People generally have a high level of literacy. People and businesses have good digital competences and have generally embraced digital technologies. In Denmark there is a strong tradition of collaboration and finding new and practical solutions between public authorities, and across the public and private sectors.

Furthermore, the public sector began introducing IT solutions many years ago. This 'first mover' advantage enabled Denmark to build a secure and robust digital infrastructure which allows individuals and businesses to complete efficiently their business with the public sector over the internet. All of this enabled a huge digital transition in recent years.

The business and growth policy of the government is not only to render electronic services to the public but also to create good framework conditions for commerce and industry to contributethe growth in Denmark through the promotion of digital solutions in Danish businesses.

Long term digital strategy

The e-Governance initiatives of Denmark are rooted in the belief and vision that public sector digitization creates value and growth, it provides efficiency improvements and it secures the confidence of Danish people in the digital society.

The Digital Strategy 2016-2020 sets three ambitious, but realistic, goals for the development of a more digital public sector in the years to come.

1. Digital solutions to be easy-to–use, quick and ensure high quality

The Danish public should see that public–sector digitization adds real meaning and value of their lives. The public sector must offer high-quality digital services and digital welfare solutions. Digitization must make it easier for people to help themselves, and improve the quality of public services. Furthermore, digitization is aimed to contribute to a more cohesive and efficient public sector.

2. Public sector digitization to provide good conditions for growth

Digitization will make it easier to run a business and will contribute to the government's goal to reduce the administrative burden on the business community by DKK 3 billion by 2020. The ambition is that the administrative burden on businesses from reporting to public authorities is to be removed through automatic business reporting. All solutions aimed at businesses will be integrated in the Virk.dk portal, and businesses will meet a public sector that fully supports their digital transition. The business community will have access to more public sector data that can form the basis for new business opportunities and innovation.

3. Security and confidence to be in focus

The great confidence Danes have in each other and in the public sector is the foundation of Danish welfare. The sense of security is to be safe-guarded in an ever-more digital society.

Therefore, focus is to improve information security in the public sector and enhance the digital competences of citizens and of businesses. Moreover, Denmark aspires to be an inclusive society in which everyone can participate, both those who are ready to digitize, and those who cannot use the digital solutions or who do not have access to them.

Action Steps taken or under progress

Efforts for Unified data: The IT solutions and processes of a number of authorities in Denmark were earlier designed to match the internal needs and organization of the authority rather than the needs of citizens and businesses. Much data were stored differently and defined differently from one public authority to another. This made exchange of data across sectors or administrations very difficult. This in turn made it unnecessarily complicated for different authorities to collaborate to deliver the best and most efficient services to individuals and businesses.

Therefore, extensive development work was required so that citizens and businesses can be rest assured of the service they receive is coherent and that the IT systems function optimally.

Building on earlier successes: Over the past 15 years Denmark has undergone a unique transition to digital public administration, communication and services. A number of solutions originating from previous digital strategies have now become routine. Benchmarks have been established in the digital delivery of public services.

Unique Identification for Citizens: With Nemkonto (a mandatory citizen's account for payments from the authorities), the authorities now know which account to pay benefits into. Furthermore, with the secure identification solution NemID everyone has a secure means of personal identification and authentication online. Digital registration of property rights makes it easier to buy and sell property. Several common, cross–sectoral web portals have been established such as a web portal with access to personal health data (sundhed.dk), a single–point of access to all digital public services (borger.dk), and a public services web portal for businesses (virk dk). Furthermore, a digital income registry has been established so that, in a number of areas, individuals are no longer burdened with reporting and documenting changes to their income in order to receive benefits.

Diverse application: Some of the most recently introduced initiatives include mandatory digital post and mandatory online self – service for individuals and businesses. Telemedicine solutions for people with chronic disorders and digital learning tools and materials are becoming more wide spread throughout Denmark. Furthermore, much public – sector basic data is now available online and free of charge for individuals, businesses and authorities alike. All of this makes up the solid foundation which the public sector will develop further up to 2020.

Allied support systems: New initiatives have been envisioned and more cohesive user pathways are being created. Better technical support for citizens and businesses is envisaged. All communication from the public sector is to be made mandatorily digital soon.

Process Re-engineering (GPR): Better use of data and quicker case processing are core concerns. Time is one of the important service parameters in a digital society. Simpler rules, better processes and reductions in the administrative burden is envisaged to make the public sector more efficient and easier to use for the individual person and for businesses. The huge amount of data already under the charge of the public administration was envisaged to be used more extensively to benefit citizens and businesses wherever possible within the framework of legislation. Digitization is aimed to provide good conditions for growth and better digital environment conducive to the business community. Public sector data is to be strategically positioned as growth driver.

Leveraging proven solutions: All public authorities are now required to use all relevant public sector solutions, to avoid developing parallel systems and to promote reuse of pertinent data.

This will help to ensure that citizens experience a collaborative public sector.

New Partnership models: The Digital Strategy runs up to 2020, and in it the central, regional and local governments create the foundation for the Danish public sector of the future. The strategic digital initiatives make it possible for the public sector to make joint investments in areas which are particularly complex and in which there are interdependencies across different authorities and sectors.The individual authority has a responsibility to realize the digital potential its own initiative and, thus, to ensure that digitization leads to the desired change. In parallel with joint public sector efforts, there are sector- specific digitization projects and strategies, for digitization provides a good balance between common strategic targets and local adaptation and priorities. Furthermore, interacting with the public sector, private businesses, trade organizations and NGOs (Non-Governmental Organizations) are also contributing to finding common solutions for the digital transition and helping to secure the foundation for a strong and secure digital Denmark.

Denmark has a long and strong tradition of common government public sector digitization. Scope, objectives and financing of digital strategies are agreed upon by all stakeholders. Thus there is a collaborative implementation of digital strategies.

Evolution of Digital Denmark

The goals that were achieved in the journey of Denmark's digital evolution:

2001-2004: 'Towards digital public sector management.'

2004-2006: 'Strategy for digital public sector management.'

2007-2010: 'Towards better digital service. more efficiency and stronger collaboration.'

2011-2015: 'The digital path to future welfare.'

Let us look at the more recent changes in detail in the following paragraphs.

Phase-1: 2011-2015

Huge transition process for citizens and companies (digital communication with the public sector) was planned. Involvement of all parts of society was the ultimate scope and purpose. Large national campaign activities were launched targeting citizens. The central government, regions and municipalities agreed on an e-government strategy 2011-2015 in order to accelerate the adoption of digital solutions in the public sector. An array of new digital opportunities has quickly transformed everyday life for many citizens and companies. The Danish public sector is a world leader in the adoption of IT and new technologies, aimed at improving welfare services. The Danish digital strategy is leveraged to capitalize on its leading position and take the next steps on the way to future welfare services.

The e-government strategy is divided into three broad segments. Each segment covers various areas and targets different groups.

Phase 1 has achieved the following to a reasonable degree of success.

1. Elimination of printed forms or letters
2. New digital welfare projects in a range of areas
3. Digital solutions for closer collaboration between (a) Citizens and government (b) Public sector and private sector (c) Within public sector organizations

Phase 2: 2016-2020

Improving digital service and user journeys will be the focus of this phase. Focus will be on the back-office process in public authorities. Building the digital data high-ways for the future will be another crucial activity in this phase.

The ultimate goal of the Danish digital Strategy is to make the public sector more coherent, efficient, and effective. It aims to make everyday life easier for the public and empowers them to help themselves online and public services are of high quality. Authorities are required to share relevant information and data, and collaborate better regarding individual citizens and businesses.

The digital strategy aspires to make it easy to run a business, and administrative burdens are reduced. Automatic business reporting has been standardized with the long-term perspective in mind. The public sector is mandated to supportthe digital transformation of businesses and makes more public data available.

Building citizen trust

Trust is the focus of the strategy. Special efforts are planned to be taken so that information security in the public sector is improved and critical public digital infrastructure is robust enough to fulfill the needs of citizens and businesses.

Digital competencies of citizens and businesses are envisaged to be strengthened. A user- friendly and transparent digital public sector is the care of the Strategy which is envisaged to ensure

1. Coherent digital user-journey
2. Better digital communication
3. Overview of own interaction with authorities and benefits
4. Better user-support for citizens and businesses
5. All communication from public authorities is digital

Better use of data and quicker case processing is targeted, which involves

1. Clear legal frameworks for digital administration
2. Moving forward with good basic data
3. Correct payments and better data on the individual citizen

Better and more coherent welfare services are envisaged which includes

1. Coherent welfare service journeys for citizens
2. Better data about disabled and marginalized adults
3. Further deployment of digital welfare solutions
4. Digital learning and teaching. Digital competencies for public employees

Better framework conditions for businesses is planned as part of the strategy which includes

1. Automatic business reporting
2. Digital tendering and procurement
3. Cloud computing in the public sector

Public data is to be fully utilized as a driver for growth under the Danish digital Strategy which includes a focus on

1. Open public data
2. Smart city partnerships
3. Infrastructure for positioning and navigation data

An efficient and effective utilities sector is part of the strategy which involves

1. Common data on topography, climate, and water
2. Open data on energy supply
3. Sharing of data on underground infrastructure
4. Overall ICT architecture for data on waste

With focus on retaining and building public trust, the public sector protects takes on the vanguard role to protect the data of citizens. This will include well-managed information security in all authorities, common standards for secure exchange of information, digital identities and rights management. 'New generations' of 'Easy ID', 'EasyLogin', and Digital Post and secure ID solutions for children and young people.

Sample results with digital post and NmeID

The following paragraphs give details of actual

implementation with respect to various initiatives quoted above

The population of Denmark isabout 5.6 million and public sector involvement is prominent in most life events of the citizens. There is a very high degree of trust in public sector. There is a high degree of internet penetration, usage and competencies in population. 92 % of population aged between 16-74 have internet access at their home. 87 % of the population aged between 16-74 use internet every day. 95 % of businesses have interacted online with public authorities.

Denmark has been through a significant digital development. It is estimated that digitsation has freed up EUR 296 million per year.

More than 100 services have been transformed into digital self-service. 4.5 million citizens are using 'EasyID' as the key to the digital Denmark. All companies and 89 % of the citizens are receiving digital letters. Yearly reduction of administrative burdens for reporting of data and information to authorities has been phenomenal. An electronic register enables automatic payments of social benefits, including the payments of public pensions to 1.2 million citizens.

Digital welfare extends to the realm of public health relevant COPD (Chronic Obstructive Pulmonary Disease) patients get the possibility of managing their diseases from home from 2019 the latest. The municipal care sector got assistive eating devices, shower toilets and ceiling lifts. A common medicine card provides health sector professionals with information on citizens' medicine usage. User-portal have been created for pupils, parents, and teachers in primary and lower-secondary education on learning and communication from 2016-2017.

4.7 million Danish citizens from the age of fifteen are subject to mandatory use of digital letter box-digital post. By the end of 2015, nearly 82% of citizens signed in to receive digital post. Public authorities are increasingly using Digital Post.

Volume of messages via digital post to citizens and

businesses is phenomenal and is evidence to its success. There has been 47.9 million messages in total in 2014 and 88.9 million messages in 2015. 4.3 million citizens have a digital mailbox for receiving mail from the public sector.

The tools used to achieve successful e-Governance in Denmark include

1. Combination of mandatory and user-centric approach to public eservices.
2. Encouraging use of the portal by combining personal, relevant and current content, data and service.
3. Optimization of cross–public sector channel strategy.
4. Cross–public sector cooperation, joint development and reuse of content, data and infrastructure.

The public sector's role has been

1. Public portals creation
2. Delivery of e-services, e.g tax declaration and applying for universities
3. Digital ost, mail from the public sector

The private sector's role has been

1. Support by all banks for e-banking
2. Encom passes over 500 service providers: insurance companies, pension funds, pharmacies, buy'n sell-site, etc.

The OCES

The OCES – Offentlige Certifikater for Elektroniske Services (Public Certificates for Electronic Services) is a State owned OCES certificate policy framing and issuing organization. It looks into the requirements for the public key infrastructure and level of security applied for the digital signature. Supervisory authority is the Agency for Digitization. Annual report of the OCES is sent to the supervisory authority including external system audit of the CA.

OCES certificates are of many types and issued as

1. Personal certificates- PID (a unique number related to civil registration number)
2. Employee certificate- RID/CVR (employee number/ central company number)
3. Business certificate-CVR (central company number)
4. Device certificate- CVR (central company number+deviceID)

These certificates can be used for

a Access control-logon

b Secrecy-encryption of e-mails

c Signature for e-mails, documents and web-sites (non-repudiation)

The next-generation solution in the case of this project aims at one single National eID to retain wide dissemination and high volume. Focus would be on user experiences and usability more scalability (volume), flexibility (diversity of uses), adaptability (new technologies). Modular architecture is to be based on standard components. Fast and agile development is a central concern along with sharing development and operations costs, between the public sector and private sectors.

Clearly demarcated duties and responsibilities

Division of responsibilities, duties and roles in the area of e-health is an example. Division of duties follows an agreement between the government,regions and municipalities from 2010. The role of ministry of health related to legislation regulating access to health data etc. A National eHealth Authority was created that is responsible for IT-infrastructure, standards and terminologies. The role of regions and municipalities is maintenance of eHealth of hospitals and eHealth related to local health tasks. National board of eHealth has been constituted with representatives from the government, the regions and the municipalities. Its duty is to coordinate and follow the overall strategy and development within eHealth, to initiate new national eHealth projects etc.

Public joint venture with different public sector organizations and agencies cooperating with each other is an interesting area in the Danish e-health strategy. This encompasses:

1. Official Danish health portal – Sundhed dk
2. Medcom- a project organization with various projects related to health
3. Cross sectorial e-health, especially to and from GPs
4. Telemedicine
5. The Danish health data network.

A few examples of health IT strategy is as follows:

1. The shared medication record
2. National deployment of telemedicine for COPD patients
3. National deployment of telemedicine for ulcer assessment

Some challenges and benefits in implementation of health-it are as follows

1. It is entirely agreement based –no hard bat for the central government in case of lack of progress
2. Decision making and agreement on evidence can be time consuming
3. It is possible to solve classical sow and reap dilemmas-if the actors are willing and convinced
4. This achieves some degree of involvement and commitment
5. There is often doubt in the interpretation of agreements-especially in the second order

Just as with the phenomenon of globalization, digitization raises many difficult questions. In a number of areas, Denmark is well prepared for what the future will bring. However, in other areas, it has a lot to learn. The public sector must work closely with the Danish business community, stakeholder organizations, etc to establish the basis for a flexible and adaptive society, ready for an ever more digitized world.

The Digital Strategy 2016-2020 sets the course for Danish public sector digitization efforts and their interaction with businesses and industry. Jointly with the businesses and public institutions at local, regional and central-government levels, which on a daily basis takes advantage of the opportunities provided by digitization. This strategy is envisioned to help in building the foundation for a strong and secure digital Denmark.

Lessons

1. A comprehensive vision that sets forth both long-term objectives and short/medium term goals is important in e-Governance
2. Digital solutions must be user friendly to satisfy both internal departmental needs and the citizens who are the beneficiaries
3. Inter-connectivity between departments and inter-operability of information flow must be ensured and built-into overarching e-Governance plans
4. Public–private partnership, if systematically and professionally designed, could give a huge impact to e-government projects
5. Projects must be planned in such a manner that at a future date they could be seamlessly integrated with other such projects. Success of e-government projects is 'Silos' is short lived

CASE STUDY–4

Managing Socio-Cultural factors successfully

Egypt's Family Card Project (FCP) and Ministry of Justice (MoJ) Project

Note to the reader: The Egyptian Ministry of State for Administrative Development (MSAD) is the organisation responsible for the e-government programmes in Egypt since early 2004. The project of electronic government is envisaged to be one of the strategic projects for building information base in Egypt. It was also expected to pave the way for an informatics-based Egyptian society that would be able to cope with IT revolution and bridge the digital gap between Egypt and the advanced world.

Background

The vision of e-government initiative in Egypt is 'delivering high quality government services to the public in the format that suits them'. This vision relies mainly on two principles, namely:

1. Citizen centric service delivery
2. Community participation

Several projects were created under the Egyptian e-Governance programme, each directed towards a selected category of problems. The Family Card System Project (FCP) and Ministry of Justice (MoJ) project are two among these projects created to increase efficiency and provide high-quality service delivery to citizens.

The FCP and MoJ projects

The Family Card System project was one of the national projects which aim at linking various national databases of the family, using the national ID number. This is done using a smart card for each family to get various services such as subsidised goods, the pension security and access to health care funds in addition to other services provided to low-income families that deserve support. The project classified the Egyptian family into segments according to the social and economic situation of the family, to determine those in need for support and optimal support value for each segment, that commensurate with the family condition.

The major players of the family card project were

1. Database Technical Unit (DTU): dedicated to electronic database activities management
2. Distributed Team (DT): dedicated to manage the implementation of the initiative activities amongst different Egyptian governorates
3. Family Project Task Force (FPTF): responsible for DTU supervision, DT follow-up, and ensuring that the overall system components are correct
4. Project Management Group (PMG): responsible for follow-up of all project procedures, such as: financial, management, and technical issues

Studies have shown that the problems faced by the family card system were spread along the life-time of the project starting from the budgetary problems, even before the commencement of implementation. Also, studies have pointed out to the lack of cooperation between the different governmental departments involved in the project and the conflict of priorities among ministries as major problems facing this particular project.

The Ministry of Justice project was within the projects implemented by the MoJ to improve the delivery of services provided by the ministry. The project involved transformation of all courts and related agencies within a large framework rather than incremental improvements. Innovative methods, tools and techniques, are applied to themes such as modernisation through the provision of e-government services, change of organisational culture, administrative reforms or the overhaul of government service delivery procedures and the application of knowledge management processes.

With reference to the MoJ project, it was found that most of the barriers were encountered during the implementation of the project. They are mostly organizational culture related. This involved issues like the lack of motivation to use the new services, lack of awareness of the new services existence or the resistance to use them as a result of the citizens' negative attitudes towards the new technology.

The problems in the case of both projects existed before the start of their respective project implementation and had the potential to put the whole initiative at risk. Hindrances and problems also occurred after the start and during the actual implementation of both projects.

There was lack of coordination among many governmental ministries and organisations. Electronic services were not accepted as a priority for citizens, the key beneficiary from the projects. There was a vision-reality gap between what was desired and what was delivered. Although the projects initiatives provide many opportunities for their own convenience and satisfaction, but still, there is very low demand for what is supplied by these projects.

There was a failure in increasing people's awareness to e-Governance projects. In addition, the awareness barrier existed from inside the government as government employees lacked awareness regarding the potential of electronic services and the added value that they offer to society. Finally, the projects were repeatedly stuck up and delayed at operational level due to administrative problems. Some studies pointed out that the problem began with the lack of clear policies and strategies in the administrative system.

Many attempts were made to address these problems and issues. In the family card project case, two types of trainings were applied, theoretical and on-the-job training. The objective of the training was to make the employees comfortable with the automated system. The same happened in the MoJ projects where extensive and IT training courses took place to train civil servants who thought they will be replaced by younger, computer literate employees. This led to overcoming many problems at one time. It removed the fear from dealing with technology as a threat to employees, increased the human resources skills needed for the sustainability of the projects. It also helped reducing corruption within government agencies resulting from lack of monitoring and accountability methods associated with traditional, paper-based environment.

The main impact of both projects as emphasised by many studies and the general public opinion strongly suggests better management within the system, and improved public services. The new systems, along with the institutional development and business process reengineering have led to cost savings, and better efficiency.

ICTs, as the main tool utilised to reach the development goal, have many challenges to deliver, but they are not impossible to overcome. ICT, if implemented successfully can have a tremendous impact on public services. This is proved from the two case studies of Egypt.

The two projects, in their own particular ways resulted in additional benefits that range from standardisation and lower maintenance by means of solution unification for more sectors/services (one system instead of multiple systems) to easier, greater and more accurate reporting capabilities utilising one database while reducing error and increasing efficiency, credibility and accessibility for beneficiaries to their own records. The two projects also stand as good examples of cooperation between the public and private sectors for better serving the public and reducing the government expenses which can be used in other sectors.

The case of Egypt also shows the value of the 'little steps' approach to e-Governance. The 'little steps' approach holds that big projects should start with a pilot project to prove the success of the initiative even if on a smaller scale, to discover problems, rectify them and create a win-win case with all stakeholders.

Social considerations of the project should be taken into account prior to technical aspects. Citizen considerations and requirements should be taken into account from the start before planning and implementation phases. Capacity building of different stakeholders is crucial to the success of the projects. Considerable effort is required to change the citizen's culture to use new technologies for service delivery. The key performance indicators of the system should be clearly stated and fc llowed up.

Implementing electronic government projects in developing countries such as Egypt is more difficult than in developed ones. The reasons include difficult economic conditions, weak human assets in developing countries and the gap between developed and developing countries in Internet technological infrastructures, practices, and usage.

Egypt tried to overcome these kinds of difficulties as a developing country by signing agreements with multinational companies such as Microsoft and IBM to provide the latest technologies to the government. The Egyptian e-government transformation concerns focus more on cultural than administrative, political, and legislative barriers and problems.

Key benefits of family card system project include the following

1. Delivery of the services to the underprivileged citizens through a computerized application, up-to-date database and efficient incurring system
2. Monitoring, control over the infiltration and loss in supports
3. Creation of a civilised environment through which underprivileged citizens can acquire their services
4. Transparency through the establishment of clear and neutral processes for acquiring and managing subsidies
5. Employing only one card to support all support services
6. Ensuring that the citizen should not bear any extra costs.
7. Centralising the design and decentralising the implementation

8. Decentralising service provision by creating untraditional outlets to fulfil the citizen's needs
9. Applying new methods of management that consider the aspect of efficiency and guarantee the ideal usage of the resources

A methodical and well planned implementation was followed. This can be summed up as follows

1. Establishing an electronic database for underprivileged families and the transactions performed for each type of service
2. Defining the overall system technical architecture and preparing the top-level design of the system, and defining the system configuration
3. Developing applications to manage the service database to support provision of the service
4. Issuing multi-application smart cards for services delivery
5. Building the network infrastructure of the system that allows all stakeholders to communicate together
6. Building the service centres that manage the database updates
7. Building a call centre to receive the citizens' requests and complaints. The centre is equipped with a complaints management system that traces the received complaints until fulfilment. Training the system users: theoretical and on-the–job training sessions

Obstacles faced during the project were many. Some of them can be clearly identified as follows

1. Employee's culture to work manually and the reluctance to use the automated system
2. Citizen's culture used to deal with paper card and may never have dealt with electronic equipment

3. Difficulty to get acquainted with the difficulty to get acquainted with the new system
4. Conflict of priorities
5. Lack of confidence in government cooperation

The need to synchronise all stakeholders to the big picture and the projects vision, and building a sense of ownership within relevant stakeholders were top priorities. A modular approach to roll out such huge projects has proved to work best in case of Egypt instead of the big bang approach. Also responsibilities should be clearly defined and assigned. Beneficiary convenience should always be the target when developing a service. Centralisation of ICT applications can save many costs while decentralisation of service delivery is a must.

The Ministry of Justice digitalization project was also a prestigious one replete with many challenges. The project scope was defined and set to include all types and levels of judicial bodies, courts, prosecution offices and support agencies. Strategic technology partners were brought in to oversee local development partners, as well as finance the development activities. Institutional development experts were employed to analyse business processes at all judicial organisations, ahead of requirements gathering for information systems.

Scope was set for all courts to adopt a case management system, internal workflow automation system, integration with all relevant judicial/support bodies. Setting up service provision outlets (one stop shop) within courts instead of in-office services is part of this project. The Judicial Information Centre was identified as the future central hub for all judicial applications, including the judicial case database, integrating with courts, prosecutions offices and support agencies.

The project began with a well-researched and firm footing with institutional development experts presenting their reports. Their recommendations were implemented. In parallel, extensive training courses were initiated for civil servants at different judicial organisations. The development partners and System Integrators came in and developed their respective components of the project.

Some of the obstacles faced during the course of this project were as follows

1. The digital divide and computer illiteracy and resistance to change of civil servants who are end-users in the delivery of judicial services
2. The lack of qualified and skilled human resources within judicial offices structures
3. Problems with interoperability and multiple service delivery channels, as the information systems were to be integrated with numerous other agencies
4. The huge size of backlog of data and information that needs to be entered into the new information systems
5. Undependable and erratic electricity and internet connections at remote judicial offices and weak infrastructure at remote areas
6. The large number of stakeholders involved in the project was another source of communication and co-ordination problems

A thorough study of the 'as is' scenario was done and issues were systematically tackled. The groundwork was also laid by retaining the services of an institutional development expert to review and reengineer the internal processes and public services offered by judicial entities.

The project was implemented in two phases. The first phase cost was around US$6.5M. This covered the costs for all hardware, software licenses, communication lines, training and development, workplace development, in addition to project management costs. The second phase entailed the roll-out of case management and other information systems at all remaining judicial institutions. Its cost was estimated at US$18 million.

There was good and professional financial management of the Project as well. Some of the project revenue allocated for the constant upgrade and development. ICT development programmes were put in place so that information systems teams would be always up to date with the latest technologies.

Specialised training units were set up within the Judicial Information Centre for training new systems users, as well to further facilitate the use of ICT within the judicial agencies. The Judicial Information Centre that was set up was also responsible for maintaining the central national judicial database, linking all judicial entities in Egypt together. A geographically remote disaster recovery site was also set up, synchronising daily with the main site. Both the family card project and the Ministry of Justice project were a success by the skilful management of the soft side of organizational change by the project leaders.

The barriers evident in the case of Egypt's e-Governance project can be summed up as the following

1. Privacy and security risk barriers
2. Legislative barriers
3. Administrative barriers
4. Technological barriers
5. Cultural barriers
6. User resistance

(1) Privacy and security risks are a serious concerns in the era of e-services. If they are not properly managed, they could pose a threat to the viability of e-service. The justified concern about the misuse of personal information disclosed on the web, the protection of data, and the use of online financial transactions has become a significant issue in developing e-service systems, especially in the government context.

(2) Legislative Barriers arise mainly from such issues as the

lack of a suitable legal framework that addresses submission and processing of electronic documents, liability emerging from electronic documents, and proofing value of electronic documents against paper documents. For the proof-of-identity and the electronic document integrity, there is no globally accepted framework or standard for all services today. Electronic signature technology is accepted in some countries only for specific services. In addition, legal issues, such as the requirement for physical presence, physical inspections, audits, and examinations, may hinder the transition to electronic services, since some manual processes will still remain in the workflow.

(3) Administrative Barriers arise because government administrators in some cases are reluctant to promote and introduce electronic services. One main reason is the managerial and administrative issues of e-service deployment in the public sector. The development and deployment of electronic services incurs significant costs for hardware platforms, software development and licensing, and employee hiring for electronic service administration and help desk operations.

(4) Technological barriers are a major bottleneck in the implementation and maintenance of e-service systems in the public sector, especially in the developing countries.

(5) Cultural barriers are one of the biggest obstacles for e-service implementation. Some barriers may be ascribed to cultural or special characteristics of user communities. For example, specific citizen communities have a negative stance against electronic services and would only see 'traditional' paper-based service channels. In addition, e-service designs and implementations may not take into account the language literacy levels or culture background of the users.

(6) User Resistance stems from the fact that many citizens

have a minimal understanding of how government processes are executed or decisions are made. This lack of awareness can prevent the citizen from actively participating in government services. Citizens and enterprises are not always informed regarding the web addresses through which electronic services are available, or even whether an e-service exists at all. Cultural and sub-cultural barriers also exist within the organisations that need to often re-invent themselves to manage change introduced by ICT or using ICT to deliver e-Governance services to the citizens.

Such cultural factors lead to resistance to change. Resistance hinders or at times completely stops the electronic services from inside the government. The employees may resist the shift of power resulting from the introduction of e-service. Employees possessing a certain amount of tacit domain knowledge are considered to have more power within the organisation. Introduction of electronic services converts tacit knowledge to explicit, depriving these employees of their source of power. Further, this initiation will generally require structural reforms in the organisation, modification of job descriptions and change in duties. Studies in information systems have established how the resistance of users to a new system because of trust or other factors regularly hinders its implementation.

The family card system project and the judicial procedures development project are the result of the fruitful co-operation between numerous government organisations, as well as those from the private sector.

Lessons

1. Awareness about an e–government initiative and its benefits among citizens are the 'litmus test', so to say, of the success or otherwise of any e-Government project
2. Synchronization of all stake holders to the 'big picture' of e-Governance is vital

3. Confidence building measures must be initiated to build up trust levels among citizens who are the intended beneficiary of an e-government project
4. Privacy and security issues must be earnestly addressed. An breach or lacunae in the same must be rectified at once
5. Human issues that are in total to a department such as fear and resistance to change must be addressed on priority
6. Inadequate stake holder commitment can harm a project

CASE STUDY–5

Integrated Information System (IIS) for Defence Force Management in a country in the Middle East–ITPOSMO Analysis.

Note to the reader: The IIS is another interesting but not so successful case of a project to develop an Integrated Information System for Defence Force Management in a country in the Middle East. This project was undertaken in the year 1996 by the Republican Defence Force (RDF), under control of the Department of Defence (DoD), that consists of the nation's army, air force and navy.

Background

The ICT intervention was the planned introduction of an integrated information system (IIS) that would cover all branches of the Republican Defence Force (RDF). This was intended not only computerize but also integrate a variety of management information systems, including human resource IS, budget IS, accounting IS, and procurement/payment IS.

Until the mid-1990s, management of the RDF was a hierarchical activity that relied predominantly on manual information systems. As the RDF grew in size and in its gamut of activities during the 1990s, this approach became increasingly inefficient and ineffective. A right decision was therefore made to upgrade the management information systems, with a view to improving management processes, and enhancing the image of the RDF. This also coincided with a more general move to improve the functioning of the whole apparatus of government. It was hoped that the spread of IT to other sectors from here could be a definitive solution to a variety of managerial and administrative problems.

Project analysis

As indicated earlier in this section, the project is to develop an integrated Information System (IIS) for managing the RDF which includes human resources, budgeting, accounting and procurement to payment.

The main stakeholders were those in senior positions (including the Secretary for defence and other DoD senior officials; head of the RDF, Heads of the individual defence services, and other senior officers), key advisers of senior officials/officers, middle-ranking project leads involved in the IIS introduction process and field staff who will be using the outputs of the system.

This ambitious project was a failure. An analytical study was conducted that brought out the Design-Reality gap. It compared the assumptions/requirements within the application design with the reality prevailing just before that design was implemented along seven 'ITPOSMO' dimensions. The results and findings were as follows.

1. Information: The study found that the design made relatively few changes to the content of formal information that was in use within the Republican Defence Force just prior to IIS implementation. It did implicitly assume that informal information would not be used in the RDF. In reality that had been very important. The design explicitly required that information be presented in different ways to those who

do not use computers ever and that information flow in different ways. In particular, the design required a sharing of data within and between the different arms of the RDF. That was quite different to the pre-existing reality by which officers jealously guarded their data both for reasons of personal power and concerns about national security. This created a large design-reality gap on this dimension.

2. Technology: The design assumed the use of a broad range of new software and hardware, including a series of networked information systems spread across the whole of the RDF. The initial reality was almost entirely manual management information systems. Only very few PCs were in use for word processing. There was also a lack of nation-wide telecommunications infrastructure. There was even a lack of electricity in some RDF locations. This created a large design-reality gap on this dimension.
3. Processes: The study found that the design assumed significant changes to pre-existing RDF management and information-related processes. Although the basics of many management decisions were similar in design and initial reality, those decisions were designed to be made more on the basis of formal information. This required a removal of pre-existing duplications and some bureaucratic checks, and with an integrated approach to decision-making, particularly financial decision-making, that was not present in initial reality. This created a significant design-reality gap on this dimensions.
4. Objectives and values: The design assumed that the objectives of the project (automation and integration of processes) were shared by all stakeholders. In reality, during pre-IIS, some senior and middle-rank officers shared these objectives, but others did not and DoD

officials felt reluctant about the project. The design also assumed a rational, objective culture within the Republican Defence Forces. In reality, the culture was heavily personalized, with management processes strongly affected by conflicts between senior officers, some of whom belonged to different tribes. This reality also jarred with a design assumption that cross-functional team-working would be valued.

5. Staffing and skills: The design assumed the presence of a broad range of staff competencies. These included good contract design and management skill, strong technical skills from a local IT contractor; sound project management skills, IT skills among all relevant service personnel including officers and IT knowledge and awareness among all senior officers. In reality, in the pre IIS phase, none of these competencies were actually present.

   For instance, the local contractor who was the System Integrator (SI) turned out in practice to be inexperienced and lacking both managerial and technical skills. Also, most service personnel lacked cutting-edge IT skills. A few had word processing skills, but those fell below the operational skill requirements assumed in the IIS design.

6. Management systems and structures: The notion of decentralized, flexible but integrated decision-making systems was incorporated in the design. This clashed with the pre-existing reality of autocratic, hierarchical, centralized but disconnected management systems and structures.

7. Other resources: The design requirement was for budgetary expenditure of some US$5m to be spent on the IT, plus further expenditure for general staff training and IT staff recruitment, to be spent over an

> 18-month implementation period. The RDF did have such resources in reality. There was also a requirement for commitment of a considerable amount of time by senior and middle-rank officers in the planning of system design and installation. In reality, staff had some other calls on their time. Devoting the required time to IIS would necessitate the sidelining of some other duties.

It also emerged that the system implemented was a product initially designed for the private sector. Although the RDF design removed inappropriate private sector components, in practice those components were not actually removed by the initial SI. In other words, the IIS was never customized to specific RDF processes and systems. The design-reality gap on these dimensions therefore actually increased after initial implementation. The initial SI was then replaced. The new SI did attempt some of the designed customizations, bringing the design-reality gap back down to initial levels. Yet, there was not much success.

The staffing and skills gap was narrowed somewhat by IT training provided to service personnel. However, this left the gap in other competencies untouched. Finally, after a few years, and despite the obvious problems with the system, the design was expanded to incorporate two additional computerized modules. In all, after some years of implementation, the overall design-reality gap has not significantly reduced from the initial score.

Introduction of the integrated information system has been largely unsuccessful, bordering on a total failure. The system was physically implemented in terms of hardware installation but most modules have never worked satisfactorily and never been used, or were just run in parallel with existing practices but not made part of those practices. Nearly six years after project initiation, only one module of the five envisaged was in operational use. In cost-benefit terms, the project was a clear loser, with hundreds of meetings, training sessions, and other uses of staff time plus the direct financial costs all being invested with very little to show on the benefit side of the balance sheet.

With such high gap ratings on so many dimensions, it can be argued that all except 'other resources' were a contributory cause of the largely unsuccessful outcome. The greatly-elongated timescale for the project and the gradual introduction of IT means that 'technology' in practice should not be seen as a prime cause of the failure. The remaining dimensions have been grouped into three related areas as causes:

1. The project aimed was too high and was not 'grounded' in reality of the user community and the organization itself. It tried to change the entire information/ management systems and structures/processes dimensions. By changing all these dimensions - looking for a fundamentally different set of working practices, the project tried to do too much at once.
2. Like all armed forces, the RDF is a very traditional organization but also one with some strong individual personalities. The way the IIS was designed conflicted directly with both the traditional culture and the self-interests of at least some senior figures. There was thus a mismatch between the organizational culture and vision and objectives of the project.
3. There was a clear absence of key competencies. Such an ambitious project required a strong set of complex competencies that simply were not available. The staffing and skill-sets dimensions were languishing.

Any one of these could have been addressed suitably with appropriate advance planning, but together they created a strong case for failure. To reduce the risk of failure, e-governance projects must therefore reduce problematic design-reality gaps. This means either making the design more like current reality and/or making reality more like the design.

Hindsight recommendations based on studies and root-cause analysis for improvements on this project fall into two main camps. These are as follows

(1) Generic gap closure recommendations: These are approaches to e-governance projects that can help generally to reduce gaps on a number of dimensions. These include (a) scope limitation (b) Incremental approach and (c) Participation.

Scope limitation is a grounded and closer-to-reality approach. With e-governance, if one just changes one of the two elements - i.e. changing the technology but keeping working practices the same, or changing working practices but keeping technology the same - then the organization may be a little unsteady but it can still keep going. Also, with e-government, if you change both technology and working practices simultaneously without any basic ground work, then the project will often come tumbling down. The initial project should have been much more limited in its scope and ambition based on ground realities. It should initially have aimed just to introduce computers and networks to the RDF, but to leave current working practices untouched.

It could have done this in one of two ways. Either by automating some of the current administrative/management working practices, but leaving those practices as close as possible to the original form that is, retaining to an extent the same information, the same processes, the same management systems and structures, the same personnel. Alternatively, by focusing on roll-out of basic network applications like email and web access, to a broad range of locations and personnel. This would not change any of the main work of the RDF. It would result in just automating some communication and data-gathering practices. In either case, this would mean a significantly smaller overall design-reality gap.

Incremental or step-by-step approach is another way of looking at avoiding the perils of over-ambition. Instead of computerizing and integrating all modules at once across the whole RDF, the project design could have been better advised to take an incremental approach. This could have been incremental in terms of modules. Like for instance, computerizing the HR function first, then moving on budgeting once HR was successfully completed. If that still appeared too ambitious, the project could also have been incremental in terms of services. For example, by first focusing just on the navy, say, and then rolling out a module to the other services once the navy module was proven to work well. The incremental approach breaks down the overall design-reality gap into smaller individual elements.

The IIS project was conceived by a small clique of senior officers. It would potentially have been better if a broader range of stakeholders had been involved in a participatory manner in the process. In that way, a better sense of reality would likely have been incorporated into the project's design, resulting in a smaller overall design-reality gap. However, the design of this technique may itself be mismatched to RDF realities, which neither involve nor value participative approaches to any great degree.

(2) Specific gap closure recommendations: These are actions taken on e-Governance projects that can help specifically to reduce gaps on particular dimensions. The two important dimensions are (a) values and objectives and (b) Skill-sets and staffing.

There is relatively little that could be done specifically about values and objectives. The project design incorporated a very top-down approach to project implementation that overtly imposed the system on middle and lower ranks. The reality of their objectives and values could perhaps have been moved a little towards the design through clear and interactive communication that explained the value and role of the information system. The only true way to address the objectives and values gap would have been to design a quite different e-government system that did not conflict with existing motivations, interests and culture.

Global external consultants could have been roped in for this prestigious project instead of local ones. However there are two issues here. First, the fact that external consultants may quite often be poorly in touch with national and organizational realities, so their designs have a propensity to be mismatched with those realities. Second, e-Government applications in security and defence are highly sensitive. Few governments would welcome foreigners.

In the dimension of staffing and skills, a broad range of awareness-raising and training activities should have been initiated in order to address some of the competency gaps identified above. The problems of poor contract, change and project management skills were pronounced. Different skill-sets at all levels were conspicuous by their absence. Focused and need based end-user training must have been given. This ought to have been practical and experiential. RDF project thus offers many lessons for successful digitalization and also tips to avoid pitfalls.

Lessons

1. The design of the information systems must be related to both the actual and anticipated needs.
2. Infrastructure readiness must be ensured
3. A thorough GPR must precede the actual rollout of any e-government project so that legacy issues are dealt with
4. Change must be institutionalized so that personal preferences and egos of top project management do not hinder the vision and purpose of the project itself
5. The private sector partner in the rollout must be carefully selected andthe roles and responsibilities must be explicitly laid down
6. Staffing and skill set gaps must be addressed continuously till the project is stabilized

CASE STUDY–6

The PP (Power and Perils) of PPP

South Africa's 'Golaganang' (Come Together) Project:

Note to the reader: The World Summit on the Information Society (WSIS) plan of action foresees the formation of a people-centred, inclusive and development-oriented Information Society, where everyone can access, utilise and share information and knowledge. South Africa has made great strides towards meeting the commitments of the WSIS Declaration of Principles and Plan of Action to which the country is a signatory.

The South African leadership understood the need to develop an Information Society and harness the power of ICTs for economic and social development for the benefit of the country and its citizens. The need for reform and the transformation of its core activities to make processes more effective, efficient and more citizen oriented was recognized. This case gives an overview of e-Governance in South Africa and examines the ambitious Golaganang project with focus of the important issues related to public-private partnership. It focuses on issues that put the project into trouble.

Project analysis

Vision 2014 of South Africa described an 'inclusive Information Society, one in which the use of ICTs will be harnessed to ensure that everyone has fast, reliable and affordable access to information and knowledge that will enable them to participate meaningfully in the community and economy'.

The vision further aspires to move the country from being a consumer of ICT products and services to being a major player in the production and innovation of these products and services. The cornerstones of this inclusive information society are a vibrant and thriving ICT sector, an enabling policy and regulatory environment, accessible ICT infrastructure and broadband connectivity, and an appropriately skilled and knowledgeable citizenry.

The vision for e-government has been stated in a document titled, 'Electronic Government, The Digital Future: A public service IT policy framework'.This was published in 2001 by South Africa's Department of Public Service and Administration. This document strongly advocated that an e-Government initiative should address three main domains

(1) e-Government : the application of IT intra-governmental operations (Government to government or G2G)

(2) e-Service : the application of IT to transform the delivery of public services (Government to Citizens or G2C)

(3) e-Business : the application of IT to operations performed by government in the manner of G2B transactions (e.g. procurement)

In South Africa, information policies enable the sharing of information with the public and across government departments. The Promotion of Access to Information Act enables the constitutional right of access to information. A person is entitled to request information from any public or private body.

A number of policy measures have been identified as critical in creating an enabling environment for the implementation of e-Government. These include: Minimum Information Security Standards (MISS), Handbook on Minimum Interoperability Standards (MIOS), Electronic Communications Transaction Act of 2002, and the Law Commission Issue Paper on Privacy Public Service Act. The Public Service Regulations of 2001 has also enabled e-government implementation.

Mobile penetration has risen to over 50% of the population increasing opportunities for multi-access to information. South Africa has leveraged the tools of multi-access government to promote free and fair national elections in 2004. The Independent Electoral Commission (IEC) developed partnerships with cell phone service providers, which enabled voters to short message service (SMS) their identity number and in return receive a message back indicating their eligibility to vote and voting station details. Custom-designed handheld scanners captured information from bar-coded ID books and greatly streamlined the process of voter registration.

A further strategy employed to increase affordable universal access is that of granting Under-Serviced Area Licenses (USALs). The licensees are Small Medium Enterprises (SMEs) that provide telecommunication services in areas designated as under-serviced

South Africa faces significant human capital development challenges in building the inclusive information society. One of the key challenges is the shortage of skilled ICT executives in the public sector and professionals in the private sector.

South Africa has achieved a number of successes including an e-government information portal called 'Batho Pele' gateway launched in 2004, 355 multi-purpose community centres have been established to provide people in villages with access to ICT and ICT related services. This includes telecentres and cyber labs in schools. All universities in the country and about 6000 schools are ICT enabled. Nearly 800 Public Information Terminals (PITs) have been established and over 80% of health centres are connected with ICTs. All provincial and national government departments and many local governments have websites and e-mail addresses. An educational portal, 'Thutong', has been established to help educators and learners to access curriculum related information and a language portal using all 11 official languages.

The Batho Pele gateway portal was launched in 2004 as an information portal providing information on government services and other information such as legislation, policies and all other information of government.

The post office's paymaster was launched to make life considerably easier for recipients of pensions, particularly those who live in remote rural areas. Under the scheme, welfare grants and pensions are paid into a postbank account that is linked to a smart card containing a magnetic strip and a chip, which contains the beneficiary's fingerprints and photo to eliminate fraud. In the government to business (G2B) domain, the South African Revenue Services (SARS) e-filing facility provides a means to conduct transactions related to tax returns on the internet

In South Africa there are a number of examples of Public Private Partnerships in ICTs for development. The corporate sector plays an important role in providing support to community programmes.

The relationship with vendors remains problematic and change leaders must remain vigilant in not getting 'locked in' to proprietary solutions from a single vendor. Promoting the use of non-proprietary solutions such as open source software is a viable option or must form part of long term strategy, if not contingency plans in an ongoing context too.

'e-Governance in South Africa, as it is with many countries, still finds itself perched between performance and promise' as its full potential has not been reached

One of the emerging key issues of e-Governance is the manner in which public services and service delivery are planned, structured and logically bundled. A multichannel approach is required. This is necessary to ensure the availability of a right channel for each type of service. It is also imperative that service delivery is integrated and consistent across channels. The standardisation and norms around enterprise architecture is also critical for the overall success of digitalization of public services delivery.

Though sincere in intention, South Africa did face and continues to face issues in successful roll out of e-Governance. Let us take one case–the 'Golaganang' or the 'e-society' initiative. This project involved the attempt to provide general public services and public administration using ICT.It was initiated by South Africa in 2002.

'Golaganang' (meaning 'come together') was an ambitious joint initiative between the South African government and the private sector to provide public service sector employees with an affordable computer and accessories bundle. This included a multi-media PC, operating system and application software, a modem and Internet connectivity, a printer and free installation. It also included a three-year extended warranty, interactive tutorial software plus three hours basic computer skills training for the employee and one family member.

The Golaganang project was intended to be accessible to all of the 1.1 million public servants in South Africa. The project aimed to distribute Internet-connected PCs to at least 50,000 employees within the first 6 months of operation. The high income economic strata had to pay US$45 per month over a 36-month period. There would then be a sliding scale of subsidies down to the lowest earners. Those on less than US$1,300 per month had to pay just US$10 per month.

The Ministry of Public Service and Administration (MPSA) had the overall responsibility for the project. The project was an ambitious and visionary attempt to address inequalities in access to technology by providing an opportunity to those public servants that hitherto could not afford to buy their own home computers. In the process it was believed, and rightly so, that digital literacy among public servants will improve significantly and that this in turn will result in better utilisation of ICT in the execution of their work. It was expected that the cumulative effect of this would result in better service delivery to the public.

The Department of Public Service and Administration (DPSA) front-ended the project from the public sector side, with involvement also from the State IT Agency (SITA). The private sector group was led by global multinational giant in the IT sector. Other stakeholder organisations included Telkom, CS Holdings, Standard Bank and Microsoft. Obviously, all South African public servants were also stakeholders and ultimately the intended beneficiaries.

Direct costs alone of the project were around US$80m in the first six months assuming the target of 50,000 end-users was to be reached. There was also a significant additional costs of administering the project, including the donation to local schools of one PC per 20 purchased through Golaganang. A boost to local employment was expected since the PCs were to be manufactured domestically in South Africa. The benefits of digital literacy enhancement was also envisaged because of PC usage and skills build-up. Golaganang was seen as a flagship programme in the South African's attempts to champion use of ICTs in the public sector specifically, and across the society in general.

It was clear to all the stakeholders that the failure of the project will have had broad effect in damaging ICT roll out and uptake.It could also end up damaging confidence levels about large ICT projects and about the much hyped public-private partnerships. Much was at stake and thus all efforts were put in to make it a success.

Within a matter of months after its ambitious launch problems began appearing. Soon thereafter the Ministry itself in a public statement admitted to the failure of the project and the reason for the same too.

The government's approach on the Golaganang partnership was on a basis of shared risks and benefits. However, analysts have pointed out that the difficulty arose when the private sector partner and system integrator, a leading global IT giant, began insisting that government offer guarantees to the value of US$73 million to allow the project to go ahead as they were unable to carry the commercial risk.

Many held that this was against the spirit for which the DPSA and SITA conceived and presented the project. DPSA was also not in a position to offer guarantees in advance payments. Furthermore, DPSA investigated other options to allow the project to proceed. The alternative options were found to be financially not sustainable in the long term. DPSA thus informed, with understandable anguish, option has not been found. DPSA therefore decided to shelve the project till such time a best alternative has been found.

Having stated the above facts, it is only fair to touch upon the things that were positioned and poised favourably for the project. The lead private sector stakeholder initially did have a sales strategy to address e-government and as such it has aggressively targeted roll out of ICTs in the South African public sector. This goes all the way to the top as the then CEO of the lead private sector company was positioned on the South African President's ICT executive advisory council.

Addressing the digital divide is seen as the key ICT issue in South Africa. All the top change champions in the government departments were unanimously convinced of the benefits of the private sector proposal when they decided to accept it. When civil servants initially heard about the project, they were very keen on the idea, and welcomed the opportunity to extend ICT access to their own homes.

However, the Critical Failure Factors (CFFs) were the following. There were gaps in the 'trust levels' between the public and private sectors. This 'trust deficit', so to say, may have its roots in the fact that due-diligence was undertaken neither by the public nor the private sector stakeholders in the prestigious project. This public-private partnership was established on the basis of 'taken-for-granted' assumptions and a leap into faith, so to say. Too much weight was placed on 'partnership' and this resulted in the misunderstanding of finances and associated issues.

The project also lacked any notion of a pilot scheme, pilot study, or Proof of Concept (PoC). The scope was far too large and ambitious for the timescale envisaged. This was a classic case of 'biting more than one can chew'. Starting small, then grow would have been a better strategy in this case. For e-Governance projects, especially ones that may ultimately have a large scope, small starts with measureable milestones and timelines must be aimed first. Then based on the results, these can be scaled up quickly.

This does not imply that small-scale pilots must always be monitored and evaluated in great detail. It only means that there must be appropriate risk management. All that is needed is a good sense of both costs and benefits, and an ability to put some balance between both while being grounded in reality.

Lessons

1. A consultative process is important to get a 'buy-in' from all stakeholders of any e-government projects
2. Getting the right PPP strategy in place is necessary to ensure 'promise' translates 'performance'
3. Mere installation of IT or ICT technology will not ensure success of e-Governance. The efforts must translate to larger impact on the society and economy
4. A pilot project or proof of concept in one or two select locations will ensure that unanticipated problems are addressed and the larger country –wide implementations is on a firm foundation
5. Legal issues related to e-government projects must be clearly understand and built into the project

CASE STUDY– 7

Thailand's Smart Id Card debacle. A Lesson in Vision–Reality gap

Note to the reader: IT Development in Thailand's public agencies was initiated in the early 1990s. That was a time when there was no national IT master plan nor an established national IT agency. In the mid-1990s, the government promoted the use of Electronic Data Interchange (EDI) to increase efficiency and effectiveness of the government services in various public agencies such as the Thailand customs department and the port authority of Thailand. The first national IT master plan 'Towards Social Equity and Prosperity.

Thailand IT policy into the 21st century was introduced in 1996. In 2001, 'the Thailand vision toward a knowledge-based economy' was formulated to pursue the knowledge-based and sustainable economy.

Background

Analysts have pointed out that in the development of IT projects in the early 1990s, Thailand followed the distributed strategic approach. Under this paradigm each public agency individually initiated and developed its own IT projects. Studies have shown that this approach had resulted in many problems.

Some of them were:

1. Different types of legacy systems
2. Different types of data standards
3. Inability to directly exchange data because of differences in data formats
4. Each public agency collects duplicate data with other existing database systems
5. Multiple efforts in software development

To overcome these problems, a national IT master plan was formulated and established in 1996. Since then public agencies have gradually adopted the 'whole picture' approach to their own IT master plans at the ministry and department levels. The main driving force of the evolution of digitalised public services in Thailand is the active role of the National Information Technology Council (NITC) and the National Electronics and Computer Technology Centre (NECTEC). The integration of various government IT systems and the sharing of IT resources such as applications, network, information and knowledge, has become a top priority area of thrust in the development process. The expected outcome of integration, such as a one-stop service portal, government data exchange, government information services aim to increase the efficiency and effectiveness of government services and decision making, and also reduce investment costs.

With the formation of the National IT master plan, the e-Governance objectives and missions became well defined and has directed IT development in public agencies toward an integrated-government objective. Guided by the IT master plan, the government used both distributed and centralized strategic approaches together with the central IT agency to the e- governance development.

The government refined the distributed strategic approach with well-established e-government projects by forming a working group on e-government project development with the national IT master plan model and linking those systems together to consolidate information and services. This approach is proved to be a cost effective approach, as public agencies were able to consolidate their own systems, and share resources and knowledge in pursuing the same objectives.

Thailand has also attempted to utilize the centralized strategic approach, especially on the national data network infrastructure and software applications. This approach was intended to reduce IT investment cost and create a common standard of IT use amongst public agencies.

The National IT agency has played an active role in this approach. Analysts have categorized Thailand's e- governance projects in compliance with a National IT master into three groups:

1. Individual e-Government projects (for instance, the Thairegistration.com initiated by the department of commercial registration)
2. Group of e-government projects (for instance, the agriculture information project by the department of agriculture)

3. National e-Government projects (government information technology services, and government data exchange centre to name a few as examples

While all was well and efforts were systematic, let us look at the classic case of a failed project and examine what we can learn from that failure.

Project analysis

The failure of Thailand's smart ID card project has been studied by many analysts. It was found that the cause of failure came from

1. Errors in problem definition that became the starting point of failure
2. Incomplete inter-assessment that created more chance of failure
3. Uncontrolled chaos in the enrolment process

Since the movement of New Public Management (NPM) reform in countries with the first-mover ICT advantage during the 1980s and 1990s, governments have paid more attention than before to Quality of Service (QoS) or response to the needs of citizens. The notions of NPM in public administration have increasingly emphasized on professional management practices, and customer and result oriented administration. governments began trying to create better connections with its citizens, improve access to public services and respond to socio-economic development. Therefore, in the 1990s, e-government was introduced to enhance and support NPM reform. In the early days, e-government was used for information and communication technology (ICT) to produce and distribute public information through the Internet. However, the information was quite static at that time. Today, with more than a decade of experience, e-Governance has developed into a more advanced application of ICT as a critical tool, that can lead to a more responsive government that provides enhanced value at a lower cost. Some experts have proclaimed that e - governance is the second revolution in public administration after New Public Management.

The objective of the smart ID card project of Thailand that was initiated in the year 2002 was to enable every Thai citizen to use all government services by utilising one card only, which would provide a more convenient and faster service. It would have also greatly reduced the use of paper, document files and copies. The ministry of interior was responsible for initial data, which included documentation of birth date, ID number and registration of name and surname. All this data was included in the smart ID card. Other public agencies had the right to record and amend the data directory and fields for which they were responsible, based on the data standard of the card-reading machine, security system, and communication method of the card and reading machine. The planning and implementation of the system was based on convenience, safety, durability, cost-effectiveness, high quality and a uniformed standard across the same database. There was great euphoria around the smart ID card project.

A four–phase task and target was set to deal with applications and the utilisation of the smart ID card. This was as follows:

Phase 1, 2004 – Aim the smart ID card at substituting the free medical treatment card, social security card and ATM card. The smart ID card holder can access and contact electronic services of both the public and private sector via electronic machines or websites.

Phase 2, 2005 – The smart ID card substitutes the cash card, debit card, credit card and telephone card. It can also be used for recording change of address and voting in a referendum and election.

Phase 3, 2006 – The smart ID card substitutes the passport or border pass, national and international driver's licence, and national and international cash card, debit card and credit card.

Phase 4, 2007 – The smart ID cards to have alternative uses such as 'dual contact', i.e. contact and less contact.

The much hyped journey of the project began when the Thai cabinet set up a high-powered committee to integrate and reform the registration system. The mandate was for this committee to improve and develop the country's registration system as a foundation of e-government. In 2003, Thailand endorsed the year 2003 as 'the year of electronic services for citizens. The same year, the government allocated a budget of 2 billion baht (approximately 37 million pounds) for the smart ID card project. There were five ministries, six organizations and eighteen sub-projects under this project. The project leaders were led by the ministry of interior (for card issuance) and ministry of information and communication Technology (ICT) (for production of the ID card, software and hardware).

Towards the end of the very same year, the ministry of ICT reported problems with card production to the government. It was announced that the card might not be produced in time for the grand opening ceremony and launch of the project that was eagerly planned. The government responded by hiring a private company to do the job instead of the ministry.

In the early months of 2004, there was conflict in the smart ID card committee about the security of the smart card system and card manufacturing. These conflicts caused some key persons to resign. It was clear by the middle of 2004 that the goal of issuing twelve million smart ID cards by the end of 2004 for Thai citizens was difficult to be achieved. A year later, the planned issuance of the smart ID card failed again. At the same time, the government forced relevant organizations to produce the first twelve million cards as soon as possible. In Mid-2006, the auction for card production in phase two showed signs of problems, with the possibility of mismanagement in the process. A couple of months later, one thousand seventy seven card issuing stations over the country stopped production due to a shortage of material, and old fashioned magnetic cards were issued once again.

Analysts narrow down on the following with respect to the lacunae and flaws in the initial roll out of the project.

Unrealistic targets and no pilot: The government was the focal actor in what proved to be an unrealistic OPP (Obligatory passage point) set up to improve public services via smart ID card technologies. This indeed seemed acceptable in general terms. However, detailed analysis showed that achieving the OPP was seemingly unreachable.

The idea of government setting up an OPP was not based on a pilot project or feasibility study. The timeframe of three years (2004-2006) was relatively rigid. All sixty four million people in the Thai population were envisioned to have had a smart ID card in this timeframe. This was a rather Herculean task. Moreover, the card should have been multi-functional in order to access many public services.

Not engaging the stakeholders at the right time: The crux of the matter was that the OPP and its details were not revised or adjusted by the other stakeholders. Therefore, no alternative choice was provided. Some public servants are stated to have held that to improve or enhance Thai public services, the old magnetic card could function just as well as the smart ID Card, if public agencies developed their database to interface with the magnetic card. Thus there were voices of divergence and dissent. The unity of thought and agreement with the purpose of the project was missing.

Wrong technology choices: Incomplete technology assessment created more conditions of failure. The then existing technology did not fit in well into the 'actor-network' in the latter process, and was found to be incompatible with new technology. This created organizational change management problems within all agencies involved.

Not involving the players at the right time and inadequate support: As the Ministry of ICT could not produce the card independently, IT vendors were needed for taking over of this duty in the enrolment process. Some analysts named this event - 'the swift translation'. It referred to a new actor having to understand the project in a short period of time, an entity who was not part of the project from the moment of its inception. The IT vendors were thrust into the project as complete 'aliens', so to say. Once IT vendors won the bidding for producing the card, they faced new and complicated technologies due to obsolescence of former technologies. Even with new technologies, there was no guarantee of their compatibility with other pre-existing technologies already in place. The IT vendors thus produced the inappropriate specifications that could obviously not pass the security test set by the National Electronics and Computer Technology Centre (NECTEC).

Lack of continued leadership conviction: The government leadership and departmental change managers were no doubt strongly determined to run this project. However, by the time the process of enrolment arrived, its willingness of all other stakeholders had gradually weakened.

The smart ID card project was not mobilized. This reflects to the fact that it could not achieve the planned objectives. The formation of IT projects needing collaboration between various public agencies must have started with a clear objective and vision together with advice and guidelines from the National IT agency. The collaboration tasks could have been, not only in the area of technology but also in altering and updating the outdated internal organizational processes and procedures.

Laws and by-laws that each of the public agency could have been suitably amended. Enacting new electronic support laws and regulations that facilitate the proliferation of e-Governance, such as electronic signature, and security protection law could have been done.

Thus, despite the best of intentions, Thailand's ambitious smart ID card project for all its citizens ended up as a mere shadow of the hype with which it was launched.

Lessons

1. A thorough study of all related legacy systems is needed before launch of any project
2. Data standards must be revamped and re-oriented to facilitate interoperability.
3. Technology requirement must be meticulously planned during the planning process itself
4. The technology assessment must be translated to a clear and unambiguous techno-commercial specification in the tender/RFP document itself preferably in a project involving private partnership
5. A risk assessment and analysis is recommended to put the project on a firm foundation and to lay out contingency plans
6. Involvement of stakeholders from the start of the project, listening to their suggestions and

A parallel to the Aadhaar ID of India is worth recalling in this context. The idea from Thailand is very similar to that done by UIDA in India. It is a proven fact that a country of India's size and diversity is able to cover the entire country reasonably well and use Aadhaar card as a means of any governmental service to citizen and this is a commendable effort by any standards.

CASE STUDY–8

Uganda's e-government efforts–success against all odds

Note to the reader: ICT contributes 5% of GDP in Uganda. The country has a liberalized telecom market with multiple vendors and increasing telephone and internet penetration levels. It has a young and vibrant population of twenty four million with median age of over twenty one years with good English speaking skills.

Uganda offers an attractive taxation regime for ICT sector and Internet bandwidth costs are lowering with the countries access to undersea cables. This case takes a look at the challenges faced by Uganda in its e-Governance efforts with focus on the 'Reforms: e-citizen' project.

Background

The Ugandan e-government implementation structure and strategy is ambitious. The National Information Technology Authority of Uganda (NITA-U) was established by the National Information Technology Authority Act of August 2009 as a semi-autonomous body under the ministry of ICT, to promote and provide technical guidance for the establishment of e-government, e- commerce and other e-transactions in Uganda.

NITA has the mandate to focus upon and usher in the following:

1. A rationalized and integrated national Information Technology (IT) infrastructure and Systems
2. A coordinated and harmonized national IT Systems
3. A well-regulated Information Technology (IT) environment in public and private sector
4. Strengthened capacity in Uganda (both institutional and human)
5. IT research, development and innovations visibly supported and promoted
6. Information security championed and promoted in Uganda
7. Strengthened and aligned institutional capacity to deliver the strategic plan
8. Development and promote the BPO/ITES (Business Process Outsourcing/IT Enabled Services) industry

NITA-U Strategic Goals

The main objective of the IT rationalization strategy is to enhance efficiency and effectiveness in service delivery to the citizens through increasing use of ICT. The specific objectives are to

1. Standardize, streamline and harmonize the acquisition, deployment and disposal of IT services in government to eliminate duplication
2. Enhance information sharing and interoperability of e- government applications
3. Ensure integration of voice, data and video communication and enhance use of shared applications and systems across government – thus reducing cost of communication, improving transparency, information security and accountability
4. Realize cost savings through economies of large scale purchase of internet bandwidth and licenses for software and applications
5. Rationalize use of available IT skills and consolidate IT skills development in government rationalization of ICT services in expand this

Project analysis

Vision statement of e-government of Uganda was designed to usher in an integrated smart one-government by providing quality services with accessibility, enhancing competitiveness by integration, information sharing through interoperability and boosting efficiency by expandability.

The mission statement of e-Governance of Uganda: 'Integrating Uganda to provide quality services to citizens, and to improve the national competitiveness through administration innovation, and to reform unnecessary processes based on interconnected government and safe society'.

An e-Governance readiness survey was conducted in 2012

and an e-government master plan was put in place. Challenges faced by Uganda in implementing e- governance were as follows

1. Each MDA had implemented their own systems
2. There was no interoperability between systems in MDAs
3. The important national ID project that was already taken up among other projects, was not yet completed
4. There was no centralized hosted and shared services in place yet

These concerns were systematically addressed and certain results were obtained. Some examples of e- governance services in place are

1. E-Tax – Uganda Revenue Authority
2. Integrated Financial Management System (IFMIS)
3. Integrated Personnel and Payroll System (IPPS) – Ministry of Public Service
4. Utilities – Umeme (Electricity) and National Water
5. Case Management System in Judiciary
6. Uganda National Examinations Board (UNEB)

Many MDAs have implemented their own systems to automate and monitor their internal operations.

Uganda runs a decentralised system where local governments implement central programmes. Local government councils also draft their working budgets for the financial year with funds provided by the central government under the directions of the ministry of finance planning and economic development.

One of the most successful digitalisation and e-Governance programme to date is the Uganda Revenue Authority (URA) which adopted the e-tax register in 2010. At the nineth eLearning Africa conference hosted by Uganda, it was officially announced that there has been remarkableimprovements in collection efficiency since e-tax was launched.

The case of 'Reform: e-citizens (Listening to citizens)' project by electoral commission of Uganda, which was launched in 2001 is discussed in detail here.

This was a citizen service aimed at taking photographs of all citizens of voting age using digital cameras. The photographs were then to be loaded onto a single voters' register database. The database was supposed to be maintained on a mainframe at the interim electoral commission headquarters, which would be connected to district electoral commission offices through the Internet. The database would be used as the basis for voter identification at polling stations for the 2001 election.

The visionary purpose behind the application was to weed out impostors who voted in the names of the dead and absentee voters. This was also to discourage double registration of voters, which was rampant in the country. One key stakeholder in the entire 'reform' process was the interim electoral commission. All citizen-voters were stakeholders being affected by the registration process and all politicians and political parties had a stake in the registration system.

A total sum of roughly US$22m was spent on equipment, consultancy services and operations in implementing the project. There were no formal benefits because the system was not put to use for the 2001 elections as it was intended. The acrimony which arose out of the electoral process led to a number of court cases.This project was a failure. Things went wrong at an early stage with the hardware.

There was criticism that the tenders for procurement of the digital cameras were not structured well nor facilitated wider participation from the private sector. This led to problems with the equipment delivered, and with reports that a number of the cameras were stolen from what should have been a safe government store. Secondly, on the implementation front citizen photographing did proceed, but took place within a very short time and many people were not captured by the system. There were complaints from all over multiple agencies intervened in the workings of the computer system. Thirdly, when sample voter registers were produced by the system, they were found to be erroneous. In many instances the photographs did not correspond with names of voters. The entire exercise had to therefore be suspended.

Old voter registers were used to conduct presidential, parliamentary and civic elections in the country in 2001. There have been suggestions that the system may be used for the 2006 elections. However, the work of the electoral commissioners was later wound up. No action has been taken to revive the system.

Some of the lessons that can be learnt from this failed attempt are the following. Such pan-national level projects must be planned meticulously and systematically. The 'big bang' or 'big results' approaches of suddenly introducing new technologies and processes are quite likely to fail if enough ground work on all fronts is not done involving all stakeholders.

In projects that touch the broader issues of governance, the participation of all stakeholders, including civil society organisations should be encouraged right from the inception of the project, even from its conceptual stage. Such larger and broader levels of participation will bring to focus long term objectives for improvement of the governance processes while balancing them with short term or immediate objectives.

Lessons

1. Procurement process related to e-government projects must be very carefully and transparently planned
2. All stakeholders, even the civil society organizations if necessary, must be consulted right at the inception of the project
3. Realistic timelines must be set given the complicity and scope of the project

4. Adequate and realistic budget allotments and grants must be made and expenditure is to be monitored regularly so that there is neither a cash crunch nor unutilized funds
5. Staffing in e-government projects must be done to fit the skill set requirements of the project
6. Provisions in contracts must encourage genuine and experienced private sector partners

CASE STUDY–9

Lessons in improvisation and 'kaizen'. Sweden's Citizen Contact Centres (CCs) project:

Note to the reader: The e- governance efforts in Sweden started in 1997 with the introduction of a modest project named 'Government e-Link' which was aimed to enable the secure electronic information exchange within the public administration, as well as between public bodies and the citizens and entrepreneurs.

The year 2000 was the landmark year in terms of Sweden's digitalization journey when its full-fledged e- governance policy was formulated. The same year a '24/7 Agency' concept was introduced as a guiding principle for the networked public administration. According to this, the administrative departments as well as the services they provide had to be made reachable at any time and place, through the combined use of the Internet, phone lines and regular brick and mortar offices.

This case gives a snapshot of the evolution of e-Governance in Sweden with special focus on the successful Citizen Contact Centre (CSC) project.

Background

The entire system drew its strength from the fact of the relative autonomy that many government agencies in Sweden were enjoying at the time in relation to the government departments. Despite tangible achievements such as the creation of an access gate to all government eServices for citizens – the 'Sverige.se' portal (now closed down), this governance equation reached its limits. A lack of coordination was evident at all levels be it organisational, financial or legal. This was among the other drawbacks that led to the partitioned and duplicated development of the public eServices during the initial years of Sweden's digitalization strategy.

Learning from these mistakes and experience Sweden's e-Governance policy underwent a self-critical review which resulted in the 'action plan for e-Government' in 2008 whose central goals was to rationalise policy governance. It aimed to make the Swedish administration the 'world's simplest administration' and to take public services delivery to a higher level than that of mere provider–customer interaction. This streamlining effort was continued with the establishment of the 'e-government delegation' a vanguard institution to drive digitalization of public services delivery.

Since then, Sweden has been on the track of what it calls the 'third-generation e-government' a concept formulated by the 'strategy for the government agencies work on e-government' document prepared by the e- government delegation.

The salient features of the third-generation e-Governance are as follows

1. A simplified infrastructure for the electronic authentication of anyone wanting to make use of e-government services requiring such authentication
2. Different government agencies to create synergy by jointly developing shared public eServices
3. The re-use of infrastructure solutions
4. Common technical support for the development and implementation of the abovementioned shared services of different government agencies
5. Transparent funding mechanisms and updating of legislation and regulation

6. A positive approach to the use of open standards and open source software in the public administration sphere
7. The possibility and facilitation for citizens and businesses to have a say, through electronic media, in decision making processes regarding e-government

According to the United Nation's 2008 e-Government survey, Sweden is internationally acknowledged as one of the most successful e-governance countries and the world leader in terms of e-Government Readiness. As for the eigth EU Benchmark, it places the country among the top five European Union members' States in the area of e- governance.

Instead of keeping a single electronic citizen entry point to the public administration, the Swedish government made the choice of web portals entirely customised and dedicated to a given theme (e.g. taxation portal, health portal, employment, social insurance, etc.). For example, businesses reap benefits from a one stop shop for entrepreneurs called 'verksamt.se'. This portal gathers company 'life-event' procedures thus re-organising the public services provided by three government agencies in a user-friendly way.

Some of the other significant achievements of Sweden in the area of e-Governance are

1. Electronic Invoices – All government agencies have been handling invoices electronically since July 2008
2. E-Legitimating – A popular electronic authentication infrastructure that enables the citizens' and businesses' access to secured public eServices
3. A set of well-established public electronic procurement portals

The ministry for local government and financial markets holds the leadership over the Swedish e-government policy. Among other tasks, the e-government delegation co-ordinates the work of the government agencies and departments by defining working lines, monitoring their application, and reporting to the ministry for local government and financial markets. The delegation acts as an intermediary between the central government and the local governments, which steer their own e- governance initiatives, to ensure a healthy and mutually beneficial collaboration in the best interests of the country's overall public administration.

The leadership and change champions of Sweden had to face and overcome many hurdles in its journey to attain the status of excellence in digital delivery of public services. They realized that policy documents alone will not overcome the age old gaps between the three layers of public administration containing nearly six hundred independently managed agencies.

Some of the pain-points encountered and learnings in the attempted paradigm shift were as follows

1. Unrealistic time scales
2. The realization that governance is not possible without an enterprise architecture
3. The truth that modeling of the needs of the end user cannot be left solely to individual agencies
4. The need for clusters and federations to be defined by means of federation level agreements in addition to service level agreements
5. The problem of low adherence level to EU's directives (e.g. Services and Public Information Re-usage will be rewarded with low e-gov EU ranking)
6. The realization that there are very few mandatory standards and profiles for Swedish agencies and no Swedish National Interoperability Framework existed.

To compensate for the unrealistic time scale and to secure public value, it is an urgent need for forums with reference to e-gov discussions, architecting work and information exchange to be established.

Project analysis

Many studies and reports have focused on challenging organizational issues faced during Sweden's digital transformation. Let us look into a few of those encountered when Municipal Contact Centres (CCs) were implemented in Sweden. The CCs project typically exemplifies the organizational and human angle ofe-governance issues. Two cases of implementation of CCs in Swedish municipalities have been compared anddiscussed to from an organizational perspective by school of business, Economics and IT of University West, Sweden. The study established that the implementation strategies varied between the cases and affected the pace of implementation, attitudes and motivation, the mental constructs and understanding of the implementation.

The financing of the ICT enabled CCs and recruitment strategies created problems, but in somewhat different ways and different phases of the process in each case. The potential of using authenticated and registered information as a source for planning and decision-making was not fully utilized in the municipal organizations. Some statistics were produced and some data was churned out.

A useful lesson that can be learnt from the CSC implementation in Sweden is the organizational learning strategies involved. This consists of a combination of formal and informal learning strategies and flexible co-operation among the employees in the CCs which contributed to continuous learning processes and a good co-operative working climate. There was a need for continuous updating of individual skills and skill-sets in both cases, but with slightly different focus, related to the organization of the work.

Two main challenges for the case administrators at middle management in the back offices were to adapt to a more process-oriented organization of their work and to co-operate more with their colleagues both in the back office and at the front end CC.

They now had the possibility to plan their administrative tasks in a more effective and efficient manner than before. Initially, many case administrators were afraid of losing their jobs and work tasks to CCs, contributing to negative attitudes towards. This hampered and showed down the learning process in taking part in the implementation process.

e-Governance research and studies have predominantly focused on technology as an enabler to increase public sector efficiency and improve internal management capabilities and administration in terms of productivity of government performance. The case of e-Governance success in Sweden has proved that introduction of e-Governance also means a fundamental organizational change in public institutions requiring new skill sets, attitudes and competencies. The main focus for public service organizations in Sweden initially was on improvements of front-end services to citizens, neglecting the importance of also aligning back-end aspects. Implementation of CCs is an example of a relatively recent local e-Government initiatives in Sweden that integrates back office too. Sweden has learnt from its own errors and mistakes of its past. CCs today are not only for local e-government front-line service delivery, but are also actively involved in dynamic organizational settings, developing practices and management in municipal public administration. These processes involve as integration of both front-line and back-office practices.

A call centre is a place which responds to phone calls from people and is dependent on the use of ICTs. It can be an internal function of an organization or an outsourced function. The use of the contact centre concept in Sweden is an extension of this function of call centres, focusing not only on phone calls, but also other contiguous work tasks. The traditional model of a call centre is thus transformed when CCs were established in Swedish municipalities.

The main difference between a call centre and a contact

centre is that while a call centre is focused on incoming and outgoing voice calls, a contact centre is able to manage customers with both voice calls and data applications like e-mail, web-based chat/instant messaging, and in some cases will include the capability to share web pages sent to and from the customer. The fully functional contact centre takes advantage of customer needs for text and visual communications in addition to phone calls. Typically a contact centre also uses a 'blended agent' who can manage multiple forms of voice and data-centric customer communications.

Because of technological trends, businesses are turning to contact centres as their mode of customer interaction. While call centres are still a viable form of communication, contact centres offer additional pathways of interaction that customers may find convenient.

Every citizen receives the same qualitative level of service regardless of social or economic status. The development of contact centres in the public sector is especially influenced by aspects such as increased service and availability from a citizen perspective as well as internal efficiency. The CC is thus a front office for citizens and businesses, and the main communication mode is by phone. But the CC also requires developed work processes for the back office in order to contribute to increased quality and efficiency for the organization. Usually the CC has extended opening hours compared with the normal opening hours for the municipal offices. Some CCs also have an office open for personal visits by citizens and businesses.

Sweden is ranked the 10th most competitive country in the world according to the World Economic Forum 2014- 2015 report that compared one hundred forty two economies. Sweden is also a favoured destination for complex and high-value-added contact centres. The country excels in contact centre assignments focusing on qualified and personalised customer care. Being advanced users of IT, Swedes have successfully integrated contemporary leading communication technologies into daily business life. Sweden has proved that a regional contact centre with multi-country responsibility can help you reduce costs, drive sales and build customer loyalty

As discussed in the chapter on change management implementation of e-Government does not simply mean installation of new technology or even implementation of new technology solutions. Implementation challenges invariably also involve changes in work practices, work cultures, behaviours, power structures and learning processes. Implementation of local e-government such as CCs is characterized by huge and complex change processes that require new competencies both for employees and management in the municipal organization, as well as for citizens and businesses. The extended use of ICT support for municipal service production and re-organization efforts in Sweden have contributed to more efficient procedures, but has also put demands on continuous learning processes in order to meet the new requirements.

The Swedish multi -level government system is based on three levels: national, regional and local. This approach is meant to strengthen the local autonomy of Swedish municipalities. On the local level, there are two hundred ninety municipalities in Sweden that provide services such as building permits, environmental permissions, matters regarding social services and schools, healthcare, day-care and welfare. They are governed by elected local officials and have a high degree of autonomy. The internal work of these municipalities is differently structured due to variations in geographic location, population and social structures of the inhabitants and economic conditions. The municipalities in Sweden account for 70% of total public administration and they are considered to be the closest to citizens' needs in terms of public service.

The Sambruk

The notable and interesting thing is that these municipalities do not have a statutory obligation to set up offices like CCs or similar service locations for their inhabitants. However, it is mandated by Swedish law that all Swedish municipalities should provide individual service, such as for instance, to meet visitors and to answer telephone calls from citizens. The service should be of as high a quality as possible from a financial resource perspective. The municipalities are free to interpret their responsibility to provide services in very different ways.

About eighty of the municipalities are members of 'Sambruk'. The Sambruk is the association of Swedish municipalities for joint development of e-services. The aim of Sambruk is to create a foundation for effective development programs, comprising both the technical and functional aspects of e-services, as well as the re-engineering of internal business processes. Through synergy and co-operation within Sambruk, the municipalities have access to intellectual capital vastly greater compared to that which a single municipality could develop.

Challenging issues from a management perspective in the Swedish CCs were also many. The implementation strategies The complex change process did reinforce changes in the power structure of the organization and resulted in power struggles among different 'communities of practice' and professional groups in both cases. This initially led to negative attitudes towards the CC and hampering a learning process towards common mental images and goals.

There are documented common risks with work in call centres as being monotonous, stressful and lacking variation. This can also be relevant in part for work at CCs. Many studies and practical experience has shown that those who receive formal training are likely to remain longer in their jobs and do not ask for a transfer or quit. Trained employees also believe that their employers see them as important and valuable members of an organization, further developing enhanced loyalty levels.

In a later phase of the implementation of the CCSs there

were major problems related to the fact that the department of social services was supposed to contribute financially to the activities of the CC, but had difficulties finding relevant work tasks to transfer to the CC. There was, for instance, no special response group for social services at the CC and the demands of integrity, security and competence were not easy to deal with. There were very negative attitudes towards the CC from the social services due to this situation. This way of funding the CC was made in line with the new public management idea of taking the costs where the benefits appear in the CC. The respective department within the municipality therefore had to 'pay' for the e-government reorganization and CC implementation. It thus seems to be important to anchor the applied financing models regulating the contribution of financing from the back offices at an early stage of the implementation process. There was also a realization that it was vital to specify what work processes should be transferred to CC related to the financing models.

The information systems for handling of matters was another pain-point and problem area in CCs in general. The electronic information systems for handling of matters were not fully developed in either of the municipalities initially when the CC was implemented. This caused many and conflict situations between stakeholders. The leadership team and the management seemed to underestimate the inconvenience and impact of such problems.

Choice between formal and informal learning strategies was another interesting area in the CC implementation. The study of municipal CCs in Sweden found that both of highly formalized and rule-based learning and more informal strategies for the employees were used at the CCs. According to the formalized strategy, checklists and other documented information were used when questions from citizens are answered by the employees at the CC. According to the informal strategy there were few checklists and little formal, documented information. Instead the employees at the CC search for relevant information on the web, or use their own knowledge born out of past experience.

The element of Public-Private Partnership (PPP) at a very rudimentary yet fundamental level came into play here. An employee responsible for the coaching and training of service administrators was recruited externally. The manager generated work descriptions and competence profiles for the service administrators. These were used as a basis for the competence development programs.

Another important challenge from a change management perspective was to choose a relevant implementation strategy. The implementation strategies varied in each case, and affected the pace of implementation, attitudes and motivation aspects. This 'awareness' and 'knowledge' phases of ICT driven change management is vital. The implementation could initially be carried out quickly using a top-down strategy. However, this 'drill-down totally' approach led to problems of negative attitudes and lack of motivation due to lack of intellectual involvement, empathy or volitional participation. There were problems with understanding the implementation due to lack of relevant information. A more bottom-up strategy with greater participation by the employees would have indeed taken more time to carry out, but would have contributed to a better understanding and empathy with the objectives of CCs and e-government.

The financing strategy of the CC was another challenging issue for the leadership and management. The financing of the CC caused troubles for the contributing back-office departments in both cases. The lesson that could be learnt from this is that it is important to anchor the applied financing models regulating the contribution of financing from the back offices at an early stage of the implementation process. As stated earlier, it also could have been better to specify early on what work processes should be transferred to CC.

It is also a challenge to organize the work in the CC in order to meet efficiency aspects as well as quality aspects from citizen and employee perspectives. There were combinations of formal and informal learning strategies in the CCs which did contribute to continuous learning processes. The flexible and close co-operation among the employees at the CC contributed to a good co-operative working environment facilitating the learning processes. However, in both cases there was a need to have continuous updating of skills, although there were different competence needs related to the organization of the work. It can therefore be seen that the ICT backed CC implementation in Sweden was indeed a success, but not without its share of hurdles and problems. There are lessons to be learnt by others from that experience, as Sweden itself learnt and improvised on its e- governance journey.

Thus, in spite of being a pioneer in the domain of e-Governance, Sweden did face problems in its roll- out but kept the learning cycle on and improvised in the spirit of 'kaizen' (continuous improvement) in all its e-Governance initiatives.

Lessons

1. The attitude to adapt to the new ways of working by employees at all levels in the organizational hierarchy is important for any successful e-government project rollout
2. Comfortable and efficient end-users/government employees will result in satisfied end-beneficiaries/ citizens
3. The government and citizen contact points must be designed to be user friendly and scalable to future citizen needs
4. Coordination and co-operation within different divisions/sections of the department/organization embarking on an e-government project is important. The project leaders/ change champions must ensure this

5. While absolute perfection is an ideal in any e-Governance project, it is worthwhile to learn and improvise as the project goes along

CASE STUDY–10

Leveraging technology innovation to improve healthcare through better stakeholder (patients and healthcare employees) engagement.

Note to reader: In the recent past, most healthcare and life sciences organizations, particularly in the West, have attempted to increase 'stakeholder engagement' by use of technology and innovation.In the USA for instance, this is in line with government regulation and mandatein the healthcare sector. Stakeholder engagement is being done using social media and online patient communities. It is also being done by utilizing wearables and mobile, encouraging health technology literacy and by incorporating patient-generated health data in conjuncture with clinical data.

The focus on engaging both patients and employees to drive better health outcome is not new and many organizations and governments across the globe have taken steps in that direction. However, the cases presented below with reference to onelarge hospital in New York and a pharmaceutical major that partnered with Microsoft are unique because they extensively employed technology and organizational innovation in such stakeholder engagement projects.

Background:

The Ministry of Health and Family Welfare in India has undertaken various initiatives using ICT for improving efficiency and effectiveness of the public healthcare system. The ministry is continuously working on planning and introducing more ICT initiatives.

These initiatives are grouped under 4 categories: (1) e-governance: ICT for delivering government services, exchange of information, services like government- to-citizen, government-to-business, government-to-government etc. (2) e-Health: Use of ICT for health services like for treating patients, conducting research, educating health workforce, tracking diseases, and monitoring public health (3) m-Health: Medical and public health practice supported by mobile devices for patient monitoring devices, Personal Digital Assistants (PDAs), and other wireless devices (4) Tele-Medicine: It is the use of telecommunication and information technology to provide clinical healthcare from a distance. It is also used to save lives in critical care and emergency situations.

The ministry is progressively using ICT to make government services and information available to citizens and business groups in a convenient, efficient and transparent manner and also in improving transactions with other government departments and agencies. In line with the 'Make in India' and 'Digital India Program', the ministry has undertaken various initiatives with focus on online services through different technology platforms.

Health is a unique area, where private and public sectors must work jointly to attain the goal of accessible health for all and effective delivery of healthcare services. The Involvement of private sector, public private partnership, research and preventive healthcare are the major focus areas under the new health policy.

Increased private sector participation will certainly improve access and equity by bringing in much needed resources for healthcare and by allowing government to increase focus on underserved populations. Apart from encouraging the private sector to pro-actively participate in serving citizens more effectively, the government could also imbibe some of the best and successful practices of the private sector into its own departments and institutions. The case below dwells into the important and emerging aspect of stakeholder engagement in this context.

The most common and viewof patient engagement is that healthcare providers and patients work together to improve health of the patients. The fundamental assumption is that a patient's greater engagement in healthcare contributes to improved health outcomes and innovations in information technologies can support and accelerate that engagement. Patients want to be engaged in their healthcare decision making process and those who are engaged as decisionmakers in their own case tend to be healthier and have better outcomes. Similarly 'engaged employees'are more productive, more in alignment with the culture of the organizationand are more satisfied in the work they are involved in.

Engaging Patients at New York Presbyterian(NYP):

Patient engagement is an emerging ICT based paradigm in the healthcare industry. Many hold that the future of healthcare is being shaped largely by this patient engagement phenomenon. Patient engagement refers to the tools and methods taken by caregivers, healthcare providers and patients to promote informed decision-making and behaviors to facilitate improved health outcomes.

Medical care providers are today increasingly aware of the value of having patients engaged in their own health. While the concept of patient engagement may not be new, what is new is the pivotal role of technology in this multifaceted process.

The data given below lends further support to the high level of impact technology in this context:

1. One in twenty Google searches is for health related information
2. Eighty percent of Internet users seek online health information
3. Seventy seven percent of patients use a search prior to booking an appointment
4. Sixty six percent of Internet users look online for

information about a specific disease or medical problem

5. Forty four percent of Internet users look online for information about doctors or other health professionals

Some of the latest technology based areas that focus on patient engagement are- managing patient health data, managing communication with physicians, self-care at home, health education, and management of finances related to health. From wearable technology and medical devices to patient portals and personal health records, all innovations are aimed at enhancing the overall patient experience.

With the introduction of health information exchanges, health records in electronic formats and patient portals, patients are becoming more engaged in their health. Healthcare institutions are trying to be receptive to these developments and integrate these changes while seeking to adapt to this new and rapidly evolving ecosystem.

The generally accepted benefits of improved patient engagement include:

1. Costs rationalization -Technology can help improve workflow through the use of shared information. This can reduce or eliminate paperwork, assure accurate information and provide patients with a better experience

2. Increased communication-Through the use of technology, healthcare workers, physicians and patients can seamlessly communicate with one another more often and provide updates or changes on the patients' condition

3. Increased patient satisfaction-With increased communication and more information regarding their health, patients are more confident regarding their condition and diagnoses

NYP hospital is affiliated with two Ivy League medical schools-Columbia University's College of Physicians and

Surgeons and Cornell University's Weill Medical College. They support over two million inpatient and outpatient visits in a year, including two lakh visits to its emergency departments. They have about six thousand affiliated physicians and 19 thousand staff.

This hospital and its affiliated medical colleges set out on a on a journey to improve patient satisfaction and to better engage the patient to drive improved patient outcomes. In order to do this, they developed a unique service to (1) Improve the way caregivers and patients communicated (2) Provide patients access to their medical information connected to their Electronic Medical Records (EMR)in a quick and easy way and (3) Put ina platform that is flexible enough to deliver differentiated services to the patients at their bedside as the healthcare systems evolved.

NYP Hospital was faced with two major challenges in this context:

(a) How to increase patient registration into their patient portal tied to their EMR, which will lead the hospital to engage the patient better and which is a requirement to meet 'meaningful use' of core criteria of the US government.

(b) How to improve patient satisfaction while the patient is still in the hospital as opposed to surveying them post discharge and thereby having a lagging indicator of satisfaction.

A few years preceding this,the hospital care team developed MyNYP. org–a patient portal based on Microsoft HealthVault which allowed patients to view their medical records, create reminders and appointments online. Extending this, they now had the idea to bring a tablet to the bedside. The entire care team was already tracking themselves electronically and now all of that information was immediately available to the patient as well through the tablet. With the windows tablet in their hands while at the hospital, patients could access their medical records, know their care team and even call or page them. With the click of a button they could also, in real time, record their physical condition, provide feedback and access entertainment. Figure 1 depicts what the user experience looks like.

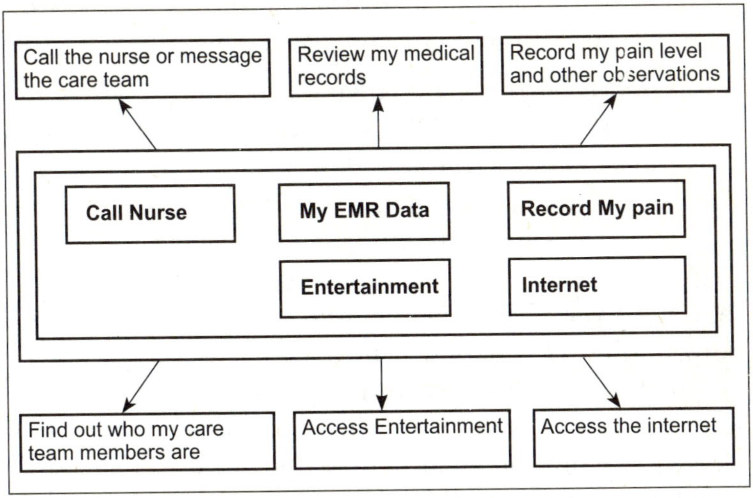

Figure 1 User experience

This distinctive project of NYP hospital drove up registration in the patient portal. This not only helped the patients but also the NYPhospital to meet regulatory requirements in accordance with the meaningful use guidelines.

In addition to driving better patient experience and fulfilling mandatory requirements, this project also saved significantly on operational expenditure. Reports show that by reusing its existing infrastructure, NYP is spending less than five hundred thousand on software development, whereas a significant nurse call system upgrade could cost close to 40 million dollars.

In the year 2015, NYP's'Patient Tablets' were ranked 6th in the USA in Information Week Elite 100–a list of top business technology innovators in the US.

It goes without saying that all these technologies and techniques would be rendered futile if the patients do not have interest in taking an active role in their health. Healthcare personnel must therefore encourage patients to learn to utilize tools and technology that produce improved health results. All stakeholders must be willing to participate and embrace the shift to technology in order to achieve better outcomes. This brings us to the issue of employee engagement.

Employee engagement at Sanofi:

The Dale Carnegie Training Course for driving employee engagement states, "The one thing that creates sustainable competitive advantage – and therefore ROI, company value and long-term strength – is the workforce, the people who are the company. And when it comes to people, research has shown, time and again, that employees who are engaged significantly outperform work groups that are not engaged."

Employee engagement in the public sector is of special relevance in the context of digital delivery of services to the citizens. Gallup Consultants (2006)[1] proposed that employees could be divided into three types with regard to their level of engagement- the engaged, not engaged and the actively disengaged.

The nature of the three types of employees is as follows:

1. Engaged employees work with passion and feel a profound connection to their company. They drive innovation and move the organization forward
2. Not engaged employees are essentially of the 'checked out' kind. They're sleepwalking through their workday, putting time, but not commitment or passioninto their work
3. Actively disengaged employees aren't just unhappy at

---

1 "Gallup Study: Engaged Employees Inspire Company Innovation: National Survey Finds that Passionate Workers Are Most Likely to Drive Organizations Forward", The Gallup Management Journal, http://gmj.gallup.com/content/24880/GallupStudyEngaged Employees Inspire Company.aspx

work. They also, more often than not, act out their unhappiness. These workers undermine what their engaged co-workers accomplish.

Gallup conducted an exploratory and analytical study of a large Indian'Navaratna' Public Sector Unit in the power sector in this context and came up with interesting insights. These are summed up as follows:

1. Motivation, encouragement and meaningful task - In this study it was observed that the most important factor for the enhancement of performance and engagement of the employee was the motivation given by management and meaningful task assignment. Employees were motivated to perform when they were appreciated and identified for their specific task.

2. Recognition and support -This study showed that the second important factor for employee engagement was recognition and support. Employees were motivated to perform when they were appreciated for their good work and were ready to perform when there was support from the superiors to showcase their skills. They were encouraged to take initiative when they were provided with material and equipment that they required to perform their jobs.

3. Cooperation- It was established that employees were committed to perform when they were in the midst of a friendly work culture.

4. Feedback and opportunity - It was observed that one of the ingredients that was required for the engagement of the employees was the platform providedtodiscuss their performance, and learn from such discussions.

Employee engagement essentially means engaging them in the decision making process. Much research has been conducted in this area. Surveys and studies have shown the following to be some important benefits of employee engagement:

1. Sense of ownership - Employees feel that they are a valued part of the team
2. Pro-active contribution to problem solving - Team effort and team spirit is build up by engaging employees in decision making
3. Sense of responsibility –Employees are more responsible and receptive to suggestions and constructive criticism

As discussed in the section of change management, merely introducing ICT or installing high end devices will not magically result in generating intended outcomes. The 'soft side' of bringing any change through technology is very important to the success of any ICT based changed intervention in any organization. The 'soft side' of change is the human side.

Technology must first be accepted by the end users of the same. A high end computer for instance, could remain no more than a glorified typewriter, if technology is not accepted. Technology must also be used appropriately after being accepted. This was very much evident in the case study No.1 that dealt with the systemic and structural changes in the organization that had to be made along with the introduction of ERP in BSNL.

Over and above this, the unique experiment of creating cross functional 'quality circles' and 'focus groups' were also discussed. In the present case of Sanofi, a similar exercise was adopted and this led to the success oftechnology driven change.

'Sanofi' is a global life-sciences organization with over one hundred thousand employees and a presence in more than a hundred countries. Sanofi Pasteur-their vaccines division is a global leader in producing vaccines that help people around the world fight more than 20 infectious diseases.

Sanofi has manufacturing sites in over 40 countries which are subject to rigorous quality requirements throughout the manufacturing processes, as expected of any pharmaceutical manufacturer. Manufacturing vaccines is a complex and highly regulated process. Most pharmaceuticals spend between 50 to 70 per cent of their resources on managing quality through the manufacturing process. This is because assuring quality of drugs to the citizens is a mandate of every government and the moral responsibility of every pharmaceutical company.

The Sanofi team, looking for improvement in this space, decided to implement a quality improvement program driven by what they called 'corporate activism'. They started to work with fifteen industrial sites and their business partners to shape the policy to comply with Good Manufacturing Practices (GMP).

According to Sanofi's leadership team "This method redefines quality from an imposed set of rules and regulations to a shared passion among all employees that equates to a new quality mindset." Sanofi Pasteur chose Yammer as the platform for this change.

They implemented a simple and intuitive social collaboration platform that cuts across the multiple generations of the workforce and turned hierarchies into networks. This platform was ubiquitous and accessible anywhere at any time and allowed employees at all levels ideate on quality improvements.

As a result, they started to see the 'native knowledge' from people on the ground emerge and drive quality improvements. It is reported that today the company is saving hundreds of thousands of dollars through simple ideas to reduce waste. They are seeing improved workplace safety with 10 per cent less workplace injuries. Of course, the government regulations are being more effectively and efficiently adhered to.

What's more, studies have shown that the employees had started connecting at all levels around the topic of quality and were using it to share wins. This experience with an innovative technology combined with a leadership team that fostered collaboration proved that the more people share their solutions, the faster they could use those solutions to deliver quality in what they do. This ultimately meant meeting statutory requirements for the benefit of the citizens.

This initiative caught on across all the global divisions of Sanofi. For instance, Sanofi Circle of Hong Kong was formed in 2014. This Sanofi Circle consisted of five small circles: family, innovation, wellness, corporate social responsibility and health, safety and environment, representing the core values of the company. All circle members had volunteered to serve during their non-work hours and each circle was led by a leader elected by others. Under the principles of Sanofi Circle, the company funds all activities proposed by the circle, while circle members will be responsible for devising the overarching strategy, planning for the year-long activities, budgeting, event promotion and logistics co-ordination.

Lessons:

1. Unique solutions to complex problems require an interdisciplinary approach. Let us take a look at what NYP did in order to be able to provide a consumer like experience on a tablet in a highly regulated and sensitive setting and manage it like an enterprise device. They had to have experts who understood regulatory requirements around personal data that may remain on the device once the patient is discharged. They also had to essentially wipe the device clean of any personal data while 'resetting' it to a default state. Apart from this, they had to make sure that the devices were physically sanitized,given the hospital setting and the risk of Hospital Acquired Infections(HAI). This meant that the team had to invent new protocols to manage them like a medical device. The core technology itself needed to have experts who understood how to monitor, manage, patch and keep the devices up to date.They needed Unified Communications experts who knew how to hook up the tablets to NYPs existing infrastructure, and application

developers who understood the needs of a patient and how to make the user experience simple and intuitive; They had to have the technology provider - Microsoft in this case, take feedback on a relatively new platform, incorporate and evolve it quickly. They had a core account strategist and a dedicated team to work as part of the NYP team. They had to bring together a services organization who knew how to engineer the application and provide ongoing maintenance. This interdisciplinary team could only function as a unit where there is strong leadership, clear shared vision of the 'end state'-putting the patient first.

2. Simplicity is the quintessential key while driving engagement. In any digitalization or change initiatives backed by ICT, we may have to engage a broad constitution of population and build a solution that may require multiple generations working together. This includes people from varied cultural, ethnic and technical backgrounds and who have had varied levels of exposure to technology. Thinking of and planning around overall end user experience is key for success.

3. During the past few years, digital technologies in the healthcare segment have transfigured and transformed the tools used to seek and store information, communicate, prevent and treat diseases. They have expanded their reach, qualitative richness, ambit of participation, transparency and accountability while also lowering costs. Health outreach is rapidly evolving from being top-down to a participatory approach. Likewise, health promotion has rapidly advanced from a'curative' perspective to 'prevention and promotion'.

4. Increasing digital literacy and smartphone penetration has brought in transparency and empowered people to

gain more access over the management and treatment of their own health. People today want to make conscious and well-founded choices before they agree to measures that affect their health and the lives of their near and dear. Healthcare providers, in both the private and public sectors, must acknowledge and accept technology as a force for good rather than as an intrusive obligation or burden. They must enhance engagement to build trust, improve treatment compliance and adhere to government guidelines.

CASE STUDY–11

The Gujarat model–360 degrees citizen centric e-Government is good governance.

Note to the reader: According to a number of surveys, Gujarat leads in the arena of successful e-government project implementation. Dataquest-CMR e-Readiness Assessment of Indian States as early as in 2013 for instance, placed Gujarat as one of the leader state in India in this criteria. All departments meticulously prepare their IT action plans, which have a one-year short term focus and a five-year long term perspective.

Background

The first major step towards e-Governance in Gujarat was the initiation of Gujarat State Wide Area Network in 2001-2002, followed by establishment of a server farm. The establishment of Department of Science and Technology (DST) in 2002 was the next major step. Departmental level capacity building started with the creation of Chief Information Officers (CIOs) and system managers at the departmental level for smooth implementation of IT strategies and e-Governance projects in 2003.

The evolution of e-government in Gujarat can be seen in following phases

1. Informative phase: (2002-2004): Broadcasting and

dissemination predominantly using websites was the focus

2. Interactive phase (2004-2006): Query from database and two way communication such as enquiry based exam results, was the focus
3. Transactional phase (2006-2008): Delivery of services to the citizens was the concern. This includes paid services, one day governance centre's, city civic centres. An example of this is e-Dhara
4. Transformational phase (2009-2012): The aim was ubiquitous and 24x 7 government. This phase consisted of online portal for citizen centric services, one stop shop for citizen centric services, collaborative and shared data
5. Convergence vision phase (2012-onwards): This phase is distinguished by (i)Converged infrastructure (ii) Mobile and telecom governance. (iii) IT and infrastructure optimization, (iv) Cost efficiency and reconsideration. (v) Virtualization and cloud computing

Many studies have established that the Gujarat e-Governance has emerged as a potent tool for any citizen centric, transparent and effective governance system. It is based on the fact that e-Governance is incomplete unless government services are made available to the citizens in a problem free and 24x7 manner.

The vision and its components

e-Governance in Gujarat is predicated upon the vision and visionary maxim of – "Minimum Government, Maximum Governance". This also sets the overarching theme of e-Governance policy of the State of Gujarat (2014-2019).

This vision consists of three components.

1. To bring about ICT-enabled all-round sustainable development and inclusive growth of the State

2. To provide transparent, affordable and efficient public service delivery closer to the door-step of citizens; and
3. To ensure the socio-economic empowerment of all (with special emphasis on women, youth and the marginalized) through Digital Inclusion

Each of these components together are aligned to Digital India programme that envisages to transform India to a digitally empowered society and a knowledge economy.

As is the invariable case with all successful e-government projects that make up overall effective e-Governance, the Gujarat model of e-Governance is an outcome of a strategy of ideas of various stakeholders. This can be seen from the comprehensive and overarching objectives and action plans to achieve it are stated below

To broad-base and institutionalize 'Digital Gujarat' towards the fulfilment of the larger vision of 'Digital India' by giving thrust to the following areas

1. Proactive participation in implementation of the key components of 'Digital India' namely broadband highways, universal access to mobile connectivity, public internet access, e-Governance: Reforming government through technology, e-Kranti-Electronic delivery of services, information for all, early harvest programmes, electronic manufacturing and IT for Jobs
2. Across-the-counter delivery of nearly five hundred services through multiple channels in a phased manner
3. Creation of e-Gujarat as an integrated portal
4. Enhanced focus on mobile governance in service delivery
5. Citizen engagement through social media
6. Promotion of digital literacy in the state
7. Skill up-gradation for gainful livelihood

8. Further strengthening cyber security measures
9. Promoting GIS and analytics for creation of a holistic Decision Support System (DSS)
10. Augmenting last mile connectivity to bridge the urban-rural digital divide with focus on next generation data centre and augmenting GSWAN (Gujarat State-Wide Area Network)
11. e-Connecting all government departments, societies, boards and corporations under their administrative control, ULBs and PRIs
12. Incentivizing innovation and new initiatives
13. On demand availability of IT Infrastructure, platforms and common applications through cloud computing
14. Encouraging PPP models to the extent feasible

The success of e-government projects in Gujarat is largely due to clear formulation of a strategy for their implementation and actionable sub-plans that are amenable to constant measurement and evaluation. These are built into the objectives and form the following broad focus areas:

1. Public service delivery
2. Connected government
3. Integrated application systems
4. Participatory and democratic governance
5. Capacity building
6. Guidelines and enabling framework

The e-Governance vision follows a well-articulated and structured paradigm in Gujarat. An IT committee for each department sketches out its IT plan headed by respective Department Secretary. Each department is horizontally connected with Department of Science and Technology (DST) thereby following uniform and interoperable standard for all applications as well as ensuring unified infrastructure and hardware system. State level apex committee have been formed for state wide roll out of the projects.

The task of the apex committee is explicitly defined and includes

1. Identification of project priorities
2. Designing and approval of detail scope of work, SLA, RFQ, RFP with the help of consultant and IT committees
3. Selection of technical standards with the help of consultant
4. Bid process management by consultant as per respective GRs
5. Finalization of successful developer/ service provider by IT committee.

The innovations bouquet

Major e-Governance initiatives in Gujarat can be grouped into the following segments

- Infrastructure Initiatives
  - (a) Gujarat State Wide Area Network (GSWAN)\
  - (b) Gujarat State Data Centre (GSDC)
  - (c) Sachivalaya Integrated Communications Network (SICN)
  - (d) Bhaskaracharya Institute for Space Applications and Geo-informatics (BISAG)
  - (e) Jan Seva Kendra
  - (f) Aapno Taluka Vibrant Taluka (ATVT)
  - (g) EGram-Vishvagram
- Applications G2B
  - (a) E-Procurement

   (b) Value Added Tax Information System (VATIS)
   (c) Extended Green Node (XGN)
   (d) Drugs (Allopathic) Manufacturing License System DMLA
   (e) Investor Facilitation Portal (IFP)
   (f) Commissioner of Geology and Mining Applications.

- Applications (G2C)
   (a) State Wide Attention on Grievances by Application of Technology (SWAGAT)
   (b) Hospital Management Information Systems (HMIS)
   (c) E-Dhara& E-City
   (d) E-Mamta
   (e) Online Job Application system (OJAS)
   (f) E-KrishiKiran
   (g) Targeted Public Distribution System.

- Applications (G2G)
   (a) Integrated workflow and document Management System (IWDMS)
   (b) Integrated Financial Management System (IFMS)
   (c) E-Guj Cop
   (d) Information security Management System for GUVNL(ISMS)
   (e) Revenue Case Management system (RCMS)
   (f) Works Monitoring System of Roads
   (g) Buildings Departments (RNB-WMS)

Successful projects

Out of a wide range of spectacularly successful projects, a few are presented below as examples only that are not only worthy of emulation by other states but are also setting global benchmarks.

Gujarat State Wide Area Network and Gujarat State Data Centre are core and critical infrastructures responsible for the delivery of e-Governance services.

Gujarat State Wide Area Network (GSWAN) connects all the government offices and buildings in State capital on gigabit backbone. It is the core Infrastructure component for e-governance implementation in Gujarat that has established new benchmarks in connectivity. GSWAN is one of the largest IP based Multi Service (Voice, Data and Video) IT infrastructure connecting 33 districts, 248 talukas to state capital Gandhinagar. Conceptualized in the year 2000, GSWAN was country's 1st robust State Wide Area Network and biggest in Asia. It Provides seamless connectivity of government functionaries at different levels across state, district and taluka centres. The Sachivalaya Campus Area Network (SCAN), having 7000 fast ethernet input/output ports, connects all the government offices and buildings in state capital on gigabit backbone. Among its unique features are state of the art grievance redressal system with IVR (Interactive Voice Response) facility, help-desk call-centre, on-line ticket log management for all government employees. Over four thousand five hundred district/taluka government offices of thirty two government departments and semi government offices have been connected with GSWAN Gujarat State Data Centre.

GSWAN has been a backbone for various e-Governance initiatives in the State. It's bandwidth has been scaled up from 8 Mbps to 34 Mbps for state capital - district centre and from 2 Mbps to 10 Mbps for district centre – taluka centre. Internet bandwidth has been augmented from 16 Mbps to 90 Mbps.

Leveraging this drive, the state government aspires scale the existing network to state-of-the-art carrier grade MPLS based centralized, secured and scalable information highway (GSWAN 2.0) to provide seamless connectivity across G2G, G2B and G2C.

The next version of GSWAN will feature seamless voice, video and data over the same IP backbone to serve all government offices. It will be fully IPVG enabled with bandwidth on demand.

Departments would be selectively allowed to explore different options for connectivity beyond GSWAN network to enable last-mile connectivity. The State leadership plays a proactive role in improving the communication and connectivity across the state by leveraging National Optical Fiber Network (NOFN) in addition to National Knowledge Network (NKN) framework. Existing GSWAN connectivity would be extended to gram panchayats through NOFN.

An ISO 20000 and 27001 certified Gujarat State Data Centre (GSDC), set up at Gandhinagar provides common/ shared infrastructure to various departments to host their services or applications leading to ease in integration and efficient management, ensuring that adequate and optimal use of the resources. All the e-Governance applications and websites of the state are required to be hosted at SDC.

Looking into the future, or rather 'leaping' into it, 'virtualization' and cloud computing are stated to be used to ensure on-demand availability of IT infrastructure and common applications. The SDC shall further be equipped with adequate Disaster Recovery (DR) frameworks including - near and far DR sites to ensure uninterrupted business.

The GSDC has the distinction of being India's first State Data Centre to be operational under National e-governance plan. GSDC consolidates services, applications and infrastructure centrally to facilitate government departments in establishing a transparent and efficient public administrative department through e-governance at a low-cost. It has been connected to all the government offices through GSWAN and is operational since 2008.

Another instance of a successful e-government initiative – the e-Gujarat (eDistrict MMP) is also presented here. This ambitious project encompass service delivery channels comprehensively cater to various services being delivered to the citizens. The e-Gujarat integrated state portal was envisaged to function on the following broad framework:

a. Strengthening e-enablement: Implementation of unified state portal for delivering services of various departments of the state government

b. Improving efficiency: Reduction in service delivery time by simplification of processes

c. Fostering integration: Enablement back-end (workflow) automation for various services

d. Promoting digitization: Undertaking digitization of state-wide legacy data/records to enable delivery of services across the counter

e. Institutionalizing electronic signature: Delivery of e-certificates for services

f. Widening reach: Making services available to citizens at their nearest locations

It aspires to create a digitally equipped society where all the possible ICT channels like service centers, self-help kiosks, web portals, mobile service delivery applications, etc. are utilized. Cross-departmental service delivery using digital mediums is envisaged.

Just as successfully done in Sweden, Gujarat has established Citizen Service Centers (CSCs) as physical access centers for citizens. Over fifteen thousand CSCs, which amounts to one center for approximately every 4000 population through various departmental initiatives have been established. The total number of CSCs targeted to be increased to over twenty thousand by 2019 to deliver nearly five hundred services closer to the door-step and meet the following service levels

1. Availability of government to Citizen (G2C) services within two kms

2. Waiting period at service counters to be less than 30 minutes

These objectives are envisaged to be realized by scaling up the following service delivery channels

1. eGramVishwagram: The number of eGram centres currently operational across all gram panchayats are envisaged to be further strengthened. In order to increase the service portfolio, eGram centres would be integrated with GSWAN network to improve the last mile connectivity.

2. AapnoTaluko Vibrant Taluko (ATVT): The ICT infrastructure and the basic civic amenities at the ATVT centres will be augmented to improve the citizen experience. Service offerings through these ATVT centres will be enhanced to include majority of citizen services.

   This initiative was launched in 2011 to bring all local government activities under one roof. ATVT is an online system to strengthen the administration at the Taluka level for better implementation of government schemes and addressing the applications and grievances of the people. A cluster level monitoring approach is used in ATVT model.

   Nearly one hundred eighty services of different departments are being delivered under one roof from a single window. Applications for assistance under various services are collected and processed at the Taluka level itself. This does away with the need of time consuming , costly and cumbersome travel of citizens to district headquarters for paper work formalities. Services provided by ATVT include one day services like Issuance of certifications such as income, caste, residence, senior citizen, renewals such as arms license, ration card, birth date change etc. SMS alerts are sent to applicants on receipt and approval of their application along with online status tracking.

Studies have concluded that ATVT governance is phenomenally empowering citizens and is proactively facilitating to shape the course of their lives and business.

3. Jan Seva Kendra: The ICT infrastructure and the basic civic amenities at the Jan Seva Kendras will also be augmented to improve the citizen experience. Service offerings through these Jan SevaKendras will be enhanced to include majority of citizen services.
4. City Civic Centres: The urban local bodies will further scale up their centres in line with the e-Nagar programme of Urban Development and Urban Housing Department (UD&UHD).

Spectrum of services at a Glance

A quick view of the kaleidoscope of various services cutting across different areas are indicated below. These are only samples and there are many more in practice in the state. The idea of giving a glimpse is to highlight the depth and breadth of possibilities in the area of service delivery, use of technology and implementation possibilities.

The mass acceptance of mobile devices such as laptops, mobile phones, etc. has fuelled the demand for mobile governance. All the departments to leverage high mobile penetration in Gujarat for providing services to the citizens, which will also help to bridge the last mile gap, especially in rural areas.

GIS Based System: Bhaskaracharya Institute for Space Applications and Geo-Informatics (BISAG) is a state level nodal agency to facilitate use of spatial and geo-spatial technologies for the planning and developmental activities of the Gujarat Government. It has developed centralized geo-spatial database and Decision Support System (DSS) which gives integration of whole-of–government with most government activities now being GIS based.

BISAG has developed e-Map services for visualization, interpretation and integration of remote sensing data with departmental data including maps. Geo-spatial databases which include terrain characteristics, administrative systems, city and village maps, ports, forests, etc. are created using conventional, maps high resolution 2D and 3D Imagery and official datasets. This ensures that micro planning of various government schemes and public services are done through GIS data lead to inclusiveness. Many Studies have established that the integrated centralized database not only saves time but also leads adoptability and affordability to government and citizens and efficient allocation and use of resources. BISAG won the National Award on e-Governance 2012.

Satellite Communication (SATCOM) is yet another e-Government project empowering citizens by using satellite communication to ensure reach of education skill development and awareness about various government schemes across the State. SATCOM has been operational since 2006.This ICT initiative facilitates regular and direct communication between government departments and users using satellite communication. Studies have established that this initiative has resulted in better planning and feedback mechanism to the system.

SATCOM provides services to government departments for telecasting educational skill development, training and awareness programme through TV broadcast. The project services are currently used by over 25 stakeholder departments to reach a wide panorama of beneficiaries ranging from farmers, youth, school teachers and private sector employees. A number of studies and research reports have established that this project has helped to touch upon the primary rural issues like school availability, addressing farmer concerns, health programs, solving the problems of tribal communities and rural women by interaction with the heads of the Government at the highest levels. It was established beyond a doubt that the travel cost for creating awareness and training programs for departments has been reduced because of this project.

Online Grievance System: (SWAGAT) The most innovate and path-breaking e-Governance project in the direction of democratic empowerment of citizens is the State Wide Attention on Grievances by Application of Technology (SWAGAT). It is a unique online grievance redressal program through which the Chief Minster directly addresses the issues of citizens from of Gujarat. Operated by Chief Minister's office, SWAGAT, is one of the country's first ever state-wide online grievance redressal program. It is aimed at transparent and speedy redressal of citizens' grievances. Structurally it is a 4-tier system at gram, taluka, district and state levels. Grievances submitted are first resolved by authorities at the respective level and thereafter all pending grievances are reviewed by the CM on a particular day of every month. Concerned stakeholders are present along with the CM for direct interaction with aggrieved citizens. Studies and reports establish that this led to enhanced transparency in governance. Reports and studies have established that SWAGAT has led to phenomenally strengthening public accountability and has increased citizen's satisfaction as grievances are monitored at the highest level. SWAGAT has won numerous awards. Some of the top ones include the national award on e-Governance 2011, United Nations Public Service Award 2010, and the International Award Manchester University 2004.

e-Gram: The eGram is another spectacular success story worthy of emulation. It can be summed up in the maxim "While the world becomes global village e-Gram panchayat turns villages global". Under this project, village panchayats have been equipped to provide the e-services through VSAT broadband connected PCs along with printer, UPS, web cam, VoIP phone in order to bridge the digital gap between urban and rural Gujarat.This resilient eGram VSAT network also known as 'Awan Network' is Asia's largest public domain network. Over fourteen thousand village panchayats are equipped to provide the following services. G2C Services such as (i) Basic certificates (ii) Land records (iii) Utility bills (iv) e-Ration card and e-Gram mail. B2C services include (i) e-Ticketing (ii) Utility bill payments (iii) Market linkages for agricultural commodities (iv) DTP. Another unique feature of this project is that the e-Grams are being operated through Village Computer Entrepreneurs (VCEs) on a revenue sharing basis under PPP model.

Online Recruitment for Government services: In the area of government recruitment, the Online Job Application System (OJAS) ensures and facilitates a transparent recruitment process for Government jobs. This was launched in the year 2012. This unique ICT initiative has rendered the long drawn and time consuming government recruitment process much more simplified time saving, cost effective and transparent. OJAS makes the entire process of recruitment easy end to end right from an applicant starting from filing online application, validating and verification, interview schedules receipts, and SMS based alerts to getting the appointment letter. OJAS is also used for Teachers Eligibility Test (TET). Lakhs of applications have been processed online till date for various positions in the government. OJAS has helped the agencies to speed the recruitment process and reduce complexities with improved data security.

e-Land records (e-Dhara): Another pioneering initiative is the e-Dhara Easy. It is a transparent and secure way to access and maintenances of village land records. After digitizing all land records, e-Dhara Kendras(e-DK) have been setup at taluka mamlatdar offices to take up day to day activities of land records such as mutations and issue of Record of Rights (RoR). Workflow based software (BhuLekh Soft) has been implemented since 2004-2005. By integrating BhuLekh Soft with the e-Gram Vishwa Gram (eGVG) project, that provides broadband connectivity through VSAT to village panchayats, farmers can get RoR copies from the village panchayat itself. The e-Dhara e-project has been successfully implemented in all districts and talukas of Gujarat.

On the lines of e-Dhara, the e-Jamin project was initiated for integration of all stake holders with land records and as a starting point, registration is linked with e-Dhara for auto mutation and notice generation after successful agriculture land registration. This project has won many awards and accolades including the CSI-Nihilent Award 2006 (second Runners-up) and Microsoft Award 2006 (Service Delivery Category).

e-Procurement: To streamline and ensure transparency in tendering and procurement, a resilient e-procurement system was introduced in the year 2007. This was also to overcome challenges of the cumbersome traditional procurement process like tiresome paperwork, inadequate transparency, delay in tender finalization etc. The entire e-procurement has been designed as a web based application that caters to all services from Notice Inviting Tender (NIT) stage to issuance of Letter of Intent (LOI). e-procurement has been made mandatory for multiple items across many government departments. This initiative has brought in qualitative benefits and have overcome the challenges of traditional system along with cost savings through higher competition and demand aggression. It has also led to shortening of the average tender processing time drastically thereby making the procurement process more efficient.

e-Health services (e-Mamta): This is another quintessential initiative of Gujarat that is intended to harness the benefits of ICT to improve effective and efficient delivery of health care services that are available. The system aims at registering individual pregnant mothers and children of the age upto 6 years and adolescents along with their full details to ensure complete services delivery of Ante Natal Care (ANC), child birth, Post Natal Care (PNC), immunization, nutrition and adolescent services and to track the left outs of these services. Studies have established that this project helped immensely to minimize mother-infant mortality rate by providing vital health services at pre and post delivery time. It provides real time reports and better analysis with interdepartmental co-ordination. It also aims towards realizing priority issues in health. The project has won many awards and accolades including the national award-2012, eWorld forum Award 2011, outstanding performance in Citizen-Centric Service Delivery (Silver) Award and the Social Innovation Honours - 2012.

Internet connectivity is being introduced in the e-gram villages in a phased manner through the Bharat Sanchar Nigam Limited (BSNL) Network, which in turn enables linkages with the Gujarat State-wide area network (GSWAN).

Gujarat has been effectively using video conferencing to conduct various e-Meetings across the departments, thereby saving precious travel time and costs. All the officials are encouraged to optimally use video conferencing facility in their day to day administration.

Wi-Fi hotspots are being created as per relevant guidelines preferably on a PPP mode at various public places, educational campuses, tourist locations, business hubs etc. in a phased manner all over the state.

Departmental actions put in place

In the overall matrix of usage of IT, the emphasis is on reusability, replicability, interoperability, scalability and convergence while developing enterprise-wide applications. Departments are expected to ensure interoperable framework across other departmental applications in the interest of seamless data exchange for convergence and synergy. All government departments are required to revisit their IT action plan and prepare a roadmap coterminous with this Policy. Up to 3% budgetary allocation of the departments is expected to be earmarked towards IT.

Each department's IT Roadmap is mandated to encompass components such as: (a) Software application (b) Client side hardware (c) Networking and connectivity (d) Central IT infrastructure (server, storage and licenses) (e) Use of mobile governance and social media (f) Legacy data digitization (g) Training and capacity building.

To make the internal functioning of departments more agile in terms of human resources management, a project named 'SAATHI' was launched by the general administrative department. The system provides facility to create an integrated state-wide employee human resources database with modules for employee administration, leave management, payroll processing, transfers and posting, recruitment and training, retirement processing, etc.

All departments shall ensure that they follow the general approach of GPR approved by the state e-Governance apex committee for e-Governance applications. It enumerates the following key aspects of the approved GPR approach that shall be given due attention to bring about the necessary changes in the governmental processes, thereby taking full advantage of technology

1. Simplification of the application forms to seek only the necessary information required for the service delivery
2. Minimizing the requirement of submitting supporting documents to the extent possible and collaborative use of other online database
3. Digitization of legacy data for facilitation of delivery of 'across the counter' services
4. Acceptability of scanned documents, which shall be verified by designated government officials, to be used to create digital repository of citizen documents. Such documents shall not to be asked again from citizens for newer services. Some of these documents would have a life span based on their validity.

5. Delegation of powers for faster application processing and improved service delivery levels.
6. Standardization of the output formats issued by the system.
7. Reduction in number of scrutiny levels those which do not add any value to the overall application scrutiny.
8. Improvements in certain processes/documentation to reduce citizen hassles like replacement of 'legal affidavit' by 'self declaration'.
9. Application of 'rule of precedence' to simplify the requirements for availing of a service based on previously delivered successful services to the applicant / applicant's family.
10. Use of electronic signature to accord approval and issue electronically signed certificates / licenses, permits, etc, within the provisions of various Acts.
11. For internal government communication/administration, Gujarat has already taken several key steps in this direction by pushing applications like IWDMS, IFMS etc. Increasing adoption of these applications with further BPR and rollout of new applications like HRMS, Asset management.

Enabling structure for e-Governance: (including legal provisions)

A State e-Governance Plan Apex Committee (SeGP) under the chairmanship of Chief Secretary has been constituted to provide strategic direction and oversee timely implementation of all e-Governance projects. The functioning of this committee is also to oversee compliance to this policy by all the line departments.

The provisions of Gujarat (Right of Citizens to Public Services) Act, 2013 is designed to be implemented across the

State government departments. Due impetus is given to the Gujarat Information Technology (Electronic Service Delivery) Rules 2014 wherein all government department and offices must notify the services which will be delivered through electronic mode and the timeframe for the same will also be defined. All the government departments are expected to adopt and deploy uniform electronic authentication framework in a time-bound manner to ensure secured delivery of public services to the intended recipients. All state government websites are web portals are in the process of being integrated with web analytics tools.

Gujarat's e-Governance policy urges all departments to optimize the use of appropriate Business Intelligence (BI) solutions to undertake data analysis and data mining. Government data is considered as state asset and may be used by various departments to create their own Decision Support Systems.

The state portal and government departmental portals are envisaged to be made mobile compliant in due course from the effective date of notification of the policy. A mobile application store is to be created with easily downloadable applications, to avail of various public services through handheld devices. The mobile applications will be developed by the departments using open standards.

The e-Governance policy recognizes that security of critical information infrastructure is vital for the sustenance of e-Governance initiatives. A cyber security cell for the protection of state's critical information infrastructure for countering cyber attacks has therefore been constituted. Steps are being taken to

1. Assist all relevant state entities for countering cyber attacks by providing cyber security implementation guidelines in line with guidelines issued by Indian Computer Emergency Response Team (CERT-In, Govt. of India), National Critical Information Infrastructure

Protection Centre (NCIIPC) under National Technical Research Organization (NTRO, Govt. of India) and Implementation of ISO 27001 (Information Security Management Systems) standards and controls from time to time

2. All Government applications (including hosting of websites) to be deployed in public domain only after security certification is obtained
3. Information Security awareness workshops to be held at regional levels
4. Ensuring security and privacy of sensitive personal data of citizens in accordance with the applicable Acts

Taking perhaps the first of its kind initiative in the world, the policy re-affirms its commitment to environment protection by introducing eWaste management guidelines. The disposal of obsolete ICT equipments shall be made strictly in accordance with the laid down rules. All the concerned stakeholders are required to adhere to the Green IT Principles and ensure savings in energy and printing.

Participatory and democratic 'Good Governance' is at the core of Gujarat's e-Governance strategy. Digital literacy for self-reliance is the driver of that core. This includes the following policy goals and objectives:

1. It will be ensured that the children completing elementary education get an exposure to basic computer skills in school
2. Suitable training for the rural and urban population will be imparted to ensure that within next five years every family in the State has at least one e-literate member preferably female
3. Departments will be further encouraged to maximize the use of SATCOM facility subject to relevant guidelines

to impart quality distance education and awareness targeted to various segments of population including women, farmers, students, healthcare staff, etc

4. The e-literacy drive in the State will be facilitated to develop more IT skilled citizens by opening IT training centres in districts preferably through PPP mode. These training institutes would impart short term IT courses
5. IT fairs will be organized by GUJCOST in various parts of Gujarat to demonstrate the benefits of IT to its citizens
6. Appropriate financial assistance will be provided to Below Poverty Line (BPL) tribal students of Gujarat in pursuing IT/computer science degree from technical universities
7. Employability of the students will be improved by carrying out appropriate changes in the curriculum
8. eMPOWER: The state government has initiated a platform known as eMPOWER to train the youth in the field of IT.

Considering the nature and formidable scale of IT initiatives in Gujarat, the policy plans to undertake following capacity building measures

1. Creation of an e- governance division at state level
2. Formation of an e-Governance academy and an e-Governance - Centre for Excellence (CoE) at state level. The academy is expected to give due impetus to research in e-Governance domain for identifying innovative methods to improve governance
3. Creation of Project e-Governance Mission Teams (PeMTs) in all citizen centric departments to fast track e-Governance initiatives

4. Strengthening of district e-Governance society structure
5. Organizing regular e-Governance trainings for all the concerned government employees in different departments to provide exposure and develop an aptitude to get accustomed to the use of e-Governance

The state government proposes to setup an 'e-Governance campus' to further promote and institutionalize e-Governance in the state as also in the country. The same will contain under one roof

1. Prototypes and virtual tour experience of unparalleled success stories of e-Governance
2. Next Generation ICT Infrastructure (SWAN 2.0, SDC 2.0 etc.)
3. National e-Governance Academy
4. Centre of Excellence and digital library for e-Governance best practices
5. Cyber security cell

Insummary, it is worth referring to the numerous studies have concluded that the comprehensive nature of Gujarat's e-Governance model is comparable to the best-in-class globally and also worthy of emulation both nationally and internationally.

Lessons

1. Establishing the overarching vision and aligning it with execution is fundamental to the success of any e-government project
2. The focus must be both on the 'e' part (technology) and the 'governance' part of the equation. While most e-Governance projects fail on this count, Gujarat was able to integrate both and succeed spectacularly
3. Every e-Governance project was 'institutionalized' on a firm foundation. This ensured that the overarching

vision and focus on 'good governance' was the driving force behind all departmental heads, project leaders and change champions.

4. The Gujarat model establishes that both the 'big bang' approach and the relatively incremental but steady approaches to e-Governance projects can go hand-in-hand and can intact rein fare each other
5. The service delivery channels to achieve the purpose of e-Governance can be numerous, but then must be synchronized to deliver maximum output and intended impact.
6. The skill and expertise with which an e-government project is planned determines its success

12

m-Governance (Mobile Governance)

Introduction

It can be defined as the strategy and its implementation involving the utilization of all kinds of wireless and mobile technology, services, applications and devices for improving benefits to the parties involved in e-government including citizens, businesses and all government units[1]. These technological developments are leading to newer ways of dealing with the stakeholders that make it easy, accessible and also more convenient from time to time.

It becomes imperative on the part of the governments to adopt and develop, ways and means of harnessing the potential of these to reach out to the citizens. India is a country with a large population of the citizens living in the rural areas. While the government is addressing to fill the gap in infrastructure challenges connected with IT penetration in rural areas, the wireless technology comes handy in the interim. Use of the mobile wireless technology not only enhances the 'reach' to rural

---

1 Ibrahim Kushchu, From E-government to M-government: Facing the Inevitable

areas, it also helps to provide a transparent governance in the hands of the citizen. Realizing the importance, potential and the ease of use, Govt of India has earnestly embarked on the journey already and has announced the framework for mobile governance.

Government of India, in its framework for m-governance[2] "to utilize the massive reach of mobile phones and harness the potential of mobile applications to enable easy and round the clock access to public services, especially in the rural areas"

Drivers for m-Governance (enablers)

As indicated earlier in this section, the technology and the services are the main drivers for the emergence of mobile governance. Some of the key factors are depicted in the Figure 1 below.

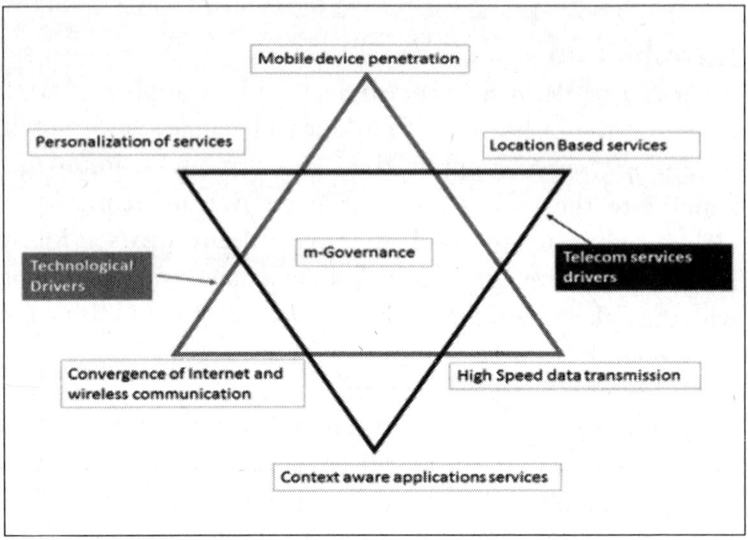

Figure 1. The key drivers for mobile governance from technology and telecom services

---

2 Framework for mobile Governance, Ministry of Communication and IT, GoI, FMG: 01, Version: 1.0, January, 2012

The mobile device penetration is a major factor to reckon with. As per the TRAI (Telecom Regulatory Authority of India) press release published in November 2016, the number of wireless subscribers stood at 968.8 million and the growth rate of around 21 % month on month[3]. Such increase in the wireless subscriber base puts the government at ease to deal with the citizens in rural areas, in a way. This is mainly because the basic connectivity to the rural areas remain a major challenge. Though there are plans and actions in place to address this through digital India initiatives – broad band connectivity – it is yet to realize the full potential. Given the current scenario, the mobile penetration proves to be a boon for the government to reach the masses at rural India.

The convergence of internet and wireless technology is another major development that is changing the way one leads the life. This helps to provide the "anywhere- anytime" connectivity to the people at large. This had been made possible by the advancement in device technologies of mobile phones, the increased developments on the wireless technology etc.

The ever increasing speed of the data transmission is the third dimension that is paving the way for a better connectivity. The high speed transmission helps to deal with massive data exchanges, helps the people not only to communicate with less time but also in high volumes.

On the services side, personalization has created strides. Thus, the owner of the device and the way it is configured helps to 'personalize' the services offered. There is so much of development in the application services that the location based services and context aware applications have replaced the mundane and run-of-the mill type applications. Thus, with so much of intelligence built into the services there is a huge scope for the providers to harness the potential to roll out

3 Telecom Regulatory Authority of India (www.trai.gov.in) Press release 09/2017, dated 1st Feb, 2017.

the 'services on demand'. This is a model which was hitherto unheard of. The 'services on demand' is one of the main mantras of digital india program released and implemented by Government of India.

Thus as given above in the Figure 1, the combination of advances in technology and availability of services on wireless have provided a compelling proposition to move to mobile governance. This emerged to be a natural choice for many Governments across the world.

e-Governance and m-Governance

e-Governance in India is about just over two decades. The penetration and drive is visibly seen on the last recent few with several state governments jumping into the bandwagon due to the push by the Government of India. Some states which have been the early birds of e-Governance – for example the State of Gujarat, Andhra Pradesh, Karnataka, Kerala, Telangana (due to its historical connection with undivided Andhra Pradesh), and Rajasthan have already embarked on migrating to m-Governance.

However it is to be recognized that there will be co-existence of e-Governance and m-governance for some time to come. This is inevitable because of the large size of data transmission needed in certain applications, non-availability of m-services across the spectrum and readiness of mobile infrastructure etc.

In case of the 'late-starter' state governments, it may be worth the while to go directly to mobile applications and provision of services in the mobile model. But it is to be remembered that these have to meet certain guidelines and characteristics. These are indicated below.

Desired Characteristics for m-Governance

Based on a survey conducted in Europe, where mobile government is already in vogue, the following factors have been identified based on the research of Al-Khamayseh, S et al[4]. Though the survey may have been from Europe, at a broad level, these are very much contextual to India as well. The factors prioritized are given below

1. Privacy and security
2. Infrastructure
3. User needs and preferences
4. Quality and user friendly applications
5. e-Government
6. Acceptance
7. Cost
8. Standards and data exchange products
9. Coherent m-Governance framework
10. High mobile penetration
11. Infrastructure management
12. m-Governance awareness
13. Access
14. Strategy
15. IT literacy
16. M-Governance portal and exclusive gateway
17. Partnership with private sector
18. Legal issues of telecommunications services

The m-governance applications and services should follow the guidelines released by the Government of India from time to time. However there are several aspects and characteristics that have to be met anyways.

---

4 Al-Khamayseh, S., E. Lawrence and A. Zmijewska: Towards Understanding Success Factors in Interactive Mobile Government: University of Technology, Sydney, www.mgovernment.org/resources/euromgvo2006/.../2_AlKhamayseh.pdf

Based on a recent study on m-Governance conducted in India and a paper published[5], the authors have identified the top five factors affecting use of mobile government services in India.

1. Availability of e-Government strategy
2. Availability of e-Government
3. Access to users
4. Improve awareness
5. Ensuring quality of mobile government services

There are a few other factors additionally to be under the consideration as well for effective m-Governance

a. The mobile service applications need to be of medium complexity (not too simple or too complicated for operations)
b. User-friendly
c. Back-end support and systems
d. Privacy
e. Information Security
f. Accessibility

Advantages of m-Governance

It is important to recognize that technological advancements are independent of user's choice or convenience. That is, just because a technology device is very advanced, the customer need not buy it or use it. The driver for the customer to turn to a technology device or solution is, their convenience, ease of use and comfort. Everything else becomes secondary for them. Thus, just because mobile technology is advanced, it does not have to be 'accepted' by the citizens or other stakeholders – they

5 Mamta Sareen (India), Devendra Kumar Punia (India), Lovneesh Chanana (India), Exploring factors affecting use of mobile government services in India, Problems and Perspectives in Management, Volume 11, Issue 4, 2013

need to see the 'benefits'[6].

In the context of m-Governance, this means that citizens need to see an advantage in doing transactions with governmental authorities with their mobile phones instead of using e-Governance based solutions or personal consultations at government offices. However, m-Governance provides several benefits for citizens compared to other approaches. The most important ones have been summarized in a report[7] and are briefly described

1. Smartphones and comparable mobile devices are usually always carried and always on. Hence, these devices provide users the capability to communicate everywhere and anytime. In the context of m-Governance, this means that citizens are able to continuously access m-Governance services independently of the current time and their current location. This is a significant advantage compared to classical e-Government based solutions that usually require citizens to sit in front of a PC and hence bind them to fixed locations. Compared to paper based administrative procedures in offices of public administrations, m-Governance services – and of course also e-Government services – have the benefit to be accessible independent from office hours.

2. The 'always-on' characteristic of mobile phones makes not only m-Governance services, but also citizens accessible anytime. Mobile phones can therefore be used to speed up the information flow between different parties involved in administrative procedures. For example, mobile communication networks can be used

6 Jennie Carroll: 'What's in It for Me?': Taking M-Government to the People, BLED 2006 Proceedings, Paper 49, 2006.

7 Mobi Solutions Ltd: Mobile Government: 2010 and Beyond, White paper, 2010, http://www.mobisolutions.com/

to broadcast urgent informational messages from the government to the people.

3. The simplicity of using mobile communication technologies can improve several processes in terms of efficiency. This way, the usage of mobile technologies in governmental and administrative processes can help to save time and money.
4. Mobile phones are usually very personal devices. While for instance computers are often shared within a family, mobile phones usually belong to one person only. Hence, when used within m-Governance, these devices provide more personalization opportunities for targeting users.
5. Smartphones and similar devices support different forms of interaction. For instance, many mobile phones may be alternatively controlled via voice. Likewise, mobile communication itself can be based either on voice or alternatively on text messaging. These choices between different types of interaction and communication can assist disabled people to access administrative and governmental services.
6. In several developing regions, mobile penetration exceeds Internet penetration. Hence, mobile phones are the only available means for people to get in contact with administrative agencies and bodies electronically. In these areas, missing infrastructures often inhibit the application of classical e-Governance services. In contrast, m-Governance solutions based on available 2G mobile networks are feasible and an easy method for governments to get in contact with their citizens. m-Governance is therefore a solution to the digital divide and can even strengthen democracy.

The above mentioned benefits of m-Governance affect

both citizens and governmental institutions. If developers of m-Governance solution manage to ensure that all participants realize these various advantages, m-Governance can become a great success. Thus, the various benefits of m-Governance are of course also important drivers for its success.

Enablers and success factors for m-Governance

It is a well-known and recorded fact that the mobile user population is increasing world over and no country is an exception. India is also in the race with a huge addition of mobile phones. All businesses and other providers of services are vying with each other to extend their offerings to the customers through mobile devices - be it a bank or a utility provider. So it is possible to come to conclusion that the mobile services are here to stay and it is a matter of time before it is all pervading.

In this condition, it is important for one to understand the need for congenial conditions for growth. Some of these are listed by Karen et al[8] being presented here:

Infrastructural investment: Infrastructural investment is a key success factor for m-Governance, especially in developing countries. This so because of the vast expanse of area to be covered and also the geographic conditions apart from general poor connectivity issues.

1. Regulatory and political environment: Applicable and appropriate legal framework has to be in place. This framework has to ensure that m-Governance services are based on a solid and unambiguous legal basis. Additionally, an appropriate policy framework for the telecommunication sector can allow for competitive market situations, which in turn may lead to better services for citizens.

8 Kavita Karan, Michele Cheng Hoon Khoo: Mobile Diffusion and Development: Issues and Challenges of M-Government with India in Perspective, Proceedings of M4D 2008, Karlstad University, Sweden

2. Awareness and acceptance: While the development and rollout of m-Governance services can be done, there is a need to create awareness of the same among the user communities. That is to be followed by acceptance of offered services by the stakeholders. Hence, in order to avoid frustration on both sides – Government and the users- new m-Governance services need to be well introduced and participating parties – i.e. citizens and employees of administrative bodies – should be provided with related information and training. This needs to be done by providing more than adequate communication, training and publicity in multiple languages to reach the masses. Only if all participants are familiar with the available m-Governance services, they will be willing to use these services and can benefit from them. Awareness and acceptance are therefore critical factors for the success of m-Governance initiatives.
3. Security and privacy: Security is an important requirement for any ICT system that deals with secure or privacy sensitive data. m-Governance services are no exception because of several reasons. The aforementioned point has emphasized the importance of acceptance of m-Governance services by citizens. Crucial conditions for the acceptance of such services are security and privacy. m-Governance services won't be accepted and used by citizens if they do not trust them. Users want to be sure that their personal data is processed securely by these services and not misused for any other purposes.
4. Equitable access: Equitable access to information is 'one of the most vital principles in the emerging global information economy'. This is also reflected in one of the nine pillars of Digital India as "Information for all". With the fast growing mobile penetrations,

mobile communication technologies and especially m-Governance services have the power to contribute to the equitable access of information.

Future of m-Governance

According to the white paper 'Mobile Government 2010 and beyond'[9], m-Governance will support and lead to the following future trends

1. Raising efficiency: The increased usage of mobile technologies in governmental processes will improve their efficiency
2. No citizen left behind: m-Governance will help to make governmental services accessible to all citizens, regardless of gender, age, nationality, income, or disabilities
3. Customer expectations: With advancing technologies, user expectations are usually increasing. m-Governance will help to satisfy rising needs and expectations of citizens in the context of governmental services
4. Collaboration: As access to information and services is nowadays available almost everywhere and any time, collaboration between different organizations becomes more and more important in order to assure transparency and accountability and to remain collaborative and responsive
5. Accessibility and broadband availability: Accessibility and broadband availability have been identified as crucial factors within the public sector. Mobile technologies in general and m-Governance services in particular can help to achieve these goals

---

9 Mobi Solutions Ltd: Mobile Government: 2010 and Beyond, White paper, 2010, http://www.mobisolutions.com/ files/Mobile%20Government%202010%20and%20 Beyond%20v100.pdf, (accessed on

7. Multi-channel delivery: Multi-channel accessibility has been identified as key for successful e-Government. Mobile government is therefore perfectly suitable to supplement e-Government services by offering a second mobile communication channel.
8. Strengthening participation and democratic decision-making: Thanks to m-Governance, citizens can be mobile without losing the opportunity to participate in governmental processes.
9. Development of mobile government in rural places: In developing rural areas, mobile penetration usually exceeds Internet penetration significantly. Hence, mobile technologies allow governments to offer governmental services also to citizens who have no Internet access.
10. Location awareness: The usage of global position information in mobile processes has been identified as important future trend. As modern mobile phones are often equipped with integrated GPS modules, such location based processes are expected to further gain in importance in future.

Besides these expected future trends, the study 'Mobile Government 2010 and Beyond' identifies the following challenges for a future success of m-Governance

1. Physical limitation: Physical limitations of small screen sizes and limited text input of mobile phones may restrict the amount of exchanged information
2. Cost: As m-Governance is a supplement of e-Government but no substitution, development, operation, and maintenance of m-Governance services cause additional costs
3. m-Digital divide: One of the greatest benefits of

m-Governance is its capability to reach also those who are not able to use classical e-Government services because lack of Internet infrastructures. Thus, m-Governance can help to narrow the digital divide especially in developing rural areas.

4. Mobile mind-sets: It is presumed that a lot of people associate mobile devices with fun and entertainment. It may be difficult to motivate these people to use their devices for serious services such as m-Governance.
5. Privacy and security: In order to assure user's trust, there needs to be an assured data and privacy during m-Governance procedures.
6. Responsibility managing exponential amounts of information and data overload: Mobile technologies allow users to be connected anytime and everywhere thus the system design should take care of the load of managing huge amounts of data processing.
7. Resistance to organizational change: Common habits, fear of new or unknown technologies, as well as security and economic factors pose serious threats to the success of future m-Governance services. Hence, it is crucial to strive for broad acceptance of offered m-Governance services. This can be achieved by motivating all participants involved in m-Governance services and to point out the various benefits of mobile applications.
8. Lack of clarity around forward planning strategies: To guarantee success of m-Governance, it is crucial to do a pragmatic planning that takes into consideration the different needs and requirements of different regions and countries
9. Lack of mobile technology standards: The white paper 'Mobile Government 2010 and Beyond' identifies

the lack of mobile technology standards as a serious problem. As expected each government agency may invest in different mobile systems to fit their specific needs, thus making interoperability between different isolated applications an issue

10. Global standards: As there are currently several different global standards and specifications, interoperability between country specific solutions are often an issue.

Case Example from India: MyGov

MyGov is the mobile Governance initiative from the Government of India. The citizen-centric platform empowers people to connect with the Government and contribute towards good governance[10].

MyGov platform is a unique path breaking initiative which was launched in 2014. It is a unique first of its kind participatory governance initiative involving the common citizen at large. MyGov is for 'Creating a participatory digital democracy, leveraging technology to enable every citizen to contribute ideas and efforts for nation-building, transforming these ideas into action and recognizing individual contributions'. The idea of MyGov brings the government closer to the common man by the use of online platform creating an interface for healthy exchange of ideas and views involving the common citizen and experts with the ultimate goal to contribute to the social and economic transformation of India. MyGov platform has been more than successful in keeping the citizens engaged on important policy issues and governance, be it Clean Ganga, Girl Child Education, Skill Development and Healthy India to name a few. There is no doubt that this platform has made inroads in diminishing the gap which has traditionally existed between the citizen and the government.

---

10 https://www.mygov.in/overview/

MyGov platform has become a key part of the policy and decision making process of the country. Where the platform has been able to provide the citizens a voice in the governance process of the country and create grounds for the citizens to become stakeholders not only in policy formulation and recommendation bit but also implementation through actionable tasks. Given the importance of this platform in transformation of India through participatory governance, the platform has been constantly undergoing upgrades to ensure an enhanced level of user experience. The major attributes of MyGov includes Discussion, Tasks, Talks, Polls and Blogs on various groups based on the diverse governance and public policy issues.

MyGov has more than 1.78 Million users (as of Jan, 2017) who contribute their ideas through discussions and also participate through the various earmarked tasks. In addition to this the platform gets more than 10,000 posts per weeks on various issues which are analysed and put together as suggestions for the concerned departments who are able to transform them into actionable agenda.

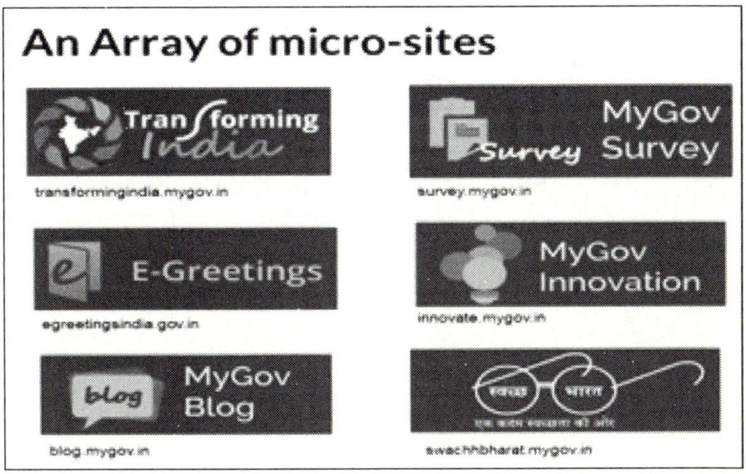

Figure 2 Some applications in MyGov (as of Jan 2017).

With these impressive numbers, one has to say this is just the beginning and there is a lot more to come on this platform in future. MyGov is an initiative which should culminate into a mass movement towards self-governance or 'surajya'. As further progress is being made under the umbrella of Digital India, utilizing the technology to further revolutionize the public service delivery and citizen engagement, MyGov platform is all set to become a key agent for this change taking inputs from the citizens, the ultimate beneficiary and leverage their collective feedback to improve policy change and implementation. Figure 2 gives a bird's eye view of some apps that are provided in MyGov.

Summary

It is natural to expect e-Governance to graduate to m-Governance – as the technology evolved. This helps to reach the 'unreachable' citizen in the farthest corner of the country. This is the power of democracy that needs to be exhibited to put the real government in the palms of the common man in the remote rural village. The journey has just begun and there is a lot to unfold.

13

Moving beyond m-Governance –The Digi-Road ahead!

Introduction:

Technology is here to stay. Technology is a leveller in this world which makes life simpler for everyone, in its own way. Harnessing the power of technology provides convenience, good experience and above all transparency for demonstrating good governance. Thus the governance has moved from e-Governance to m-Governance and beyond. The path beyond m-governance is evolving and is a continuous process. The following sections provide possible and potential scenarios of use of technology for governance. While some of the scenarios described are already a reality, some others may be in the testing stage or proof of concept stage. Irrespective of the stage in which they may be, it is certain that technology evolution will drive the governance in the country, be it at state level or at national level.

It may be a huge task to provide a laundry list of all possibilities of Internet of Things (IoT) in a book of this nature. Thus the authors are attempting to do the following

1. Provide an introduction to the concept itself (Internet of

Things – IoT) and how it works

2. Enumerate a few examples of the application of IoT – current scenarios
3. Potential use of IoT by various departments of the government. This is expected to serve as a pointer to the administrators and policy makers to take this forward and make it a reality

In a similar way, there is evolution in the business scenario as well. Newer models of collaboration between business entities, element of financial engineering and several other innovative practices are evolving, based on the situation and the need of the customers. Thus in order to travel in the Digi-Road, it is not enough only to have advanced technologies, it is also very important to look at alternative business models.

This chapter provides a glimpse of some possibilities. By no means are these exhaustive – at best these can be considered as thought initiators for furthering.

Internet of Things (IoT)

The advent of Internet has changed the way people live in the last three to four decades progressively. Coupled with this advancement, the wireless connectivity fuelled the application areas and expanded the reach further. Thus, as such Internet of Things is not a new concept, in itself, per se. But it is the application of the ideas and the way it is used for various applications have made this a hot topic of discussion.

The premise of IoT is very simple – if all objects of daily life are 'identifiable' and wireless 'connected', then they could communicate with each other and could be 'managed' by a computer. This is the concept of IoT. The concept was tested in 1999 and subsequently an article was published, which stated 'If we had computers that knew everything there was to know about things—using data they gathered without any help from us-we would be able to track and count everything, and greatly reduce waste, loss and cost. We would know when things needed replacing, repairing or recalling, and whether they were fresh or past their best. We need to empower computers with their own means of gathering information, so they can see, hear and smell the world for themselves, in all its random glory. RFID and sensor technology enable computers to observe, identify and understand the world—without the limitations of human-entered data.'[1]

In simple terms to understand IoT, it has the following components and characteristics

1. IOT is a real time – as things happen, data is collected and shared
2. It has a sensor and a (wireless) communication.
3. The collected data is pre-processed and shared with the main computer
4. In a way, IoT 'connects' the physical world to the virtual world and provide useful information for appropriate decision making. (for example a health band tied to a person can collect data about the person's BP, heart rate etc, which will be processed by a computer and the person may be 'informed' of any deviations or warnings to take care off)

In essence, the IoT offers collection of small amounts of data frequently from a large number of sources and transmitted, processed and provide them for ease of decision making.

Figure 1 gives a pictorial representation in simplified form for digital government that includes IoT as an integral part.

As can be seen, digital government provides services to the stakeholders based on information collected from the 'things' (IoT) and processing them through the re-engineered

---

1 1 http://kevinjashton.com/2009/06/22/the-internet-of-things/

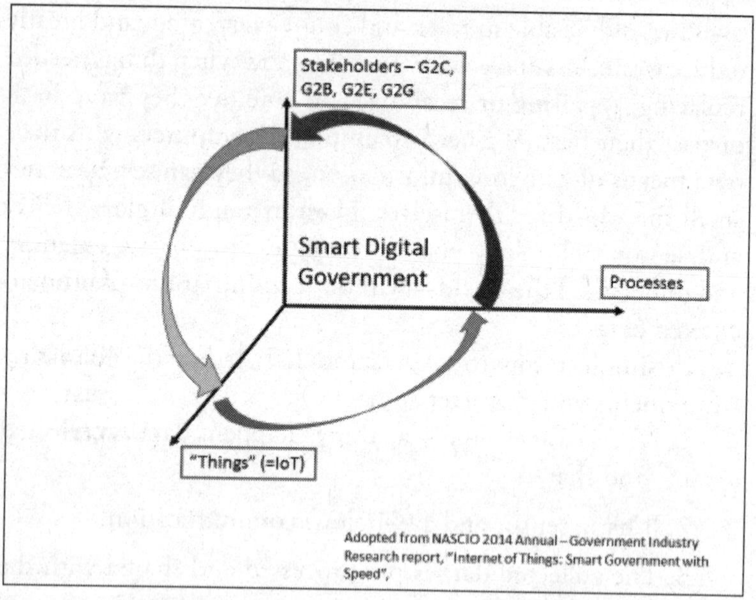

Figure 1 Representation of Digital Government

government processes in an effective, transparent and faster way.

There are three C's of IoT. [2]

Communication: IoT communicates information to people and systems, such as state and health of equipment (e.g. it's on or off, charged, full or empty) and data from sensors that can monitor a person's vital signs. In most cases, access to this information was not available before or it was collected manually and infrequently. Using IoT devices, it is possible to know the location, (using Global Positioning Systems – GPS), and other vital parameters of interest as designed in the IoT at a central location on a real time basis because of the communication capability. The communication can be achieved through short range wireless or long range wireless (GSM, GPRS or 3G etc).

Control and Automation: Due to the real time communication

2 Introduction to IoT – Lopez Research, Part 1, November 2013.

from the devices, it is possible to control and automate the device from a remote location. In a connected world, one will have visibility into a device's condition. In many cases, one will also be able to remotely control a device. For example, one can remotely turn on or shut down a specific piece of equipment or adjust the temperature in a climate-controlled environment. Thus once a performance baseline has been established, a process can send alerts for anomalies and possibly deliver an automated response.

Cost Savings: Many companies will adopt IoT to save money. Measurement provides actual performance data and equipment health, instead of just estimates. Businesses, particularly industrial companies, lose money when equipment fails. With new sensor information, IoT can help a company save money by minimizing equipment failure and allowing the business to perform planned maintenance. Sensors can also measuring items, such as driving behavior and speed, to reduce fuel expense and wear and tear on consumables. New smart meters in homes and businesses can also provide data that helps people understand energy consumption and opportunities for cost savings.

Thus, the IoT provides not only real time visibility of what is going on, but also helps to understand the details for effective decision making and subsequent application.

It is strongly believed across the indistry that 'the IoT will play a major role in the transformation of India into a digital economy - as the catalyst that empowers our citizens by providing them with transparent governance and services (education, health, legal, financial and safety) at their fingertips. At the heart of this transformation will be a re-engineering and digitising of government processes, using IT and supporting database and cloud infrastructure to simplify, improve and optimise the various government functions'.

It is precisely these characteristics that help the government to seamlessly 'connect' several dots to provide an effective and transparent governance to its citizens and businesses. Coupled with e-Governance or m-Governance, use of IoT will enhance the Governments overall performance by many fold. The use of IoT in any area is limited by the ingenuity of the designers. However, in order to make the case for IoT in government, a few sample used-cases are cited below. For ease of understanding these have been classified under several categories:

Agriculture	Transportation	Defence	Healthcare
Infrastructure	Public distribution	Logistics	Smart Cities
Oil, gas, and mining	Banking	Connected Home	Food Services
Utilities	Hospitality/ Tourism	Manufacturing	Smart Buildings

Examples of application of IoT

Given below are some example cases of use of Internet of Things in various fields[3]. As this is an emerging field there is a lot of information getting gathered and shared. Many of the points or ideas mentioned are tried and tested in some part of the world. These may have to be studied for the Indian application and adopted appropriately.

Agriculture including livestock health

India is largely an agriculture based economy and use of IoT will benefit the country hugely. Figure 2 is an indication of very few areas where IoT may be used in agriculture.

The figure is only a sample representation whereas the applications could be many more. A forecast by the food and agriculture wing of the United Nations (FAO) says that the food production worldwide should see a 70% increase by 2050 to cater the ever growing population[4]. If this has to be achieved,

3 http://www.libelium.com/resources/top_50_iot_sensor_applications_ranking/

4 http://iotindiamag.com/2016/08/smart-farming-iot-agriculture/

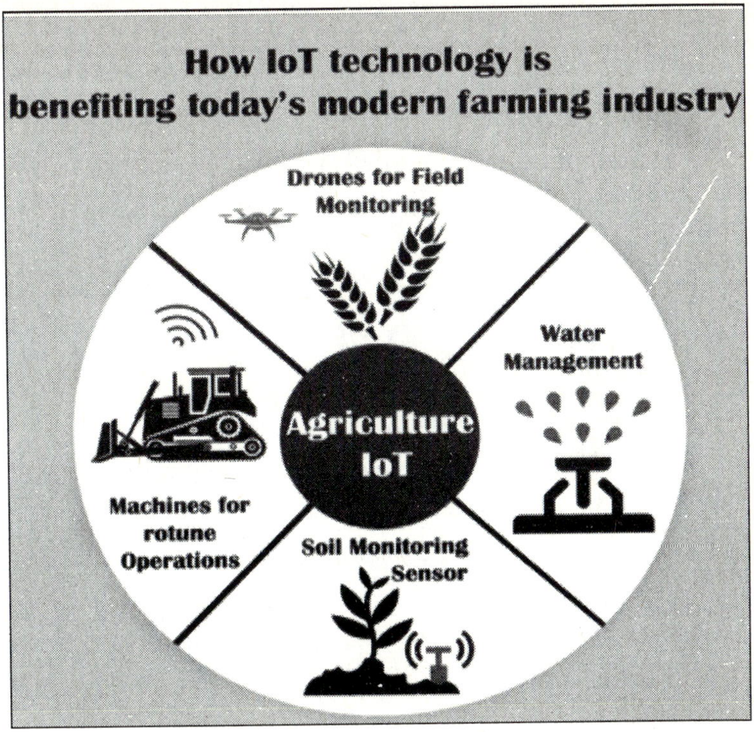

Figure 2 Use of IoT in agriculture

the traditional methods followed hitherto may be inadequate and use of modern and effective methods will be called for. IoT could provide a link to achieve this effectively.

Agriculture related

- Soil conditions and fertilizer usage
- Monitoring and control of water and moisture levels
- Equipment control and monitor
- Field monitoring over large areas (using drones)
- Climate monitoring and control of equipment
- Predictive analytics for crops (based on data of previous years and comparison

- Monitor storage conditions of crops
- Energy consumption levels in the farm land – for watering and other use
- Monitoring and control of water quality for better yield
- Monitoring the level of chemicals in water used for agriculture

Livestock related

- Tagging the livestock – keeping count and the herd together
- Tracking the movement for effective gazing
- Offspring care and growth – monitor, control and growth for the young ones of animals
- Detecting toxic gas levels – ventilation and air quality in the farm land
- Fish farm monitoring – controlling water quality for better yield

Health Care

- Fall detection – assistance for the aged, when the fall
- Patient surveillance – monitoring of critical parameters for critically ill
- Monitoring of pregnant women – their vital parameters and seeking timely assistance
- Child care – monitoring
- Remote medical support for rural areas
- Early detection of childhood diseases
- Drug preservation and control

Environment and Emergency Management

- Monitoring the mines for gaseous emissions and emergency control

- Weather warning systems
- Sensors for warning of emergency situations – Tsunami, cyclone etc
- Rainfall monitoring and control systems
- Air and water quality management
- Dust or pollution monitoring and control systems
- Peripheral intrusion detection and warning system
- Detection of hazardous gases and warning system
- Detection of flood and warning system
- Detection of radiation system
- Forest fire detection
- Detection/forecast of landslide and avalanche (Himalayan range)
- Snowfall detection and warning (Himalayan region)
- Early detection of earthquake

Transportation

- Tracking of vehicles (global positioning system GPS)
- Fleet management
- Logistics of spares and service
- Planned maintenance and control for least breakdown /preventive maintenance
- Traffic congestions and early warning for re-routing
- Passenger Load factors and planning of optimized services

Energy (Electricity generation and distribution)

- Smart Grid – monitoring generation, transmission and consumption
- Leakage detection

- Monitoring solar energy generation
- Monitoring wind energy generation
- Optimization of usage and distribution
- Preventive maintenance.

Transportation Infrastructure

- This covers mainly in this case road and rail transportation system. Similar aspects and additional areas could be considered for air and sea travel
- Monitor road/rail conditions
- Monitor and control flow of traffic in high ways and in major cities
- Emergency detection and response
- Disaster management and control
- Detect and communicate extraordinary situations

Public Distribution

This relates to the distribution of essentials to the public by the government through the ration shops

- Stock monitoring at warehouses and re-order
- Movement of stock for distribution and control
- Monitor and control disbursement at the ration shop – monitor and control with information appropriately (to the public and to the officers as needed)
- Monitoring the measurements being disbursed. (ensuring accurate weights)

Thus the limitation of application of technology is only in the ingenuity of the people involved and not by any other

Moving towards Digital Government–"The Digi-Road"

Once many of the above are implemented and used by the stakeholders, the government would be moving to the so called 'digital government'. Figure 3 gives a depiction of the trajectory

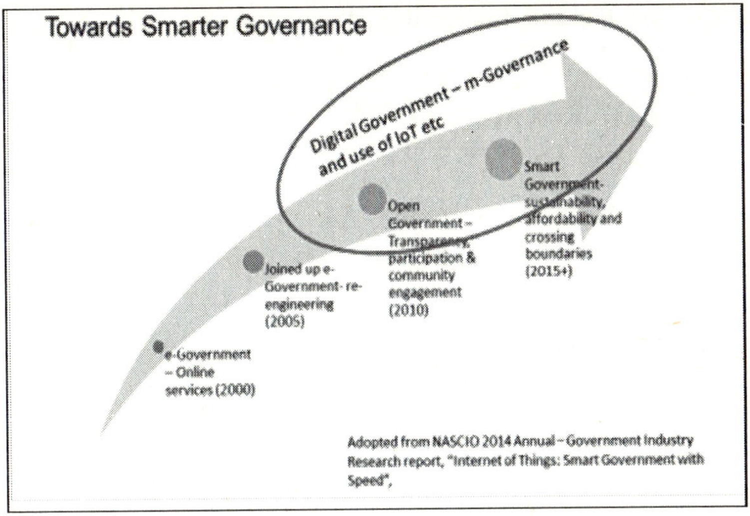

Figure 3 Trajectory of e-Government to Digital Government.

of e-government becoming digital government.

Following six characteristics are listed by Accenture[5] in its publication

- Seamless citizen experience
- Empowered and informed decision making
- Increasing engagement
- Flexibility for future
- Improved operational efficiency
- Delivering on Mission

These characteristics enable the government to become digital and also help the citizens and businesses to experience the benefits in the larger context. However the road to Digital Governance is also paved with certain challenges. These have been listed in a report by Deloitte Consulting in their report[6]

---

5 https://www.accenture.com/au-en/insight-digital-government

6 https://www2.deloitte.com/content/dam/Deloitte/au/Documents/Economics/deloitte-au-economics-digital-government-transformation-230715.pdf

These include, but not limited to

- Policy bottlenecks and bureaucratic inertia
- Budget and capability constraints
- Digital exclusion and divide
- Lack of competition
- Privacy and security
- Transitioning Govt staff to new roles

Evolving New Business Models

It is not only enough that emerging technologies are used for digital governance, but also innovative ways of business models. These innovative business models should be able to address the classical 'limited budget syndrome', leverage the strengths of all parties involved by synergizing in exemplary models and so on. A move towards this model may be the evolution of a Public-Public Private Partnership.

As is well known, the emergence of PPP model was necessitated by the need for sharing the risks and also harnessing the strengths of the private parties for public service delivery. There is much talk and hype about PPP the world over in the context of e-Governance projects and the philosophy of e-Governance as such. What is being ignored is the power and potential of Public-Public Private Partnership (PPPP) let us brand this as P4.

The P4 model (Public-Public Private Partnership) needs to evolve to leverage and synergise the strengths of the departments' to provide service delivery on top of the PPP model. This is explained in detail below.

There must be professional approach in the implementation of e-governmenance projects just as, relevant BPR principles of the corporate sector have been adapted and adopted into GPR. Proved and tested principles and practices of project planning and management from the corporate sector must be infused into the government's e-delivery of public services.

The Public-Private Partnership has immense tangible and intangible benefits to the former. Apart from the practices and skill sets of private sector, the project leaders or change champions will need to imbibe the attitudes native to the private sector for greater success in their attempts in the government. Some of these include a die-hard adherence to timelines, uncompromising achievement of milestones and cost consciousness, to name a few.

A word of caution here. The PPP pact must be water- tight and based on a clear convergence of purpose and vision. Many e-Governance projects suffered due to lack of the above and end up in endless finger pointing and blame games. The first and biggest victim of such avoidable situation is the e-Governance project itself.

The genesis of the P4 model is to leverage the competencies of different departments for the integrated public service delivery. This involves bringing together a couple of departments to provide the expertise, insights and consultancy in defining, designing and oversee execution of major service delivery projects.

There is also another reason for the P4 model to be applied. Across the world, be in the developed or developing nations, each public sector agency or department has immense resources and infrastructure. In most case there is underutilization of capacity, if not a near idling of it in some functional areas. Out of the three M's-Money, Manpower, Material- that must be managed by leaders in any organization, there will always be a relative abundance of one over the other. In the e-Governance context, one division of a department may have more of one resource than the other. This is a model of applying the under-utilized resources for the benefit of an e-Governance project. From the larger Ministries point of view different departments may likewise display such an imbalance. More often than not, these are ignored or not even taken cognizance of.

Therefore, taking a comprehensive view and rebalancing of

resources within divisions and between departments within a ministry may result in their optimal utilization. Such Public-Public Partnerships can and must be between ministries too. For instance, a ministry launching an e-Governance project invariably needs connectivity that can be provided by the Department of telecommunications. Any such project could also seek support of the IT department that can be retained to as the government's technology consultant when interacting with the private sector right from the Request for Proposal RPF stage itself. This model is pictorially represented in Figure 4.

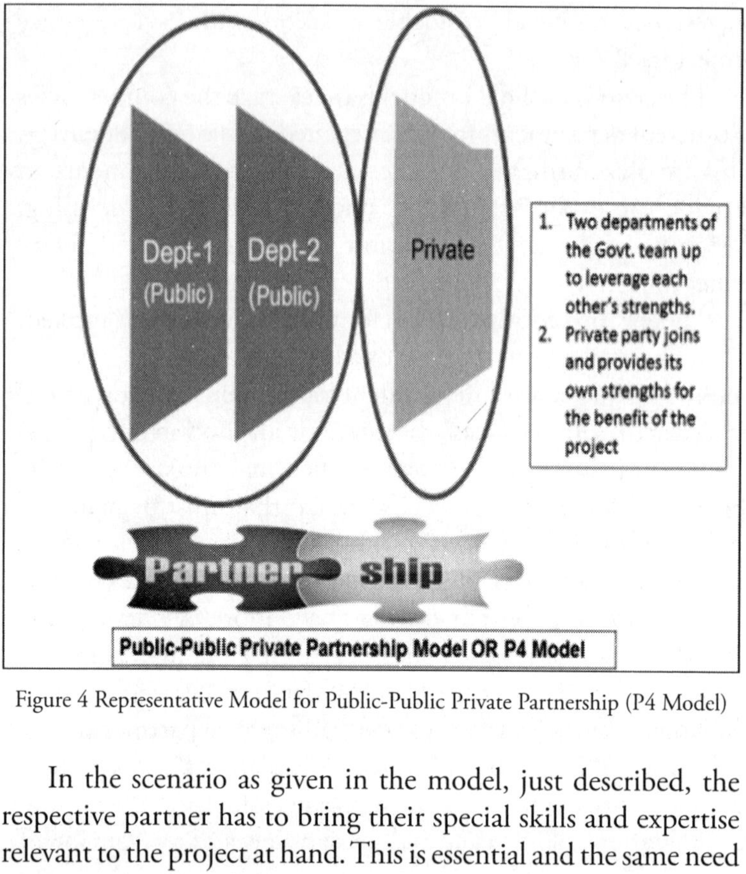

Figure 4 Representative Model for Public-Public Private Partnership (P4 Model)

In the scenario as given in the model, just described, the respective partner has to bring their special skills and expertise relevant to the project at hand. This is essential and the same need to be signed off at the beginning of the definition of roles and responsibilities of each player. Else, it will result in the classical syndrome of 'too many cooks spoiling the broth'.

A conceptual model of who needs to bring what is given in Figure 5.

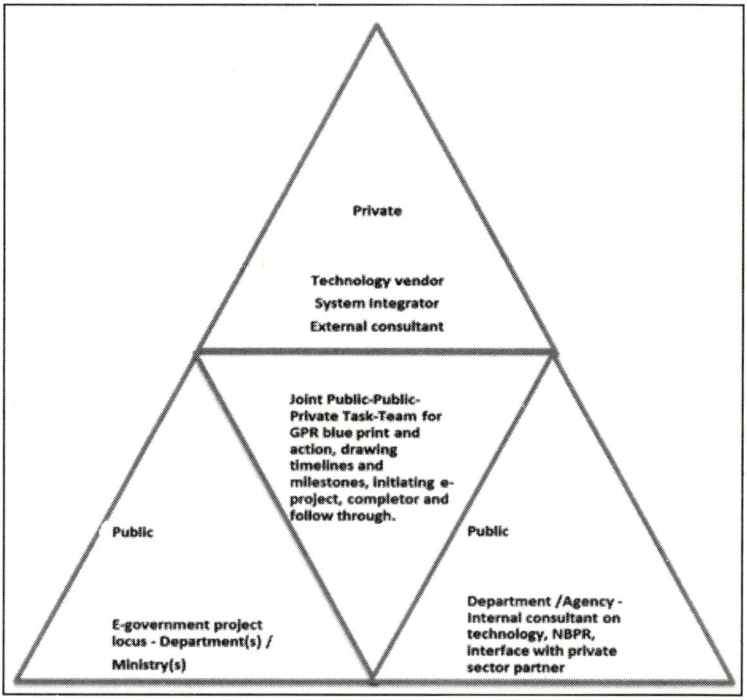

Figure 5. Conceptual model of P4 – who's who.

The basic premises of this model

Even currently such a model may exist but loosely. For example, a department of the State Government using the services of NIC or STQC is actually under the P4 model, strictly speaking. However, the responsibilities, accountability and the outcome from the players are loosely defined – leading to the classical 'finger pointing' exercise or a sub-optimal outcome if at all.

In the P4 model suggested by the authors, the main objective is to fix the responsibility and define a measurable outcome from all the parties involved. This makes it not only mandatory for all the players to 'own' and be accountable to the outcome of the project – but also helps each party to go 'that extra mile' to make it happen.

An example may help to clarify this further and bring home the point.

The following is given applying the above conceptual model, though the initiators or players of the project may not have thought it that way.

Smart City project with BSNL[7]: (Example of a potential P4 model project)

To manage this large-scale urbanization, cities are turning to digital technologies to integrate information and communication systems into various technical systems and infrastructure. This is the bedrock of smart cities.

BSNL has an important role to play in 'smart city vision' by virtue of its (1) Robust connectivity (2) Resilient technology (3) Vast network, (4) Converged solutions and (5) Commendable human resource with expertise and skill-sets required.

Building Blocks of Smart City

The key building blocks of Smart Cities are generally agreed to be the following:

Smart Energy: This includes smart grid, smart metering, gas distribution and renewable energy

Smart Mobility: This includes mass public transport, traffic management, electric vehicles and intelligent congestion charging

Smart Water: This includes water distribution management, grey water recycling, storm water management

Smart Public Services: This includes public safety, health

---

7 'Smart City project – Chennai Telephones' - Publication of BSNL, Chennai telephones 2017-18

care, education and public lighting

Smart and affordable buildings and homes: This includes efficient building and homes

Smart integration: This includes integration of information between different city departments for real-time visualisation, management and analysis of incidents across the city.

There are seven pillars of Smart City. These are described below:

Integrated Management and Command Centre (IMCC)

This is envisaged to provide a single interface to view all integrated city level information. These command centres do not imply that only one will be applicable to a city. In reality, many smaller ones could feed requisite information along its various nodes.

Services and Applications across various verticals

These have been classified according to the Infrastructure segments identified by the MoUD. It covers vertical solutions or applications and include among others

i. Smart Mobility – ITS, Vehicle telematics, insurance, fleet management, connected cars

ii. Smart health care

iii. Smart living - home automation,

iv. Smart utilities

v. Smart governance – the software and solutions that can be used by the various departments for smart governance

vi. Smart manufacturing – predictive maintenance

Communications Network

Communication Networking technologies provide the infrastructure of the smart cities to ensure that all the devices, computers and people have convenient, reliable, secretive communication paths with each other. These include

i. Wired network
ii. Wireless networks
iii. Satellite networks
iv. Transmission protocols (MQTT), M2M connectivity
v. Networks that can be called MAN, WAN, PAN, HAN
vi. Dedicated resources that could be allocated for critical communication or communication during emergencies or disasters

Devices and Chipsets

The space for devices is diversified and includes a gamut of routers, computers and other networking equipment. For narrowing focus and since M2M is the focal concern and area of core competence of BSNL, the focuses could be on sensors, RFID tags, chipsets, mobile devices, embedded software, etc. that facilitate the 'sensor web' in cities. Also, devices need to be compliant with IPv6 addressing.

Data Centre, Cloud, Analytics and Backend Platform Infrastructure

Cloud computing is the delivery of computing or storage as a service rather than a product. In cloud computing, shared resources, software, and information are provided over a network (typically the internet). Enabling access to a common group of fundamental application services on a cloud infrastructure enables different city applications to leverage and build on the value provided by each other. This includes

i. M2M platforms
ii. Service enablement solutions, application services and device management software
iii. Big data platforms
iv. Hybrid cloud infrastructure
v. Data as a service

Open Data and Analytics

One of the key enablers for smart city applications is analytics over data to derive new insights that can be used for making smart decisions that change the life of people for the better. The analytics can range from understanding the current state of a system better quality of (example: water usage), predicting a future value of interest, do a root-cause analysis of an event (example: traffic situation) or even perform what-if-analysis for different parameters. Enabling appropriate data sharing protocols, standards and schema that enables such building of analytics application would also be of interest.

Machine learning and other statistical analysis of data for developing predictive models over data that can reused across different applications may also be interesting to pursue.

i. Analytics necessary to derive intelligence and implement it

ii. Statistical Analysis libraries

iii. Data Sharing protocols and best practices

City Assistance tools

The following are some of the important ICT models and tools that are aimed complementing the Smartness of Cities:

i. Urban Design models and tools

ii. City Simulation

iii. Capacity Building Models and tools

iv. Testing and Certification

Information and Digital Security

Security of Smart City is a very important and integral part of the foundation of Smart City. It touches every aspect – the devices themselves, the communications part, the data part, the application part and the storage and services part. Besides information security, security as a topic also encompasses privacy of data and physical security.

As can be seen from the above report published by BSNL,

there are ample opportunities to marry the ICT and the services/data of various departments to enable the Smart City. This is precisely where the P4 model can take shape and help achieve the desired outcome.

In summary, moving to Digital Government in India is a certainty and an achievable goal in the near term (3-5 years) provided the right steps are continued to be taken at the right levels and implemented seamlessly – be in terms of technology or in terms of business models for implementation.

The journey has begun right earnest and actions being taken are in the right visionary and strategic spirit.

Let the journey continue!

14

Practical insights for change champions and project leaders

Introduction

Numerous studies on e-Governance have been made on both successful and not so successful projects, by the State Governments, Central Government, the National Institute for Smart Government (NISG), UNDP etc. This book has also presented comprehensive case studies and listed out learnings from each of them. We sum up below a few important and overarching suggestions to make e-Governance projects a success.

Ten Points to remember and practice

The following are some basic 'must do' principles, which are by no means exhaustive. They are pointers based on practical experience and case studies.

Understanding the Vision and aligning with it

In general e-Governance projects are conceived in line with an overarching vision. Thus it is important for any project to be in line with the overall Vision – at the Government of India and at the state level. The economic and national developmental goals take precedence over everything else. Thus when conceiving a project on e-Governance the change champion or the project leader must keep the overarching vision in mind and work further.

Building a Guiding Coalition: (involving the right stakeholders and engaging them)

The ICT backed digitalization and e-Governance strategy must be carefully introduced after a through consideration of the soft side dynamics of the organization and its divisions. It is reiterated again that this vital yet unfortunately often 'taken- for- granted' or ignored side - includes people, attitudes, organizational culture, and communications

In the initial phases of project conception towards digitalization and e-Governance, the leaders must create a sense of urgency to change. This urgency to change and embrace ICTs out of the awareness and desire to change. This sense of urgency must be existential and personalized. Each employee must passionately feel to need to adapt to the new processes and be at ease in using the new technology. ICT interventions must make each job easier and smoother.

Sponsorship by the top management sets the tone for 'leadership by example'. This also involves the skilful formation of a 'guiding coalition' which is a huge and crucial responsibility of leaders as a charge champions in digitalization and e-Governance initiatives.

The team must become self-propelling and empowered at a certain point in time. The leader who had been 'hand holding' it thus far must transmute gently and imperceptibly into the role of a mentor and a guide.

Buddhism has the concept of 'Sangha' which denotes a cohesive, like minded and well-knit group. What distinguishes the sangha is the bond of empathy among its members. It brings about a 'we' feeling and a sense of altruism.

This is the spirit of togetherness expressed by the protagonists in the movie 'Three Musketeers' when they say 'all for one and l one for all'. The leaders must confront with and resolve many individual, inter-group and intra-group conflict situations. It would, of course be far better to pre-empt and nip such situations in the bud, so to say. Preventing such conflict situations from arising would be better than any post-facto cure. However, it may not be possible to 'resolve' all conflicts as it is an organizational situation. Attempt must be made to 'manage' the conflict by addressing it openly and making appropriate decisions in the overall interest of the project. This needs the people involved to be communicated with in time and genuinely.

The leaders and change champions may often be required to play the role that Ben Hur did in the famous historical block-buster movie by that name. In that memorable 1960s movie, Ben Hur who is travelling across far and wide in search of his family, meets a wealthy Arab Sheikh. The Sheikh is an avid lover of chariot races and has a magnificent stable of 4 horses nameed Altair, Amtares, Aldebaras and Rigel. He loves them and cares for them as his own children. Despite his best efforts and recruiting numerous trainers, the horses fell short of expectations.

The keen eye of Ben Hur an avid charioteer himself, detects the problem and he offers astoundingly simple solution. He notices that each horse had a unique quality that was mis-matched in its role to be played in the race. For instance, the one that was recklessly fast was placed at the inner end of the ring while the more sturdy and stable one was at the outer edge. He simply re-organizes the horses and goes on to win the prestigious chariot race.

Like Ben Hur, the leader of an e-Governance project must have a keen eye for spotting unique capacities and capabilities of his team-mates, especially his deputies, and nurture the same. He also needs to realign their individual roles and role-sets to bring out the best in the team as a whole.

Re-constructing e-Governance project planning and strategy: The long distance rally-cum- sprint race.

In the arena of digitalization and e-Governance, the e-Governance champions must play the role of not just the captain of a ship but also that of its designer and navigator. The design is important for the ship to primarily stay afloat and then surge ahead. Navigation is vital to take the ship and its occupants unscathed through both pleasant and turbulent waters. Both the designing and navigation have to do with planning and strategizing. This is exactly the case with digitalization and e-Governance initiatives.

Sri N Chandrasekharan, the recently appointed Chairman of the multi-billion dollar conglomerate Tata Sons is an avid long distance runner. He also proudly calls himself a 'long distance thinker'. In an interview, he explained that every leader must think long distance in the leadership journey which is both a long distance rally and also a sprint race against time. Every leader, especially in the arena of e-Governance, needs to possess both endurance to go through the long haul grind and also the swiftness to maintain time schedules in project completion. This is an unenviable balancing act. Short term milestones and long term goals must be meticulously strategized planned and achieved.

e-Governance champions/project leaders must choose between two broad approaches of e- governance Implementation.

1. 'Vanilla' implementations (pure play solution from bought-out applications)

2. Customized implementation (bespoke applications)

In vanilla implementations, departments adopt standardized business processes as embedded in the ICT software systems. An envelope is the ERP system. Computer software, and sometimes also other computing-related systems like computer hardware or customization, are called vanilla when not customized from their original form. This means that they are used without any customizations or updates applied to them

However, customizations in ICT systems are required when the existing business processes cannot be fit into or mapped with the standardized processes provided by the ICT system. Government enterprises, irrespective of their size, are generally more resistant to change. They require huge customizations which in turn increase investments.

Thus balancing between the two approaches to quickly put together a working solution is different from thinking long term and brining a sustainable solution. These two are NOT mutually exclusive. So the officer in charge of an e-Governance project must think of quickly putting together a workable solution, needs to keep in mind futuristic aspects like scalability, flexibility and portability for expansion and sustenance.

Engaging Stakeholders and communicating

The importance of involving all stakeholders and establishing a clear communication between them is vital to the success of any ICT driven digitalization or e-Governance project.

This takes precedence over other technical or resource related aspects due to the emotions of people involved (employees) or the lack of digital literacy at the user level.

Identification, classification and communication with stakeholders on a continuous basis becomes mandatory. This is an often missed out area and realized late in the game, when it becomes too difficult to recover or repair. Care must be taken to appoint specific people to deal with identified stakeholders.

It is commonly known that people are ready to take up anything, provided they are informed and involved in the process. So by applying this simple and easy to do – but often missed out – step, any e-Governance initiative may be successfully completed.

Keeping the Big Picture in perspective

It is very important to keep the overall big picture in mind while planning for e-Governance applications. The major points to be kept in mind are already indicated above – namely the vision, the needs of the stakeholders, setting up a team to work on etc.

The softer side of the picture is equally important for the success of the e-Governance initiative – that is as the technology evolves and matures, different aspects have to be integrated into the service delivery platforms.

Keeping JAM is very important. Leveraging Jan Dhan, Aadhaar and Mobile applications (JAM) is the need of the hour. After a few months or years of application of these some other aspects will emerge and they become mandatory requirements. So the leader needs to keep an open mind and provide flexibility through the developments as they happen.

At the core level of the e-Governance application program, there has to be consideration for the (a) Main services (b) Application (c) Data and (d) Technology to be kept in mind. These will help the e-Governance application not only robust but also provide a three hundred sixty degree view of the citizen. An appropriate framework for the application design needs to be chosen and driven for implementation.

Avoiding the Vision - Reality gap and Bridging it in retrospect:

Sun Tzu, the medieval Japanese battle strategist, said that a battle is either won or lost even before it begins. This statement may sound metaphysical but it is in fact so intensely practical. The 'vision' of spectacular victory in a task will result in as equally spectacular spectre of failure if ground realities are not taken into account in strategy formulation and its execution.

It can be said that, in retrospect, many digitalization and e-Governance projects failed 'ever before they began.' Many more are likely to fail if the gap between a laudable vision and the harsh reality is wide. The rate and the probability of failure is directly proportional to extent of the gap. In other words, the larger the gap, the more chances of failure either at the take-off (the 'hop' stage) itself or at any time later

The overarching vision-reality gap includes various other gaps as sub sets. These include

Process flaws (lack of re-engineering)

Technology choice (wrong choice)

People aspects (skills, mind-set and lack of communication)

Budgetary issues (projections and estimates)

Data base and information flow problems (interconnection of the data)

These gaps manifest at different levels in the life cycle of any e-Governance project. Addressing them is vital to any such project.

It is also important that these are documented appropriately. Ensuring that a detailed project report is prepared with relevant information helps in many ways. Historically, several projects have not seen the light of the ay, where there was no DPR. Such DPR's not only help the incumbent leader but also the successor apart from the others involved. This is just one way of letting everyone involved know about the whole plan and expected outcome.

Leading with and without authority (influencing)

For e-Governance initiatives to be successful, leadership must use its power to play not only a facilitative and transformational role, but also a 'trans-mutative' role. Power must be skillfully used to transmute the given into what is envisaged and envisioned to be in the future.

More importantly, the leader must exercise his/her influence on a host of 'others' (stakeholders) who may not play a direct role in the e-Governance initiative, but have a large contributory role, The positive involvement or otherwise of these 'other' stakeholders may not only hinder the project but also may derail it completely.

In such situations the leader must ensure identification of such stakeholders, engaging them in productive conversation and choosing the right medium to engage with them for ensuring the desired outcome. The steps taken in such cases may vary from simple discussions to an out of box thinking for keeping them engaged and positive about the project. Additionally, these negative and invisible stakeholders may create additional hurdles for execution of the e-Governance initiative. These have to be dealt by the champion of e-Governance program, innovatively. Some of the actions taken can be proactive and some may be reactive. Irrespective of the nature, the leader of the e-Governance program needs to be on his/her toes at all times and be receptive to all signals from the field.

Thus it requires multitude of leadership approaches to keep the race running steadily and in the right direction to win.

Passing on the leadership Baton

There is another very subtle gap that stares at the face of every e-Governance project, and to which many failed projects across the world could be attributed to. We call it the 'Baton Gap'. It deals with passing the baton to another colleague in the right manner and at the right time as in a relay race.

Herein is the importance of not making any e-government project 'Person dependent'. As the popular saying goes, 'nobody is indispensable'. However, there is equally popular saying 'people make the difference'. There is a need to balance between these extremes and provide a better framework for change of guard and also continuation of the projects.

If a project failed 'because' its e-Governance champion was moved out mid-way, then the problem is with knowledge transfer and hand- holding between the incumbent and the new champion more than anything else. If it failed because of the e-Governance champion was moved towards the end of the project or around the time of its completion, then it is a problem with succession planning. In short, as in a relay race, the incumbent leader must give it all he or she has while holding the baton and prepare to hand it over smoothly to the next one. The one, set to take over the baton must be, or made to be well prepared to take on the impending responsibility and be fully aware of the genesis of the project to continue and complete it.

The successful e-Gov champion or project leader can now move on to use his or her expertise, knowledge and experience in another challenging project. ICT driven e-Governance initiatives and projects are only a tool and means of organizational transformation and must not be mistaken, as it often is, as the 'end in itself'. It is also worth the while for the powers that be to check or assess the outcome of the projects that were started by an officer who was transferred in the middle of the project. This would help to not only complete it as planned but also do so with additional knowledge and expertise of the new officer-in-charge.

In summary, this requires planning, knowledge transfer, understanding the core of the project, its benefits and the issues to deal with. If a proper handholding is given, the probability of success is high.

Managing Change

Resistance to change is a major human side bottleneck in almost all e-Governance projects.

Although there are no 'magic pill' solutions to the above, there are several techniques that at least have the potential to overcome such resistance. Some of these are as follows:

- Participation: Participation is often the most effective technique for overcoming resistance to change. Employees who participate in planning and implementing a change are able to understand the reasons for the change and contribute better for the cause. Uncertainty is reduced, and self-interests and social relationships are less threatened. Having had an opportunity to express their ideas and getting aware of the perspectives of others, employees are more prepared to accept the change gracefully.

- Education, training and communication: Educating and training the employees and communicating the positive aspects of change helps very much in reducing their resistance. If open communication is established and maintained during the change process, uncertainty can be minimized. Open communication also helps to reduce the negative impacts of the undercurrents and informal channels.
- Facilitation: Several facilitation procedures are also advisable. For instance, making only necessary changes, announcing those changes well in advance, and allowing time for people to adjust to new ways of doing things can help reduce resistance to change.
- Force-field Analysis: Force-field analysis can help overcome resistance to change. In almost any change situation, forces are acting for and against the change. To facilitate the change, change managers start by listing each set of forces and then trying to tip the balance so that the forces facilitating the change outweigh those hindering the change. It is especially important try to remove or at least minimize some of the forces acting against the change. This is depicted in the Figure1 below

Monitoring and control–administering the project processes

It is very important to visualize an e-Governance project, plan for it, deal with stakeholders and manage the change. It is equally important that the project vision is translated into reality thru flawless execution. It is well known that the plan may be excellent but if the execution fails, the project is still a failure. The failure of a project can happen from multiple dimensions. Some of them are listed below

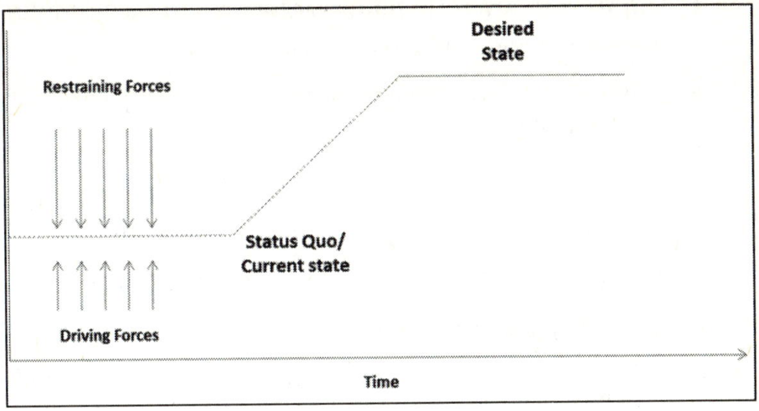

Figure 1 Force Field Analysis – Lewin's Model of Change

- Misunderstanding of the scope and expectations
- Wrong documentation of scope/inadequate scope definition
- Improper solution design by vendor/system integrator due to lack of big picture
- Lack of scalability, flexibility and portability
- Not involving the right people at the right time
- Not documenting the benefits and expectations from stakeholders
- Improper formation of DPR, RFP or contract
- Improper or no administration of contract clauses
- Not planning for vendor transitioning
- Improper exit management
- Lack of constant monitoring for progress against the plan
- Delayed or lack of decision making as needed from time to time
- Improper or untimely allocation of funds

- Untimely transfer/not filling vacancy of crucial positions connected with the e-Governance project
- Not having a Project Monitoring Unit (for large projects of reasonable size)
- Not having periodic reviews against the plan
- Not escalating issues as they appear for resolution
- Not listing all risks and planning for responding to risks
- Improper assumptions/not documenting assumptions
- Not taking into account the constraints on the ground
- Not specifying the target environment – technology and operational
- Wrong choice of technology – obsolete or inappropriate for the application
- Betting on an unproven technology ('too soon to try out')
- Handing the project to an inexperienced vendor
- Issues between the participating vendors (the system integrator, equipment supplier, application developer etc)
- Lack of passion / interest for the leader involved

These are self-explanatory and easy to identify in a project, as it is in the process of being executed. The leader must be adept at identifying them as soon as possible, put corrective and preventive actions in place. These have to be documented, and shared for a larger understanding for future projects.

ANNEXURE–1

List of major re-usable e-Governance software solutions from NIC

S. No	Product Name	Area of Governance/Details
1	AGMARKNET (http://agmarknet.nic.in)	Linking all important agricultural produce wholesale markets, state agricultural boards for exchange of market prices. System facilitates daily market rates from more than 3500 Rural Mandis.
2	MG NREGA http://nrega.nic.in	An end-to-end eGovernance system to facilitate automation of processes involved in NREGA implementation right from the registration of Job seekers, self of projects at GP level, demand of work, allocation of work, attendance, Muster roll, payment, grievance etc.
3	Open Government Platform - OGPL to Promote Transparency and Citizen Engagement (http://ogpl.gov.in/)	Framework designed to promote transparency and greater citizen engagement by making more government data, documents, tools and processes publicly available. OGPL will be available, as an open source platform.

4	E-Office (http://ftsnic.nic.in/eofficeservices)	System designed with need for effective and transparent government. The vision is to achieve a simplified, responsive, effective and transparent working of all government office. The product is standard reusable product amenable to replication across the government. The main services are eFile, Knowledge Management System (KMS), eLeave, eTours, Personnel Information System, Messaging Services.
5	PG Portal - Centralized Public Grievances Redress And Monitoring System (CPGRAMS) http://pgportal.gov.in/	An online web-enabled system over NICNET developed in association with Directorate of Public Grievances (DPG) and Department of Administrative Reforms and Public Grievances (DARPG) to enable the citizen virtually reach the concerned office to lodge a complaint.
5	PlanPlus (http://planningonline.gov.in)	To strengthen preparation of Perspective, Draft Annual and Action Plan based on decentralised and participatory Planning
6	ePOST & Instant Money Order (http://indiapost.nic.in)	ePOST is a service under which printed or even handwritten messages of customers are scanned and transmitted as email through internet. At the destination offices, these messages are printed, enveloped and delivered through postmen like other letters at the postal addresses. AND iMO service comprising counter operations, supervisory functions, pairing of booking and payment, report generation
7	ServicePlus Framework (http://serviceonline.gov.in)	Meta Data based configurable eService Delivery System
8	Training/Skill Management System (http://trainingonline.gov.in)	Facilitating capture of demand of training, training agencies registration, Training Infrastructure, Course formation, trainee's registration, certificate etc
9	National Animal Disease Reporting System (NADRS)	A system to manage the data related to animal diseases from the grass root level
10	mFMS(Mobile Fertilizer Management System) (http:/mfms.nic.in)	Mobile and Point of Sale(POS) , Web based system to track the supply of fertilizer from plant/port to whole seller, to retailer and buyer.

11	Prison Management System (PMS)	Prison Management System (PMS). This system keeps comprehensive information about prisoners, their court cases and their lodging pattern. It also records, tracks and monitors the movement of prisoners and the action taken on their court hearing.
12	e-Procurement http://eprocure.gov.in/cppp/	An open source system for the procurement of goods, services and works by government offices. End to end solution for procurement starting from tender uploading, submission, opening, evaluation and finalisation of procurement process.
13	e-Hospital (http://tsu.trp.nic.in/ehospital/)	Workflow Management system based on HL7 Standard and ISO/IEC 9126 certified for end-to –end solution for managing processes and services in hospital including tele-medicine. Implemented in DR RMH, AIIMS, Tripura etc)
14	Land Records (LIS) (http://nlrmp.nic.in/)	Workflow based system for managing Land Records, Registration, Cadastral Maps and offering digitally signed records through online portal.
15	Core Banking Solution http://ccbs.nic.in	Designed to meet all banking related requirements of all Cooperative Banks including Primary Agricultural Credits Societies (PACS).
16	e-Granthalaya (http://egranthalaya.nic.in)	Library System for automation and networking of libraries.
17	Dynamic Web Site Generator, National Panchayat Portal (http://panchayatportals.gov.in)	The product supports dynamic generation and maintenance of web sites of large number of offices on the fly. Each office can manage its own contents, layout and language without any programming need.
18	VAHAN/SARATHI (Transport)	System for computerisation of 1000 Regional Transport offices in India. The system has computerised and connected all RTOs across country for Driving Licence, Registration Certificates and issue of Smart Card based DL and RC and established national register.
19	e-Courts	System function to handle online case filing, allocation, registration, court orders and judgements accessible to litigants.

20	Pubic Distribution System	End to end computerisation of public distribution system to enhance efficiency and monitoring of distribution of essential commodities to the intended beneficiaries,.
21	e-Counselling (Admission Counselling System)	Online system facilitating students to apply for college admission and get admission based on merit parameters and reducing physical visits and mental stress.
22	e-Taal (Electronics Transaction Aggregation & Analysis Layer)	To monitor eTransactions related to eServices delivered to Citizens
23	Pareeksha	An end-to-end solution to facilitate Examination processes right from registration of applicant, issuing hall tickets, exam-centre management, attendance etc online.
24	MG NREGA http://nrega.nic.in	An end-to-end eGovernance system to facilitate automation of processes involved in NREGA implementation right from the registration of Job seekers, self of projects at GP level, demand of work, allocation of work, attendance, Muster roll, payment, grievance etc.
25	Swachh Bharat Mission (SBM-G, http://sbm.gov.in)	An end-to-end eGovernance system to facilitate reporting, Planning and Monitoring of Swachh Bharat Mission-Grameen across the country.

Source: www.nic.in (the list may get changed or upgraded from time to time.

ANNEXURE–2

General references and recommended reading

Aladwani, A. M. (2001), "Change Management Strategies for SuccessfulERPImplementation", Business Process Management Journal, vol. 7, no. 3, pp. 266-275.

Alan Levin, Providing Computers for all South African Civil Servants, http://www.egov4dev.org/success/case/mofa.shtml

Belanger,F and Carter, L (2008),"Trust and Riskin e-Government Adoption", The Journal of Strategic Information Systems, vol. 17, no. 2, pp. 165-176.

Bruke, A (2002), Organizational Change–Theory and Practice, Sage, USA.

Cameron, Esther. (2009), Making Sense Of Change Management (A Complete Guide To The Models, Tools & Techniques Of Organizational Change), Kogan Page, UK.

Chan, Kim W, & Mauborgne (2003). Tipping Point Leadership, Harvard Business Review.

Chauhan, R, Estevez, E and Janowski, T (2008), "A model for policy interventions insuppor to felectronic governance", paper presented at 2nd International Conference on Theory and Practice of Electronic Governance (ICEGOV 2008), Cairo, December 1-4.

Cordella, A and Bonina, C M (2012), A public value perspective for ICT enabled public sector reforms: a theoretical reflection. Government Information Quarterly, 29 (4), 512-520.

Ciborra, C (2005), "Interpreting e-government and Development Efficiency, transparency or governance at a distance?', Information Technology & People Vol. 18 No. 3, pp. 260-279.

Department of Public Service Administration, "South African E-government Conceptual Framework", 31 October (2005).

Department of Public Service Administration, "South African E-government Governance Framework" 31 October (2005).

Department of Public Service Administration, "South African E-government Policy Framework" 31 October (2005).

Ebbers, W E and Van Dijk, J A G M (2007), "Resistance and Support to Electronic Government, Building a Model of Innovation", Government Information Quarterly, vol. 24, no. 3, pp. 554-575.

Ebbers, W E, Pieterson, W J and Noordman, H N (2008), "Electronic Government: Rethinking Channel Management Strategies", Government Information Quarterly, vol. 25, no. 2, pp 181-201.

Ebrahim, Z and Irani, Z (2005), "e-government adoption:

architecture and barriers", Business Process Management Journal, Vol. 11, No. 5, pp. 589-611.

Gronlund, Å.(2005), "What's in a Field – Exploring the eGoverment Domain", in Proceedings of the38th Hawaii International Conference on System Sciences, Hawaii.

Grove, Andy. (1999), Only The Paranoid Survive, Crown Business, USA.

Hanseth, O, Aanestad, M and Berg, M (2004), 'Actor-network theory and information systems. What's so special?,' Information Technology and People, vol. 17, no. 2, pp. 116-23.

Hassard, J, Law, J and Lee, N (1999), 'Preface: Actor-network theory', Organization, vol. 6, no. 3, pp. 387-91.

Heeks, R.(2003), 'Most e-Government for Development Projects Fail: How Can Risks be Reduced?' IDPM i-Government Working Paper no.14, University of Manchester, UK.

Heeks, R (2003), "Most eGovernment-for-Development Pro-jects Fail: How Can Risks be Reduced?' i-Government Working Paper Series, Paper no. 14.

Heidegger, M (1978), "The question concerning technology", in Basic Writings, Routledge, London, pp. 307-42.

Halaris, C, Magoutas, B, Xenia Papadomichelaki, X and Mentzas, G (2007), "Classification and synthesis of quality approaches in e-government services", Internet Research, Vol. 17 No. 4,pp. 378-401.

Ho, A T K (2002), "Reinventing Local Governments and the E-Government Initiative", Public Administration Review, vol. 62, no. 4, pp. 434-444.

Hung, S, Tang, K, Chang, C and Ke, C (2009), "User

Acceptance of Intergovernmental Services: An Example of Electronic Document Management System", Government Information Quarterly, vol. 26, no. 2, pp. 387-397.

Jett, Hiatt. (2006), ADKAR: A model for change in Business, Government, and our Community, Prosci.

Janssen, M, Chun, S and Gil-García, J R (2009), "Building the Next Generation of Digital Government Infrastructures", Government Information Quarterly, vol. 26, no. 2, pp. 233-237.

Kashyap, Deepak (2016), Healing the Future, Viva Books, New Delhi.

Kotter, J P, & Schlesinger, L A (1972), Choosing Strategies for Change. Harvard Business Review, 57 (2), pp.106-114.

Kotter, J P (1996), Leading Change, Boston: Harvard Business School Press.

Kotter, John P (1998). The Leadership Factor, New York: The Free Press.

KenhagoTazo Olivier, Problems in Computerising the Ministry of Foreign Affairs, http://www.egov4dev.org/success/case/mofa.shtml,

Mc Kinsey Global file:///C:/Users/ITCELL/Downloads/MGI_How_IT_enables_productivity_report.pdf, How IT enables productivity growth, 2001

Mmahmudul, M, Hasan (2015),' e-government success and failure: a case study of bangladesh police, daffodil international university journal of science and technology", volume 10, issue 1-2, july

Nicolas Carrhttp://www.nicholascarr.com/?page_id=99, 'IT does not improve'

Nograsek, J.(2011), Change Management as a Critical Success Failure in e-GovernmentImplementationBusiness systems research, – Vol.2, No.2, 1-56

Parding, K. and Abrahamsson, L. (2009), "Learning gaps in a learning organization: professionals' values versus management values". Journal of Workplace Learning, 22 (5), 292-305.

Persson, A. and Goldkuhl, G. (2010), "Government Value Paradigms – Bureaucracy, New Public Management, and E-government", Communications of the Association for Information Systems: 27(1). Article 4, 45-62, July

Schwester, R. (2009), "Examining the Barriers to E-Government Adoption", Electronic Journal of e-Government, vol. 7, no. 1, pp. 113-122.

United Nations Department of Economic and Social Affairs (2003), "World Public Sector Report 2003: E-Government at the Crossroads.', United Nations Publication, New York. http://www.unpan.org/dpepa_worldpareport.asp

Vassilakis, C., Lepouras, G, Fraser, J, Haston, S and Georgiadis, P (2005), "Barriers to Electronic Service Development", E-Service Journal, vol. 4, no. 1, pp. 41-63.

Velsen, L, Geest, T, Hedde, M and Derks, W (2009), "Requirements Engineering for E-Government Services: A Citizen-Centric Approach and Case Study", Government Information Quarterly, vol. 26, no. 3, pp. 477-486.

World Bank Website (2005), "Definition of e-Government": http://www1.worldbank.org/publicsector/egov/definition.ht m (Last accessed 10 Dec 2005).

Wamoto, FO (2015), e-government Implementation in Kenya, an evaluation of Factors hindering or promoting e-government successful implementation, Volume 4– Issue 12, 906 - 915, ISSN: 2319–8656

Websites:

http://www.egov4dev.org/success/case/iecuganda.shtml

http://bbnl.nic.in - Bharat Broadband Network Limited, A Government of India Undertaking

http://www.gps.gov/systems/gps/performance/accuracy , GPS Accuracy,

http://www.jhuapl.edu/techdigest/td/td1901/guier.pdf, Genesis of Satellite Navigation,

www.nemid.nu, NemID The official Danish OCES certificate policies published in https://www.nemid.nu/dk-da/digital signatur/oces.standarden/oces-certifikatpolitikker/

www.digst.dk, Agency for Digitization

https://www.nets, danid.dk / produkter / for tjenesteudbydere / nemidtjenesteudbyder / nemidtjenesteudbyder support/ tjenesteudbyderpakken/ Documentation for implementation of NemID 9

http://www.nets.eu/dk-da/produkter/sikkerhed/NemID-tjenesteudbyder/NemID-JavaScript/Pagaes/default.aspx. NemID JavaScript site

http://www.home-affairs.gov.za/projects.asp

http://www.gcis.gov.za/mpcc/index.html http://www.dpsa.gov.za/

https://joinup.ec.europa.eu/sites/default/files/ckeditor_files/files/eGovernment%20in%20Estonia%20-%20February%20 2016%20-%2018_00_v4_00.pdf- E-government in Estonia

https://www.bloomberg.com/view/articles/2015-03-04/envying-estonia-s-digital-government

https://medium.com/sidewalk-talk/how-estonia-became-a-global-model-for-e-government-c12e5002d818#.vntq79voc

https://e-estonia.com/eu-egovernment-report-2016-how-estonia-made-it-to-the-top-well-explained/

https://ec.europa.eu/digital-single-market/en/news/eu-egovernment-report-2016-shows-online-public-services-improved-uneven

http://ipp.oii.ox.ac.uk/sites/ipp/files/documents/IPP2010_Kitsing_1_Paper_0.pdf